Nawabs, Nudes, Noodles

Ambi Parameswaran is Brand Strategist and Founder of Brand-Building.com. He spent a large part of his thirty-five-year marketing, sales and advertising career in helping build FCB Ulka into one of India's biggest ad agencies. An engineer (IIT Madras), he has done his MBA from IIM Calcutta, completed his PhD from Mumbai University in 2012 and the Advanced Management Program from Harvard Business School in 2014. Ambi is a brand advisor to several large and small companies. He has authored and co-authored eight books and over a hundred articles. He can be reached at ambimgp@brand-building.com

Also by Ambi Parameswaran

FCB–Ulka Brand Building Advertising: Concepts and Cases

Understanding Consumers: Building Powerful Brands Using Consumer Research

Building Brand Value: Five Steps to Building Powerful Brands

Ride the Change: A Perspective on the Changing Indian Consumer, Market and Marketing

DraftFCB + Ulka: Brand Building Advertising – Case Book II (with Kinjal Medh)

Strategic Brand Management
(with Kevin Lane Keller and Isaac Jacob)

For God's Sake: An Adman on the Business of Religion

Nawabs, Nudes, Noodles
India through 50 Years of Advertising

Ambi Parameswaran

MACMILLAN

Reprinted 2023

First published 2016 by Macmillan

First published in paperback 2017 by Macmillan
an imprint of Pan Macmillan Publishing India Private Limited
707 Kailash Building
26 K. G. Marg, New Delhi 110001
www.panmacmillan.co.in

Pan Macmillan, The Smithson, 6 Briset Street, London EC1M 5NR
Associated companies throughout the world
www.panmacmillan.com

ISBN 978-93-86215-13-0

Copyright © Ambi Parameswaran 2016

All rights reserved. No part of this publication may be reproduced, stored in or introduced into a retrieval system, or transmitted, in any form, or by any means (electronic, mechanical, photocopying, recording or otherwise) without the prior written permission of the publisher. Any person who does any unauthorized act in relation to this publication may be liable to criminal prosecution and civil claims for damages.

5 7 9 8 6

All logos and visuals of the ads used in this book (including on the cover) are for representative purposes only and are solely owned by the respective copyright owners.

This book is sold subject to the condition that it shall not, by way of trade or otherwise, be lent, re-sold, hired out, or otherwise circulated without the publisher's prior consent in any form of binding or cover other than that in which it is published and without a similar condition including this condition being imposed on the subsequent purchaser.

This book is dedicated to the unsung heroes
of all great advertising – The Clients

Contents

Introduction ix

Section One: People

The [In] Complete Man 3
I am a Complan Girl! I am a Complan Boy! 15
The Tingling Freshness of Teens 26
Jo Biwi Se Kare Pyaar… 38
Ab Main Bilkul Boodha Hoon, Goli Kha Ke Jeeta Hoon! 48
Twacha Se Meri Umar Ka Pata Hi Nahi Chalta 57

Section Two: Products

Only Vimal 73
Bachche Toh Bachche, Baap Re Baap! 84
Hamara Bajaj, Hamara Bajaj 97
Ghar Ghar Ki Raunaq Badhani Ho 109
Jai Jawan! Jai Kisan! 118
Har Ek Friend Zaroori Hota Hai 125

Section Three: Services

Baraatiyon Ka Swagat 139
Tan Ki Shakti, Man Ki Shakti 148
Zindagi Ke Saath Bhi, Zindagi Ke Baad Bhi! 159

God's Own Country	169
Naukri: H for Hitler, A for Arrogant	179
Kyaa Haal Bana Rakha Hai!	189
Asli Swad Hai Cricket Ka	200

Section Four: Ad Narratives

Doodh Doodh Doodh, Wonderful Doodh	213
Meri Khubsurti Ka Raaz	224
Bole Mere Lips, I Love Uncle Chipps	234
No Squeeze, No Wheeze, No Navel Please!	244
Last Word	255
Acknowledgements	263
Notes	267
Suggested Reading	279
Index	283

Introduction

Divining Societal Trends Using Advertising

I WAS LOOKING for my favourite blue jacket and could not find it in my closet. I was sure that the jacket was not with the drycleaners. Then I remembered that the previous week I had flown to Bangalore, and the flight back was terribly delayed. It had landed well past midnight. I realized that I had forgotten my jacket in the aircraft. Several phone calls later I was at the Lost and Found counter of Indian Airlines – this was in 1993; those were the days when you did not have to scratch your head about which airline to book. It took them just a few minutes to locate my jacket since I had the exact details of the flight. The person manning the department mentioned that they get on an average ten spectacles and sunglasses every few days, and enough books to open a library every few years. A dress blazer was an odditiy in the store room. I explained that I work in advertising, the client meeting had been rough and the flight was late. The executive mockingly said, 'It took you five days to figure this out? Oh, you must have been drunk; you guys in advertising drink a lot, don't you?' This was a full decade or more before *Mad Men* aired on American television and damaged the already bruised image of admen. The comment riled me up. I sat the old man down and gave him a lecture on what we do in the advertising business. He was not expecting that, but took the lecture in good spirit.

Finally, we parted as friends, me with my jacket, him with a slightly better understanding of the ad business.

While everyone is happy to speak about an ad they saw on television, their knowledge about the industry is scant. Advertising agencies have existed in the country for well over 100 years now. However, it was only in the last fifty years, or more specifically since the winds of liberalization started blowing strongly from 1991, that advertising as an industry has come into its own – truly reflecting the changing Indian consumers, their aspirations and desires.

From a societal point of view, roles played by man, woman, father, mother, grandparents, even the importance of rituals, festivals and money have changed. The rapidly diminishing effect of the deep divisions of class and caste as prescribed by the *Manusmriti* is evident in consumer India, at least in the urban markets.

Popular films, television programmes, novels, magazines and now digital media have been interesting reflections of societal changes. Be it the righteousness of the epic Indian mother (*Mother India*), the aggression of the angry young man (*Zanjeer*), to the lover boy phase (*Dilwale Dulhania Le Jayenge*) and to the NRI with a heart (*Swades*) phase, films have reflected the changing ethos of Indian society. In a similar vein, television programmes have also evolved from the days of partition drama to joint-family business sagas to saas-bahu serials to depicting IAS women on prime-time television; and as can be expected, religious mythologies continue to find their pride of place in Indian television. Several books have captured the changing chiaroscuro of Indian movies and television.

Advertising too has become a significant window to studying the transformation of Indian society, its desires and its needs. In a conventional sense, advertising has often attempted to change behaviour by introducing new products and selling them on the basis of rational and emotional benefits. At times, advertising has used social trends to sell products and services under the radar.

Often advertising has tried to stay a few steps ahead of society, thereby signalling a future trend. Sometimes it has looked at the past to hark back on an age-old ritual, custom or lifestyle to make the right connection. At a rudimentary level, advertising played a role in helping Indians discover new products and services. From the days when Dalda was demonstrated at grocery shops to the way Indians were weaned away from coal to a tooth powder to a tooth brush – ironically, today we are offered carbon-infused toothbrushes – advertising has tried to sell products rationally. Often adding a touch of emotionality as well.

While American cultural historian Jackson Lears dismisses advertising as 'the folklore of industrial society', I believe Indian advertising, considering the last five decades, provides not just folklore but also some interesting insights into a society in transition.[1]

Roland Barthes, the French philosopher, linguist and semiotician, observes that commercials for products like laundry detergent or margarine work only because they tap into ideas consumers already have. These ideas have been elevated into myths. So, while the Greeks had Homer, we have professional wrestling and Hollywood, he says. If I may add to that, we also have television commercials which in their own form have become part of urban myths.

Advertising has tried to reflect the changes in the roles of men and women since the day a pressure cooker was sold as a symbol of love to the present day when a mobile service brand offers itself as a bridge between a woman boss and her subordinate husband.

The importance of children is not to be underplayed in a country that is one of the youngest in the world. Advertising in India seems to suffer from an overdose of children who are used to sell products ranging from noodles to soap, detergents to mobile phones, even cars are within their aspirational reach.

The depiction of women has also changed dramatically from the days of the coy bride being led into the house, to the 'Mummy' who can spin magic to solve a problem to a dark-skinned woman going through the wedding ritual with her daughter eager to join her in the *saat pheras* round the fire. No other single consumer group has been depicted in such a diverse fashion.

If women have become more and more confident, men are being depicted as increasingly caring and thoughtful – even if it is wishful thinking on the part of copywriters, but there are a growing number of talented women vying for top posts in ad agencies. The days of macho men having a bath in the open with a red carbolic soap has given way to a man who helps his wife with the cooking. Not that macho men are missing. Often they are shown to be relying on the power of a deodorant or a snazzy undergarment to snag the luscious *bhabi*.

Young adults as a group too have evolved to a new level. From the days of carefree fun, today they expound new philosophies on corruption, freedom of speech and suchlike. Gender difference is getting bridged as women get their own two wheels and ask, 'Why should boys have all the fun?'

Getting a job used to be the ultimate achievement. Advertisements depicted men wearing smart formals washed with the best detergent landing the best job, and celebrating the achievement by rushing home and lifting up the devoted wife. No longer is getting any job enough. Now ads show subordinates demanding more from their bosses and even insulting them by calling them names like 'Hitler, arrogant, rascal…' when they are being unreasonably difficult.

Looking young and fair continues to be an obsession with Indian consumers and marketers. In addition there is this whole new mania about smelling good. While fairness cream advertising was once restricted by Doordarshan into describing *gori* as *nikhri* – the dictionary meaning of nikhri is improved or better, but Hindustan Unilever has been using it so consistently to promote its fairness cream that today nikhri almost means fairer to the lay public – all those taboos fell by the wayside with the opening up of television. Today, fairness obsession has even captured the menfolk. In middle-class homes, there are as many men's cosmetic products as there are women's cosmetic products, all spurred by advertising and the social pressure to look good.

When mobiles came into the country they were prohibitively expensive. One could not have even imagined that in less than ten years, it would be in the hands of every fruit vendor on the street. Advertising, and of course pricing, played a major role in the growth of mobile phones. From the days of pre-paid to free incoming calls to per-second billing, mobile marketers innovated and have not been shy of crying from the rooftops to grab the attention of the consumers.

Almost in a playback of the mobile revolution, e-commerce merchants are using high-power discount messaging to break consumer intertia in an almost perverse way. They are now driving consumers to shop from their sofasets. This battle to change consumer behaviour is being fought in the 2010s and the results will be visible in just a decade or less.

Advertising has had its share of controversies. At one time, sanitary napkin ads surprisingly were restricted to the post 10 p.m. slot on Doordarshan, though condom ads were aired at all times. When Tuffs shoes commissioned an ad that showed Milind Soman and Madhu Sapre in the nude, it led to a court case for obscenity that went on for over two decades. Fastrack, a watch brand owned by the Tatas, decided to fly a flag for the Lesbian, Gay, Bisexual and Transgender (LGBT) community by asking people to come out of the closet and embrace their sexuality. Since the days of Doordarshan, which even restricted the display of the navel of a model in a sweetener ad, we have truly come a long way.

Nawabs and other royalty too have modelled for premium suiting brands and now the new nawabs of India, its film stars and cricket stars, are endorsing apparel brands. If sarees have started vanishing from ads, we are seeing the birth of new kinds of apparel for both men and women, call them kurtis or Modi kurtas, we are bombarded with an increasing range of apparel choices.

A frame-by-frame content analysis of consumer product television advertising in India, released over the last fifty years, shows some very interesting facts. For instance, the way women are presented has changed dramatically. The number of words used in each advertisement has increased. Even products like soap have a wordy explanation.

Advertisers have at times used social consciousness as a tool to further the aims of commerce. Amul's ads celebrated the milk co-operative movement, Tata Steel proudly said, 'We also make steel' and Tata Tea issued a clarion call to counter corruption through its '*Jaago Re*' campaign.

Why is this book relevant today, more than ever? The last ten years have seen an explosion of consumer choice and media consumption. Print is under attack from digital, even though Indian language print is still vibrant and blooming. Television has been growing rapidly as well and the numbers are astounding. There were a grand total of fifty-five licensed television sets when Nehru died in 1964, about a hundred thousand when Indira Gandhi declared emergency in 1975, a little over two million when the Asian Games came to Delhi in 1982, thirty-four million families owned a TV set when Manmohan Singh opened up the economy in 1991 and when Narendra Modi was sworn in as Prime Minister in 2014, over 60 per cent of the 250 million homes in India had a television set.[2] But televison has now geared up to combat digital invasion, with consumers ready to watch television content on their mobile screens. Multiplex movie screens have opened a parallel distribution for non-mainstream films. The future holds many more surprises as was evidenced a few years ago with the monster viral hit Tamil song, 'Why this kolaveri di?'

The book is organized into stand-alone chapters with each chapter looking at the changes in society and advertising through a different lens. Each chapter may ask a few questions and present some reasons behind what is happening around us and how advertising is shaping and getting shaped by it.

The objective of this book is to provide a window to the changing Indian consumer landscape for students of management, marketing, advertising, sociology and media studies. It also hopes to make for interesting reading for the millions of consumers out there who watch and comment on advertisements. It will probably leave all its readers with some questions to answer: Where is our society headed and how can marketing play a more meaningful role in creating positive social change? And, hopefully, the next time an adman seeks to locate his forgotten dark blue blazer, the person on the other side will be a little more sympathetic and a little more aware of the troubles and travails of the Indian advertising business!

SECTION ONE
PEOPLE

The [In] Complete Man

Behind the erstwhile Moore Market in Chennai was the Corporation Stadium where I spent many an evening witnessing sports of all sorts. From the National Hockey Championships to the Ranji Trophy cricket matches, it was a part of my routine during my school days in the early '60s. The fact that my Dad's business was close by and that I loved to spend hours wandering around the bookshops at Moore Market were added advantages.

One of the most exciting things I had the opportunity of watching was the *rekla* race. While these still exist in some form in rural Tamil Nadu, they are no longer popular in the metropolitan city of Chennai. In these races, two men stood in a little chariot that was pulled by two bulls and raced around the stadium to the hooting of enthusiastic crowds. For those of you who may have seen the Hollywood movie *Ben Hur* and its chariot race, the rekla race was the Chennai equivalent. The bulls were semi-trained and the men riding the chariots were highly trained, but the races invariably ended in collisions, broken bones and more. The rekla race and *jallikattu* are very popular in rural Tamil Nadu. Jallikattu is another form of bull running where young men try to chase and catch an untrained bull and bring it to its knees. In a strange way, Indian men seemed to have a great fascination with the bull, from the seals of Mohenjo-Daro to the full-page obituary put out by a farmer on the demise of his favorite bull in the Karimnagar edition of the Telugu daily *Eenadu*.[1]

As a reflection of the ethos of those times, advertisments aimed at men had an overt macho personality. Brands like Lifebuoy showed brawny men playing football in mucky, rainy conditions only to get into a shower and bathe with the carbolic soap Lifebuoy to the tune of *'Tandurusti ki raksha karta hai Lifebuoy, Lifebuoy hai jahan, Tandurusti hai wahan'* (Health is protected by Lifebuoy. Where there is Lifebuoy, there is health). Lifebuoy ran a series of ads featuring men engaged in sports such as football set in a rather semi-urban environment. The Lifebuoy tag line from Lintas, the Lever ad agency, 'Where there is Lifebuoy, there is health' was the first ad slogan that was equally popular in urban and rural India.

Colgate toothpower in the '80s took a different angle at the brawn vs brain issue, again aimed at both urban and rural consumers. The film is set in an akhara where muscle-bound wrestlers do their daily practice bouts. A burly young man has just finished his routine and picks up a piece of sugar cane and bites into it. But his dental cavities make him cry with pain. His young sister walks up and gently chides him, *'Badan ke liye doodh aur badam, lekin daantho ke liye koyla? Bhaiya, kabhi kabhi deemag ki bhi kasrat karni chaiye'* (For your body you consume milk and almonds but you clean your teeth with coal dust? Brother, at times you should also exercise your brains, not just your body). The ad crafted by Kamlesh Pandey at Rediffusion then presented the advantages of Colgate toothpowder. Here was a brand that decided to use the Indian man's fascination with bodybuilding to its advantage by presenting its toothpowder in an interesting context.

The '70s and '80s also saw cigarette advertising enter the cinema halls of India, when bad songs in movies often drove viewers out for a smoke break. While Charminar cigarette said 'Relax! have a Charminar', Scissors said, 'Men of Action-Satisfaction. Scissors always satisfies'. Four Square launched as India's first king-sized cigarette in the late '70s offered the dream to 'Live Life Kingsize'.

When Godfrey Philips wanted a campaign for their Red & White cigarette – and I was part of the team that worked on the campaign – the agency decided to position the brand for men who did good deeds, but did not hanker after the accolades that follow. The campaign *Hum Red & White peene walon ki baat hi kuch aur hai* (those who smoke Red & White are a different breed) went on to run for more than a decade. The model chosen to play the hero in the Red & White films, Raj Babbar, went on to become a very popular film star and has successfully moved into politics as well. A similar fate awaited the Charminar model, Jackie Shroff, without the political afterlife.

While brands aimed at the lower socio-economic groups were speaking of brute strength and power, in the 1980s we started seeing brands trying to appeal to the new affluent in more sophisticated ways.

Cherry Blossom shoe polish ran a very popular campaign that said 'Something special is coming your way – Did you Cherry Blossom your shoe today?' The ad showed the beautiful face of the biggest supermodel of that era, Nandini Sen. The Hindi version of that line was also a classic, *'Chalte chalte kismat chamke'* (Your luck will shine as you walk).

Who can forget the feeling of sitting in a non-air-conditioned cinema hall at the height of summer only to see the Old Spice film showing a macho white male surfing the cool blue seas, with music set to the tune of 'O Fortuna' from the Cantata Carmina Burana. 'Old Spice, the mark of a man,' we were told. It was probably the first time opera music was played before millions of Indians – Titan introduced Mozart to millions more later in the '80s. The brand Old Spice generated great buzz in 2013 again with its 'Smell Mantastic' television commercial starring Milind Soman in a white towel.

Suiting advertising too spoke to a more sophisticated audience. Brands like Elpar presented the mythical Indian Wild West, with its protagonist lassoing horses. Vilas Kalgutkar, who played the Elpar Man for many years, reinvented himself into a highly-respected photographer in the 2000s. Bombay Dyeing used Ardhendu Bose, grandnephew of Netaji Subhas Chandra Bose, and created a series of James Bond-like films with elaborate car chases, helicopter crashes, stool pigeons, snakes, dangerous ladies and poison darts. If suitings can play the superhero card, why not an undergarment? Goutam Rakshit's Advertising Avenues created the blockbuster advert for their client VIP undergarments brand Frenchie in 1990. The hero played by Dalip Tahil combatted opponents dressed only in his night gown and a VIP Frenchie. Frenchie, which was in reality a mini brief and economical to manufacture, became a huge money spinner. Echoes of Frenchie's success can still be heard in the undergarment circles. If VIP Frenchie was sold as a symbol of sophistication, it is a pity the modern day men's undergarment advertising is nothing but celebrity six-pack parades. The first undergarment to go full frontal was Maidenform bra. The campaign 'I dreamed I ... in my Maidenform bra' ran in the US from 1949 for twenty long years, helping women live their dreams of being out in their underwear. The campaign even crowd-sourced ideas from the customers – 'I dreamed I took the bull by the horns/went walking/stopped the traffic/went to blazes/rode in a gondola ... in my Maidenform bra'. When the bra burning movement started, the campaign took a break only to come back as 'The Maidenform woman. You never know where she'll turn up'.

When the Raymond account moved to the small agency Nexus Equity, the advertising world wondered what they would pull out of their hat. Raymond had a wonderful run with Frank Simoes and his brand of sophisticated advertising. The campaigns 'Guide to the well-dressed man', 'Raymond – A new kind of an executive statement' were campaigns I had grown up with. The Indian male was changing and this was captured in the Nexus Equity campaign: 'Raymond. Suitings for the complete man'. The campaign from Nexus Equity, an agency founded by Rajiv Agarwal, Arun Kale, M Raghunath and Rajan Nair, became a defining moment in Indian advertising. It broke away from the cliché-ridden suitings advertising of smart young men with women draped over their arms, mansions, luxury sedans, horses and more.

One of my favourite ads from the campaign has a young man taking a walk in the woods with a little boy. The music that accompanied the walk was the famous Crosby, Stills, Nash and Young track 'Teach your children'. Yet another film featured a young man, ostensibly back from abroad, looking for his long-lost friend only to discover that he was now wheelchair-bound. The film ends with the two friends laughing and having fun on Mumbai's Marine Drive.

Interestingly, Levis had created a campaign for its 501 Jeans through FCB which included a man in a wheelchair. Carol Moog, who was the Professor of Psychology at University of Pennsylvania has opined '...advertising developed for Levi Strauss & Company's 501 Jeans, included a man in a wheelchair in one of its genuinely engaging, musically excellent, shamelessly imitated, sales-soaring "501 Blues" commercial. In the spot, young people are dancing, jogging, playing double-dutch and here's this guy happily popping a wheelie in his chair...'[2].

The brand Raymond at once occupied the emotional high ground of the new Indian male of the mid-'90s. The waves of liberalization were opening up new opportunities for the young men of India. They now had to find a balance to their life. Is it work or family or both? Is it money or fame or none? Is it friendship or the pursuit of material goals? The suiting brand managed to resonate with the new emerging ethos of upper-class Indian males.

Two young men are having a good time; one of them is obviously married and his wife is out for the day. In their merrymaking, they manage to spill pickles and more on the most prized tablecloth. While the friend panics, the man of the house tells him to relax. Then he goes about washing the tablecloth with Ariel, a new detergent powder which can remove the toughest stains. And lo and behold, when the wife comes back after her heavy-duty shopping, the tablecloth is back in its place, spick and span. This ad, released in the late '90s, was another milestone in the way men were presented in Indian advertising. While part of the ad was conventional in its depiction of tough stains, detergent action etc., it caught eyeballs because it showed the man, the head of the household, washing clothes. Around the same time, we started seeing ads which showed the man making coffee for his wife, serving soft drinks to his family, etc.

A new Indian male archetype was evolving around this time.

In 2005, a modest-sized FMCG player from Kolkata called Emami launched Fair & Handsome, a fairness cream for men. The Berlin Wall of skincare between men and women fell with a big crash. Emami did not shirk from spending mega

> STOCK PHOTO: Over the last few years, thanks to the availability of cheap stock photos, many brands have opted to pick photos from stock photo vendors. So a smiling kid, a smiling family, a running man, etc. are all available for ready use. But one has to be careful lest the competitor also ends up using the same image, which will definitely cause much embarrassment.

bucks in promoting their new baby. They used the star power of Shah Rukh Khan and heavy advertising to quickly ramp up the brand. Was it just a lucky break?

Hindustan Unilever for years had known that men were using their multi-million dollar brand Fair & Lovely. This was true of many of their brands aimed at women. Men were using Ponds Dreamflower Talc and Lux soap as well. Past experiments of targeting men with cosmetic brands had died with a whimper. Calcutta Chemicals had a premium men's soap brand Aramusk, which had a cult-like following, but the followers were few and far between. The challenge that confronted HUL was similar to the ones companies with large monolithic brands face. Will something that they do inadvertently destroy their own brand's equity? A newcomer has no such fears. They have nothing to lose.

Emami had latched on to a new trend, what I would call the 'effeminization of the male gender'. Globally, change was afoot. Men were becoming more grooming and beauty conscious. Global cosmetic majors like Procter & Gamble, L'Oréal and Beiersdorf were discovering a new emerging market. Male grooming products were rapidly expanding beyond the narrow band of shaving creams and colognes.

HUL was quick to counter Emami with their own men's fairness cream under the Fair & Lovely franchise.

Soon products from Nivea, Ponds, Garnier and others arrived, all of them targeting the Indian male who aspired to look fair, handsome, smart and more. The male grooming revolution also drove up the demand for deodorants, face wash, hair gels and a flood of new brands entered the market from all FMCG companies.

Godrej seem to have got it right with their Godrej Expert hair colour sachets by targeting both males and females, using an ad campaign that made one a '*Jawani janeman*' (Youthful beloved)[3].

It is not as if all products are presenting Indian men as

effeminate creatures waiting to turn fair with a head of curly black hair. We do have soft drinks like Thums Up and Mountain Dew which still evoke the thrill of adventure and action stunts. There are also undergarment brands which are trying to get scrawny young men to look tough and muscular, often with the help of a Bollywood star.

Other advertisements featuring men too have changed in the 2010s. Whirlpool refrigerators featured an ad showing a young man cooking with his wife. Act II popcorn showed a father making popcorn for his family.

Does this mean that the Indian man is finally getting off his couch and doing something useful around the house? And is he enjoying his new role?

FCB Ulka's account planning team conducts regular studies to understand the changing mood of Indian consumers. Using a technique called 'Mind & Mood', the agency teams spend extended time with consumers in their homes and places of work, chatting with them and probing them on their behaviour, habits and attitudes. The team publishes these reports as special Mood Studies in the Cogito Journal[4]. The ManMood Study done in 2014 points towards some very interesting revelations:

The study highlights seven key learnings which attempt to present a character sketch of the evolving Indian man.

1. Sandwiched Generation – lives responsibly but regrets it

The thirty-five-plus age group sees itself as a sandwiched generation which has lived responsibly. They have lived their initial years according to the advice of their parents and now are taking care of them dutifully, though reluctantly.

But in the bargain, they see themselves as cheated, since even as their parents have certainty of old-age care, they are uncertain if their own children will care for them. Their lives are dictated by the needs, desires and dreams of their children until they become adults, which, in turn, has left them with very little time to live for themselves.

2. You are only as good as the money you make

The Indian man increasingly defines himself by his possessions rather than by who he is. However, this materialistic definition of self-worth means that the goalpost of success is constantly shifting and seems ever elusive as both the list of items necessary to be seen as successful keeps increasing as does the associated costs.

3. Value of 'values' is decreasing steadily

Today, three out of four men express some level of dissatisfaction with their standard of living. In a way, for them, life has become a continuous climb to reach the ever-elusive temple of Mammon. Anything which stands in the way of making this journey easier needs to be dismantled. Hence, this generation places very little store by 'values' and tends to instead swear by 'practicality'. The worrying aspect is that they feel the need to ensure that children are brought up on a healthy dose of such practicality since good values may make it difficult to succeed.

4. Men share the responsibilities but women don't share in the pressure

The relationship between husband and wife has increasingly become a relationship of equals with both partners sharing and supporting the family. The more materialistic nature of modern Indian society is also being manifested among women and the pressure of providing for the wants of the family is being visibly felt by the man of the house.

The husband today is also increasingly expected to

contribute time towards the welfare of the household beyond just earning money – a fact he is aware of but resents because he feels that since he brings home the income, he should be freed of the other aspects of taking care of the household. But he is, slowly and surely, being forced to take a more active role in household affairs.

5. The new convention of parenting – children as assets to children as liabilities

Children continue to be seen as the most precious gift but increasingly parents know that this gift comes with an expiry date. There is an increasing awareness that their role in their child's life, once he grows up and becomes independent, may be limited. Hence, they are also preparing themselves financially for an independent existence. They see their duty as being limited to providing the best possible start for their child through the right education but increasingly expect children to shoulder the burden of expensive post-graduation degrees.

6. Money is valued for what it can do rather than for what it is

The attitude to money perhaps is one of the biggest changes in the Indian consumer landscape. This generation does not value money as an asset, but rather as an enabler. Accordingly, the attitude to money is not of conservation but of optimal utilization to achieve desires. But money is also one of the biggest stressors for today's consumers. As expenses and inflation mount, estimating the correct amount of money for a better tomorrow is becoming harder.

7. Vanity, thy name is man

The importance of grooming is being brought home to the

Indian man emphatically by a variety of factors, especially Bollywood and television. There is a significant incidence of appearance anxiety among the youth and young consumers today, who easily ascribe success to proper grooming. The repertoire of grooming products used by men, thus, is increasing exponentially the lower you go down the age ladder. Interestingly, in the less economically affluent segments, it is often the man who introduces new cosmetic brands into the household, even as the woman of the house often continues to use traditional remedies.

A more affluent situation has transformed the Indian man into a marketer's dream consumer across many categories with an ever-increasing appetite for consumption opportunities. This behaviour makes his future and retirement-related life uncertain but he wilfully turns a blind eye to the future risk and concentrates on making the most of the present.

Rama Bijapurkar, one of India's most respected consumer and strategy consultants, observes that men are a confused lot in today's India. She quotes a study by Satyam Viswanathan, to note that Indian masculinity is being pulled in three different directions, by the weight of traditional expectations, the pull of modern ways and the growing wave of emergent Indian feminism[5].

Subhas Chakravarty, veteran adman and market researcher, goes on to reiterate that the male grooming category in India was the single-handed creation of marketing pundits and advertising. There was no governmental support or societal pressure. I suspect this category is going to keep growing with newer and newer products and services being added to the male grooming repertoire.

While the Indian man is changing ever so fast, he still has a long way to go compared to his global cohorts. For instance, it is reported that in over 45 per cent of the US households, the primary job of cooking is done by the man. The same is true of child care and housekeeping. The number of stay-at-home male partners too is increasing around the world.

Indian advertising is today speaking a different language to the men of India. It is no longer wrestling and football. It also includes skincare and cooking.

I am a Complan Girl!
I am a Complan Boy!

ALL COOKING OIL brand advertising in the late '80s looked the same – kitchen, dining table, admiring mother-in-law.

An agency had been briefed about the launch of a new sunflower oil. The name was decided – Sundrop. The company, ITC. The agency, FCB Ulka. The market was dominated by groundnut oil and sunflower was a relatively unknown species. Hindustan Lever had just launched Flora, its brand of sunflower oil. While Flora was positioned as a 'light oil', it was felt that Sundrop needed to be positioned at the belly of the market, literally. Given the characteristics of the sunflower oil, it was felt that the brand could carry the tag 'Healthy oil'. So while Saffola, which was made from safflower oil, was positioned as a pricey 'Healthy oil for the unhealthy', Sunflower had to figure out an interesting space to occupy.

How to break through the clutter and stand out? How to communicate the proposition 'Healthy oil for the healthy'?

The creative team working on the brand hit on the idea of using a child as a short-code to spell health for the healthy. And then they literally made the kid stand on his head.

The cartwheeling Sundrop kid, dressed in a yellow track suit, went on to tug at the heartstrings of mothers to make Sundrop the largest selling cooking oil brand within a few years of its launch in 1989.

A few years later, Dhara did an interesting take on kids and food. A little kid sits mournfully at a small town railway station. A friendly old man dressed in khakis, probably the postman, spies him and walks past him nonchalantly. The boy, who knows the old man, is unable to contain himself and calls out to him. When asked what he was up to, the boy replies, '*Sab gussa karte hain. Mein ghar chod kar jaa raha hoon*' (Everyone scolds me. I am running away from home). The old man smiles and says that before he runs away he should consider one thing – his mother was making jalebis and by running away he would miss out on the tasty treat. The little kid sheepishly looks at the man and says that then he may postpone the running away to another day. We see the kid sitting on the bicycle as they head home. The brand message flashes. The film directed by Namita Roy Ghosh and Subir Chatterjee of White Light films for Mudra Communications was rated as one of the best films of its decade. The trustworthy postman dressed in khakhi uniform riding a bicycle has been an integral part of urban and rural landscape in India; I wonder if this cultural icon will ever be replaced by the local pizza delivery man?

The magic of the kid as kid worked for both these food brands.

Indian advertising has been using kids in their narrative since the mid-'50s. Detergents used to show kids winning cups in competitions and running home in their spotless white school uniforms. Milk food drinks like Horlicks and Bournvita too used to show kids performing well, thanks to the goodness of these brands.

Complan took it to another level in the early '80s when it featured a boy and a girl in its ad. Played by kid models who would become future film stars, Shahid Kapoor and Ayesha Takia, the ad had them singing 'I am a Complan girl, I am a Complan boy ... and we love our Complan mummy'. In a sense, it was the first of its kind where the girl child was the centre of the story line. She plays basketball, she helps her mother. But the brand could not get typecast as a girl brand, so they did have a son in the story who adds, 'I am a Complan boy'. Experts say that along with Farex, which was positioned as a 'weaning food' for infants, Complan changed the way child nutrition was perceived and promoted in the country. Till Complan came on the scene and started speaking about child growth, Indian children were growing on their own and did not need any special additive. But Complan changed that narrative. If Ayesha Takia won hearts as the Complan girl, the all-time favorite little girl was probably the Rasna girl.

Played by Ankitha Jhaveri, the Rasna girl created by Mudra Communications went on to capture the imagination of millions of Indians, old and young and made Rasna a huge success. In one of their early ads, Ankita is waiting for her dad to come home from work. The doorbell rings and she says to herself, '*Pappa aa gaye*' (Dad has come). Her mother offers him coffee. But her father says no. She offers tea, he says no. 'What will Mummy do?' wonders the little girl. She then offers Rasna to her mom, who makes Rasna for the tired father. The brand had numerous takes on the girl and her love for Rasna, for her birthday and other occasions. In a sense, the brand targeted young mothers through their kids.

Numerous other brands began using children in their advertisments in the '80s and '90s.

Kids come rushing home from school and yell '*Bhook lagi hai, Mummy!*' (Mom, we are hungry). Mother tells them, 'Two minutes'. And the brand Maggi 2-Minute

> SHOOTING BABIES: How do ad film-makers capture that particular smile? That gurgle? Baby shoots are true challenges. A full day shoot may end up delivering just five seconds of useful footage. The baby sleeps, wakes up, becomes cranky. So all baby shoots have no less than three babies as stand by.

Noodles was born with a bang. By targeting the right moment in a mother's life – when she has to prepare something hot quickly for her kids – the brand went on to create a new category. It is difficult to change food habits, and we will see that in another chapter, but Maggi achieved a miracle through a combination of kid pester power, value for money and convenience of usage.

Categories like biscuits, chocolates and toffees had traditionally been featuring children to further their cause. Be it Cadbury chocolates with their 'Sometimes Cadbury can say it better than words' stories in the '80s, or Melody which offered chocolate inside a caramel toffee, or even cream biscuits – the brands had their job cut out. Get into the house through the kids and you are safely in the kitchen and on the monthly shopping list.

While working on a confectionery brand in the '80s, I was part of a serious discussion on the role of advertising and the best time to launch a kid-focused campaign. I said that the best time to reach a kid was when she was free, maybe during vacations, in summer or during any of the other breaks. The veteran marketer T Krishnakumar, who now heads Coca-Cola's very large bottling business in India, destroyed my hypothesis by saying that the best time to launch a kid-focused product is when the kid is attending school. The argument went as follows: A child learns about a new product from the television or from a retailer. He then has to tell someone. When he goes to school the next day, he has ten or twenty eager listeners, eager to learn something new. If the kid is going to be the viral mechanism for the new product, it stands to logic that a kid does not see the ad for a new product – of interest to him – as an ad. He or she sees it as valuable information that could be traded in school.

So it was propounded that when advertising to kids, we need not apply the minimum threshold principle to advertising.

The levels of advertising for products aimed at children could be much lower. But if we advertise during the period when the kid has the maximum audience, we will be able to amplify our message that much more. As Spanish poet, philosopher and novelist George Santayana has said, 'Children are natural mythologists: they beg to be told tales, and love not only to invent but to enact falsehoods.'

There are the other categories of products that use children as an entry ticket into homes. Colgate is the biggest toothpaste brand. They realized that mothers are always worried about the brushing habits of their kids. Hence, for over five decades, Colgate advertising has always had a strong and sometimes subtle endorsement of the child in the home. While the advertising message may have focused on the dentist and the endorsement he gave to the Colgate brand, the ads often ended with a kid saying, '*Is ka swaad mujhe behad pasand hai*!' (I love its taste). The brand has a nice taste just to ensure that kids continue brushing for a few seconds more. In fact, toothpaste brands like Forhans lost out because they did not figure out the need to make their offering 'tasty' for children.

In the '90s, Colgate attempted to accelerate penetration by coming out with a sachet packet. It was around this time that shampoo brands like Velvette and Chik were runaway successes thanks to their sachet pack. Colgate came out with a small pack; featuring a camping situation, they launched '*Colgate ka chota packet*'. The effort was to accelerate the movement from tooth powders and other home remedies, like coal dust, to toothpaste. Unfortunately, the sachet strategy did not work for Colgate. I suspect consumers did not see toothpaste as an occasional use product. Shampooing is not a daily habit in many Indian homes and so a sachet of shampoo could be bought for that special occasion, once or twice a week. Consumers probably thought that if they were ready for a toothpaste, they might as well buy the big tube and not go for a small sachet. Interestingly, even in the case of hair oils, the sachet strategy has not worked as well as it has worked for shampoos, probably for the same reason.

In the '80s and '90s, another category started advertising in films and on TV, aimed at kids and mothers. This was the school accessories category. Brands like S Kumars came on TV to sell their school uniforms. So did brands like Bata with their school shoes.

The flux of ads featuring 'kids as kids' kept growing to include categories like jams, soft drinks, snacks, biscuits, sweets, etc.

In the '90s, consumer researchers coined a new term to describe why ads and brands were targeting kids. They called it 'Pester Power'. Research said that in many Indian middle-class households, children were gaining a stronger voice. They were sometimes better educated than the mother, and probably had a more working knowledge of English. All this added to their credibility in their homes. In 2010s, while kids do pester, they have to contend with mothers who are better educated than the previous generation, at least, in middle-class urban homes. I wonder if this will reduce pester power in the coming years or will the educated mothers be even more vulnerable, since it now transforms into emotional blackmail as working parents are unable to give enough attention to the child.

One of the most interesting demonstrations of the role of a kid in the purchase of a high value durable was shown in one of the early Maruti Esteem ads.

The little boy has been picked up from school by his father. His dad is enjoying the drive and asks him about his report card. The kid mutters the marks, which are not too good. But the father smiles and continues to drive. The kid concludes, 'Dad's always in a good mood when he is driving his new Esteem.' Made in 1995 by Kunal Kapoor, the film scores because of the great use of father-son bonding over a ride. Apparently, the sudden showers in Ooty, where the film was being shot, restricted the shoot time, but the director did manage to bring out the best the car has to offer.

By no stretch of imagination can we say that kids in the 1990s played a key role in the selection of which car to buy, but marketers had figured out interesting ways of reeling in the pester power and pride of ownership into their narrative.

Obviously, pester power worked best for products that were not high value and were aimed at children. So products like snacks, sweets and drinks topped the list. But researchers also found that the child could have a 'veto' in other products like soaps, shampoos, toothpaste etc. In the case of durables like cars, motorbikes, television sets etc., pester power played a smaller role, but it was rearing its head simply because the kid sometimes had more knowledge.

The narrative of using a child in an ad had changed during the 2000s rather significantly. While there are ads which still present kids as kids in shades of 'I love you Rasna', there are many more where kids play numerous other roles.

Research done in Asia speaks of how there is a new breed of mothers that is creating tremors. Called 'Tiger Moms', these mothers want the best for their kids and are willing to fight like a tiger. In China, the single child policy has also led to the rise of 'Little Emperor' kids. These kids, now a second generational product of the one-child policy, have six adults doting over them, wanting to buy them clothes, gifts, toys etc.

In India too, we are seeing the rise of the 'Nawab Kids'. These children are a product of parents who grew up in a liberalized India, who did not have to wait in a line to buy a scooter or a motorcycle. These parents want their kids to have everything that they had and more.

An ad done for Whirlpool in the 2000s captured this ethos well. The Whirlpool mom is putting clothes into the washing machine. She picks up her daughter's white skirt and holds it close to her heart and starts dreaming. Her daughter is on stage playing the key role in the school play, that of a princess and gets crowned. Her dream breaks when her family enters the room to see her dancing with the skirt.

The film was a big hit and when we sat down to analyse the reason for its success, one of the planners pointed out that the film captured the emotions of the mother of the 2000s. She is living her own childhood through that of her daughter.

Kids are today the centre of the universe for their parents. As my wise aunt used to comment, 'Those days we used to have many kids and they grew up on their own. We never realized how they grew up. Nowadays, you have just one or two kids. The attention we gave to five or six children is now focused on the one or two you have. And you people spoil them silly.'

Kids are kids no more, and mothers don't want them to be kids. The Bournvita ad released in 2013 shows a mother running with her child, so fast, so hard, that it takes him superhuman efforts to beat her. And she is happy when he is finally able to beat her. I remember my old boss, R Narayanan, challenging his children that he will give up smoking the day one of them could beat him with a better timing on their morning runs. And they did, even before they hit their teens.

Research done in 2013 by Cogito Consulting points to some interesting lessons. While the 'basic' child remains spontaneous, honest, simple, whimsical, curious – there is no getting away from the fact that the eight-year-olds of the 2010s are behaving like mini-adults. Thanks to the commercial culture and technology that propagates a different set of values, they talk and act like grown-ups. Not only do they, almost, know all that the adults know, they also want to do all that they do – late-night movies, sleep late, eat out at fancy places. Teenagers are not their role models anymore, they model themselves after adults.

While Indian kids are today more grown-up in their attitude, they are also more open to expressing their opinion with strong likes and dislikes, increased self-orientation, ready to cut the umbilical chord, greater goal orientation, increased aggression and an inherent sense of self-confidence.

In this context, it is interesting to note that India had its first Kids Fashion Week at The Grand Hotel, New Delhi in March 2015. We are already seeing cosmetics being aimed at children with endorsement from Disney and Barbie. Footwear, clothes, cosmetics, what next, I wonder.

So much focus on children is also creating its own problems for brands. The International Food and Beverage Alliance has come out with a 'Global Policy on Marketing and Advertising to Children'[1]. The policy states that IFBA members commit either to: only advertise certain products that meet specific nutrition criteria based on accepted scientific evidence and/or applicable national and international dietary guidelines – since food company portfolios vary widely, each company determines its own nutritional criteria and makes these public – to children under twelve years; or not advertise their products at all to children under the age of twelve years. The policy covers TV and print advertising, third-party Internet and now, company-owned websites – including corporate and brand-owned websites – directed at children under twelve. For the purpose of this policy, 'advertising to children under 12 years' means advertising in child-directed media where 35 per cent or more of the audience is under twelve years of age. Members also commit to not engage in product marketing communications to students in primary schools, except if requested by, or agreed with, the school administration for specific educational purposes.

Global restrictions on targeting children is set to increase in the coming years. Brazil has even considered banning all ads targeted at children. An international scan would show that there are more ads that feature children in the social sector than any other sector, given the sensitivities involved regarding products aimed at children.

Just around twenty years ago, when our agency FCB Ulka was awarded the Faber Castell advertising account, Kavita Gadkari who was the planner on the account wanted to understand how kids interacted with crayons and colour pencils. She decided to organize a kids 'come and colour' party at her neighbour's house since they had a six-year-old son. The party saw around ten kids coming in. They were given colour pencils, crayons and a large sheet of chart paper to draw what they pleased. The agency planners and creative folks were in attendance to help the kids and chat with them. They discovered that the children knew about the various brands of pencils and colours. They even knew the exact colour shades that were available in some brands and not available in others. Some loved the fact that their parents got them 'imported' crayons. The entire party was an eye-opener for the agency team to whom a crayon was a crayon and nothing more.

In the year 2014, Mahuya Chaturvedi and her Cogito Consulting team talked to kids about clothes and discovered that the passion they had for crayons had now expanded to things like clothes, shoes, cosmetics, bags and accessories. Children were now fashionistas with specific opinions on fabrics, styles and cuts. This is not true of only India. This had already happened in the USA some decades ago, as reported by James McNeal who observed that the most dramatic change in children's purchases from 1984 to 1989 was in clothing. Clothing had become the second-most purchased product category – after sweets and snacks – among children[2]. This phenomenon is set to enter India as well.

I suspect if we do a smartphone party with twelve-year-olds today, in an upper middle-class society in one of the metro cities of India, we may end up with some very insightful usage information and maybe even a riot over who has a better smartphone.

The old days of 'I am a Complan girl', 'I love you Rasna' and 'kids as kids' are passé. Welcome to the era of kids as the digital native, hyper-competitive super adults.

The Tingling Freshness of Teens

A COLLEGE ROCK music competition is in progress, a teenaged boy is singing and he notices a girl in the audience. He calls out to her and she joins him on stage, they sing together to the thunderous applause of the appreciative audience. This ad featuring teenagers catapulted a toothpaste brand on a growth path. The brand, Close Up. The year, 1986. The promise was of fresh breath that will allow you to be close to the ones you like and love.

Close Up was developed as the world's first gel toothpaste by Unilever in 1967. It entered India a few years later but languished because of its advertising that targeted older couples, walking down a beachfront, set to a soft international song. The re-launch of Close Up in fact started Hindustan Lever on its journey in the personal care category with many more successes to follow.

Close Up was not the first ad to feature a teenager. Probably the most popular ad of the 1970s featuring a teenager was the Liril ad. It launched a soap brand in 1974 aimed at the typical housewife. But instead of showing a loving couple or a star, it put a young girl dressed in a green bikini under a waterfall. It was a revolutionary ad for its time which catapulted Liril to the top position in the premium soap category, reportedly with a market share of 25 per cent. The advertisement shot in winter, live under a waterfall in South India, featured Karen Lunel who went on to become the heartthrob of millions. The film set to pulsating music played in movie halls around the country often to loud cheers from the youngsters in the audience. While the first Liril bar was blue in colour, it was later changed to green as recalled by veteran adman Alyque Padamsee. Karen Lunel was the face of Liril for the longest period, from 1974 to 1985. Alyque Padamsee observed that the Liril girl became a gateway for young women to get into Bollywood. He, however, laments that most of them were forgettable, except for a few such as Preity Zinta, Tara Sharma and Deepika Padukone[1]. The brand manager of Liril at Hindustan Lever, Diwan Arun Nanda walked out to start his own agency, Rediffusion, a year or two after Liril was launched. At least, he was bitten by the 'freshness' bug.

While Karen Lunel was having an exciting bath under a waterfall, the country was going through tremendous turmoil. Indira Gandhi had declared Emergency (1975-1977) taking away many of the fundamental rights and freedoms enshrined in the constitution of India. So in a perverse way, the Liril ad celebrated the 'Tingling freshness of lime' in a country that was no longer free.

> STARS ARE BORN: Innumerable stars are born through ad films. From the fabulous Aishwarya to Preity to Jackie Shroff to even Salman Khan, all of them faced the camera for the first time as a model.

When the Emergency was lifted and Indira Gandhi called for election, voters quickly asked for their freedom back, with lime and more. The new government that took over soon booted out Coca-Cola – and IBM, I should add – and that created a whole new game in the beverage industry.

The period immediately before and after the Emergency were testing times for the country with high inflation, high unemployment and a general state of dismay. The country that was born in 1947 and a whole generation of Indians who had idealistic fervour gave way to a new generation that was not willing to sacrifice their present for the sake of a better future. The time was ripe for the rise of a new hero stereotype, the Angry Young Man. Film historians tell us that this phase lasted almost ten years, from 1975 to 1985. In advertising, however, we don't see much evidence of anger during that period.

Demographers speak of the youth bulge triggering protests in many countries. The anti-Vietnam war protests in the USA in the late '60s was triggered by the youth bulge. A youth bulge occurs when in the general population the youth, the sixteen to twenty-four age group, become a dominant number. If a country is witnessing a youth bulge and if that coincides with high unemployment, you can be sure to see a mass-scale protest movement. In India, this bulge happened around the mid-'70s, say Isabel Ortiz and Matthew Cummins of UNICEF[2]. Chances are that if the Emergency had not been lifted when it was, you may have witnessed mass-scale protests in India as well. You could argue that the Emergency was resorted to because of mass-scale protests spurred by the youth bulge. And you could be right. In the 2010s, we are seeing signs of stronger youth presence, through candlelight marches and so forth. I think this has not been spurred as much by the numbers as by the presence of yet another weapon in their hands, smartphones.

The lifting of Emergency also saw the exit of several global majors, including IBM and Coca-Cola. Thus was born a range of Indian soft drinks. Thums Up, a carbonated cola drink, was launched by the Chauhans who owned the Parle bottling company. As a sign of things to come, the brand was launched with a tag line: 'Happy days are here again!' How true. Emergency had been lifted, the press was free again. Why not celebrate with a bottle of cola. Parle soon followed it with Gold Spot, an orange soda, and Limca, a lime-and-lemony drink.

Limca was an outstanding success and was for many years India's largest selling carbonated soft drink.

Thums Up advertisments created by Trikaya Advertising captured the imagination of a nation that was starved of Coca-Cola. Thums Up's Delhi-based rival, Campa Cola could not stand up to the Thums Up anthem. Thums Up did classic soft drink advertising showing beaches and young people having fun. The brand sold itself as 'the refreshing cola'. Its magic formula was higher carbonation as compared to Coca-Cola.

The Indian teenager's appetite for soft drinks kept growing and this was brought to the attention of the global major Pepsi. In order to enter India, Pepsi had to comply with a number of laws of the land that were in force in the late '80s. They promised to give the brand an Indian flavour, so the name 'Lehar Pepsi' – apparently the word Lehar with its other connotations in English was not loved by the American bosses of Pepsi and was soon dispensed with. They entered India through a joint venture with Voltas India Limited and Punjab Agro Industrial Corporation (PAIC), a state government undertaking of Punjab. Finally, the brand was launched in 1988 with the theme *'Yehi hai right choice, baby, aha!'* (This is the right choice, baby, aha). In a sense, they were signalling to the youth that Thums Up is an imitator and Pepsi was the right choice if you wanted a global cola beverage.

Over the last thirty years or so, Pepsi has managed to capture the imagination of the young with catchy campaigns. To their credit, the first ever screen appearance of Aishwarya Rai was in a Pepsi commercial which also featured Mahima Chaudhary and Aamir Khan. An Indianized version of the Michael J Fox Diet Pepsi commercial from the USA, Mahima Chaudhary knocks on her neighbour's door asking if he has a bottle of Pepsi. Poor Aamir had just finished his last bottle. Not to be left out of a potential date, he jumps out of the window, rushes to a store nearby to grab a bottle. After performing this miracle in a few seconds, as counted in a television spot, when he offers the ice cold bottle to Mahima, she asks if he has another bottle for her friend, Sanju. As he is perplexed about who this guy 'Sanju' could be, in walks Aishwarya, who is Sanjana or Sanju in that film. Aishwarya went on to win the Miss World crown and become the sweetheart of millions of Indians.

Thums Up came under attack and they hit back with some terrific advertising. Since Thums Up was sweeter and more carbonated, Parle decided to give the brand a more aggressive position and thus was born the 'Taste the thunder' campaign created by Ashok Kurien and team at Ambience. Ashok claims that Thums Up is the only soft drink brand in India to have retained the same tag line – and almost same campaign with/without celebrities – for twenty years. Gold Spot was sold as 'The zing thing', while Limca ruled as the 'Thirst choice for thirst'. But soon Ramesh Chauhan of Parle decided to sell his brands to Coca-Cola in 1993 for $60 million. It is reported that when it was sold, Thums Up had a market share of over 80 per cent.

Pepsi continued to focus its energy on understanding and connecting with the youth. When Coca-Cola – which had entered India as a 100 per cent Coca-Cola-owned company, when laws permitted it to do so – decided to bond with the country and sponsor the World Cup Cricket 1996, Pepsi hit back cheekily saying 'Nothing official about it' – meaning that one day cricket was not official cricket and so there was no place for an official drink. It spoke of how new-age cricket played under lights, in bright coloured clothes was not 'official cricket', so why drink the 'official drink' Coca-Cola.

One should remember that in 1991 the government of India had opened up the country for foreign investments. New products and services started streaming in. The television sector saw the entry of Zee, Star and many others. New car brands started being seen on Indian roads. Waiting lists started disappearing rapidly. Brands were now chasing consumers in category after category.

Pepsi captured the new-found energy of the young in its 1998 campaign *'Yeh dil maange more!'*. The brand spoke in the voice of the young who were standing up and wanting to be counted. The Pepsi tag line became the mantra of the youth of the late '90s and early 2000s.

The year 2002 saw Coca-Cola launch its *'Thanda matlab Coca-Cola'* campaign as well as the ₹5/- bottle. The multiple executions of the 'Thanda matlab' campaign, starring Bollywood star Aamir Khan, written by Prasoon Joshi of McCann, captured the imagination of the young. The brand, though American was reaching out to the young Indians in their own fun language. In spite of the terrific campaign, the brand could not sustain the ₹5/- price point and later even abandoned the tag line.

The angry young man of 1975–1984 was a distant memory. *Dilwale Dulhania Le Jayenge* (DDLJ) released in 1995 spelled a new era in reflecting the ethos of the young. They were no longer wanting to rebel and fight. They wanted societal acceptance. Eloping was no longer a solution to the problem. So while the heart wanted more, that more had to be got with societal approval.

> PRODUCT PLACEMENT: The growing corporatization of feature film industry, especially Bollywood, has opened up yet another opportunity for brands to reach consumers. For a fee, the hero or heroine can be made to drive your car or drink your soft drink.

Come 2000s, how are the youth being depicted in the ads? Are they all jumping around asking for 'more' or are we seeing newer shades of youth dynamics?

For instance, Center Shock chewing gum presented the youth differently. A young man walks into a barber shop, shows the aging barber a picture of an afro-hairstyled model in a magazine, and asks for the same. The hair dresser just pops a Center Shock bitter chewing gum into his mouth; and his hair stands on its end, giving him the style he wants. There were numerous such ads including the immensely memorable one by Happydent where after chewing this teeth-whitening gum, the villagers are able to light up the whole palace with their bright teeth. Written by Prasoon Joshi of McCann and produced and directed by Ram Madhwani, this ad went on to win international awards by the dozen. This ad, in fact, used the Nawabi past of India, the palaces, the chandeliers, the lamps to sell a relatively modern product. There have been many such examples of brands picking up a figment of India's past to sell a modern product. An ad for Scotch-Brite in 2015 showed a mythical God who offers eternal life to the scrubber instead of the woman in a misdirected boon.

Amid these depictions of the youth, Tata Tea, through its agency Lowe Lintas, launched its '*Jaago Re*' campaign asking Indians to not just wake up in the morning but to rise up and raise awareness about specific social causes. One of their memorable ads had a politician asking a young man for his vote. The young man asks the politician what his qualifications are, and why should he vote for him? Tata Tea managed to blend in a very relevant social message along with its core message of refreshing tea. The campaign launched in 2008 was refreshed in 2014 as the 'Power of 49', where they goaded the women of India, the 49 per cent, to get out and vote.

The rebellious nature of the youth also got its expression in television programming. The biggest of them is *MTV Roadies* which debuted in 2003. *Roadies* has now turned into a cult youth programme. The show has put an amazing 1.5 million youth through its auditions. According to Afaqs, a portal that writes about advertising and media, *Roadies* season 7 viewership in India stood at 60 million and this rose to 80 million in two years. The show has 8.8 million Facebook fans and over 300 million views on YouTube.

In 2011, Airtel captured the imagination of the young with its catchy '*Har ek friend zaroori hota hai*' campaign. The film presented how a youth is surrounded by all kinds of friends: someone who eats your food when you are not looking, someone who borrows money and does not return it, someone who is willing to help when even not asked. But the story unfolds that every type of friend is needed to make life more interesting.

The broader subtext of Indian advertising's portrayal of the youth can be seen in two very different commercials, both aired around 2013.

In the first ad, the mother is worried that the young son is spending a lot of time on the Internet. Is he looking at wrong stuff? She goads her husband to speak with the youngster. The dad gingerly sits down on the son's bed. The young lad says, 'Hi', but is still busy on the computer. The father then gently probes: 'Son you are now old enough, I thought we should speak about "sex".' To which the son replies, 'Sure, Dad, what do you want to know?' The ad by Vasudha Mishra and Chax of FCB Ulka for Tata Docomo reflected the supreme confidence of the youth of India, in a subtly humourous way.

Consumer research tells us that it is the young who bring new products and ideas into the house. While working on the brand Clairol, FCB's New York researchers came across the phenomenon that mothers often take haircare advice from their teenaged daughters. Several brands are using this insight to connect with the old and the young in India.

This is the second ad. The father is angry. He sees his son sitting with his mobile phone, fooling around, laughing. The father grumbles to his wife about his son sitting at home and wasting time. He then shouts at his son, 'I told you to go and pay the electricity bill, have you done that? What about the property taxes? And the gas bill?' To each of the questions, the son replies, 'Done, done, done.' The exasperated dad asks, 'What do you mean "done, done", you are just sitting here and fooling around with your mobile phone.' To which the smart alec son replies, 'Dad I can do all that through my phone, don't worry.' ICICI bank that offers mobile banking facility then comes with a final message about mobile banking.

Indian advertising has presented the youth of India in many different shades, not just as a fun-loving bunch of kids. The influx of technology, almost all of a sudden, has been a big challenge for the fifty-plus generation.

Jean Piaget, the Swiss psychologist, sociologist and philosopher, was the first to offer a theory of cognitive development. He presented four stages: The period of sensorimotor stage (birth to two years); the preoperational stage (two to seven years); the concrete operational stage (seven to eleven years] and the formal operational stage (eleven to sixteen years). Adding to that, David Lazear offered eight ways of knowing and teaching for multiple intelligences including Logical/Mathematical intelligence; Visual/Spatial intelligence; Body/Kinesthetic intelligence; Musical/Rhythmic intelligence; Interpersonal intelligence/Intrapersonal intelligence; and Verbal/Linguistic intelligence. I suspect the young are getting adept at managing many new things at the same time because, as Malcolm Gladwell has pointed out, they are becoming adept at thin-slicing by working with thin slices of data for taking decisions[3]. Unlike the older generation, they are able to absorb new technologies faster and integrate it into their lives that much sooner. The old theories of learning and intelligence probably need an overhaul in this new year when a two-year-old can play with a smartphone before she knows how to write with a pencil. Using developments in cognitive psychology and behavioural economics, advertisers are attempting to build better ways of communicating with the new attention-deficit young consumer.

Brands have figured out that using the teenager could be a good bridge in their own communication narrative, as nowadays, many parents seek technical advice from their kids on how to use the latest technology. The youth bulge may be behind us in India, but if the country has to progress and grow, the youth have to be channelized in the right direction; and, more importantly, the older lot has to learn to appreciate the spirit of the youth.

Market strategy consultant, Rama Bijapurkar too has written exhaustively about the changing Indian youth. She has said that while on the surface all youth across the globe appear similar, there are many differences if you scratch that surface. Indian youth are more 'affiliative' and less 'assertive' compared to youth from Russia. She has observed that each generation in every country is brought up in different cultural contexts, which shape their collective character and, in turn, their individual behaviour[4]. For instance, in my book *For God's Sake*, I have examined in detail how Indian youth are a lot more religious than their cohorts in other countries. For instance, they visit temples more often, pray more often and believe in intra-religious marriage, as compared to say the youth in Europe.

FCB Ulka's youth study, Youth Mood, captures some of the current anxieties of the Indian youth. The residual impression of the youth of today is that of a self-confident, determined and tremendously focused bunch of go-getters. But under that strong exterior, this coconut has a very tender core. It is plagued by insecurities about the future, the fear of being left out – of groups/communities – or just plain being ignored. It has shed the overtly visible, almost ritualistic demonstrations of respect for parents and elders, and replaced it with an emotional underpinning of the need for support, advice and unconditional love. This feeling emerges particularly strongly whenever their own identity or self-image is under the spotlight. They are unapologetic about being focused on their objectives, whether it is material terms, stature or relationships. However, they are mindful of certain boundaries that they cannot transgress and always seem to be wanting to come back home.

Dheeraj Sinha, an advertising planner turned author, has observed that urban upper and middle class (socio-economic classes A B & C) can be classified into three broad segments: No Strings Generation (the young, at 29 million), Transition Generation (middle-aged, at 56 million) and the Partition Generation (older, at 27 million). The No Strings Generation has a distinctly more transactional and practical view of the world than the other two generations[5].

Ray Titus, a professor at a business school in Bangalore who has worked on understanding youth behaviour in India endorses these views and also points to a research done in Australia by Mark McCrindle which says that the Gen X and Gen Y are 'up-ageing'; they think and behave older than their age, thanks to the choices they have and the access to information[6].

I submit Indian youth too are dramatically 'up-ageing'.

I was speaking with Krishna Ramkumar of Avanti Fellows – co-founded with Akshay Saxena – which was one of the winners of the Tata Salt Desh Ka Namak Award, 2014. This young man had a plum job with Boston Consulting Group in New York after he had completed his BTech from IIT Bombay. He gave that up after three years to realize his dream of creating affordable coaching for engineering admissions. He had raised some first-round funding and was confident about his future. I spoke with him at length about the risk he had taken with his career and how people of my generation did not dare take such a risk. He had a simple answer to my words of admiration, 'Your generation did not have a choice. You were lucky to get a good job. You could not give that up and there were no angel investors waiting to fund your dream. Our generation is different. We can always go back to our old employer, who will take us back quite happily. In fact, even if my venture fails, it would be seen as a positive on my bio-data. So I don't think there is any downside to my decision. In your generation, it was different.'

I was rather touched by his words. Not only was he being humble, he made me feel good. If he stands as a representative of the millions of youth who are joining the job or the entrepreneur market, our country is heading in the right direction.

Jo Biwi Se Kare Pyaar...

THE YOUNG LADY looks like a typical, demure newly-married Indian bride. Holding her hand, the young man tentatively enters a shop selling a multitude of home appliances. Obviously, they are getting ready to set up their new home. When they ask for a pressure cooker, the wizened old shopkeeper asks the man how much he loves his wife. If he loves his wife more than life itself, then he should go for a new brand of pressure cooker which has an unique new feature. He explains in a characteristically authoritative voice how the unique 'Gasket Release System' will ensure that the pressure cooker will always be safe, even if the vent on the lid gets blocked by particles. When the young man agrees to get this new brand, the shopkeeper offers the clincher, *Jo biwi se sach-much karte pyaar, woh Prestige se kaise kare inkaar!'* (How can someone one who truly loves his wife, say no to the Prestige pressure cooker!)

This television commercial, made in 1982 and directed by Prahlad Kakkar, then a confirmed bachelor, was widely aired during the early eighties capturing the ethos of a newly married couple and a young nation getting ready to set up new homes. Interestingly, the pressure cooker is one of the most commonly used household appliances in India; over 80 per cent of all Indian homes have one. The humble pressure cooker is so ingrained in our national psyche that it can be spotted in almost all NRI homes around the world. Obviously, Indian husbands, wherever they may live, love their wives a lot, at least as evidenced by the prevalence of pressure cookers, many with unique safety features.

The brand Prestige very aptly captured the emotion of a newly-married couple and in an ode to this famous '70s campaign, in 2014 they even ran a print campaign with the same line, but featuring arguably the most famous star couple of India, Aishwarya Rai and Abhishek Bachchan. Interestingly, this print ad has Abhishek saying, 'Nothing impresses Aishwarya quite like a healthy meal prepared by me.' The famous line *Jo biwi se kare pyaar...*' remains but now it is Abhishek who is doing the cooking.

How can marital love be equated to a 'gasket release system', you may well ask. And do consumers really believe such claims?

Advertising often has to marry a rational promise with an emotional one and I think the Prestige commercial did a great job of doing both.

But that ad was meant for an era that was different. Today the same ad may provoke a violent outbreak in social media. How can a humble pressure cooker be equated to true love? – would be the argument on Twitter. To be fair, there have been many claimants to the symbol of true love, including diamonds and life insurance. There will be numerous wise rejoinders including those that will take the side of the husband.

Let us now go back to 2014 and look at an ad that featured a couple once again.

It is a swanky office and in the cabin is seated a smart young lady manager. She has short hair and is wearing possibly the latest cotton saree from a designer house. In walks a young man, rather nervous. Obviously he is her subordinate and has not done the job assigned to him properly. You can see her berating him and asking him to finish the work by tonight. The clock winds down, people start leaving the office, so does the lady manager. Our young man is hard at work. The film then shows the manager at her home, preparing a wonderful dinner. She makes a video call on her Airtel mobile connection. Who is at the receiving end? None other than her subordinate who is still at work, and who is also her husband. She calls him on video chat and asks him when he would come home as dinner was ready.

This ad written by Agnello Dias of Taproot Dentsu for the mobile services brand, Airtel, presented the married life of this millennium. A working woman. A man who is a subordinate to his wife. However, the executive woman is also a loving wife; ready to cook up a storm for her hard-at-work husband, who she berated a few hours ago in office. It is not shown, but maybe she even used a pressure cooker to make his favourite dish. The advertisement was lauded by the experts as a great ode to the new Indian woman and her drive to do better than her husband. Many others lamented that Indian advertisers and agencies are still stuck in the 'wife-as-cook' mode. Senior human resource executives blogged about corporate governance issues of a husband or wife reporting to their partner. The arguments can go on and it is not our job to take sides here, but to point out how in a span of forty years, Indian advertising has moved in so many different ways in which it presents the dynamics of husband-wife relationships.

It is possibly true that in most Indian homes, the woman is the homemaker and the man is the breadwinner. But the Airtel ad presented a scenario that flipped the argument around and managed to gain a lot of social currency and talk value. In many ways it reflected the direction the society was moving in. From strict gender-defined roles for man and woman to a more confusing arrangement.

Married couples and their relationships have been fertile hunting ground for advertisers. Take for instance, the campaign for Wills Navy Cut filter cigarettes from ITC that ran for many decades. One particular print ad that ran unchanged for a decade in the '70s-'80s showed a happy smiling young couple reading a Polish joke book. The ad had a captivating slogan, 'Made for each other'. The explanation provided the link, of how the tobacco and filter were perfectly matched in Wills Filter – as it was known then – cigarettes. The campaign made the brand the largest-selling filter cigarette in India within a few years of its launch. Powered by this strong promise, the brand dominated the cigarette market like a colossus. I was told by a senior manager at ITC that at one time Wills Filter made more profits for the company than all other brands and divisions put together. It would be naïve to assume that the success of Wills was solely due to the advertising claim, as the brand also captured the imagination of a young post-freedom fighter generation with their 'Wills made for each other' couple contest. This contest, launched in 1969, ran for almost two decades and was a very eagerly anticipated event in the key Indian cities. I know of a friend who even started smoking socially in order to enter the contest!

How have society's views of married life changed over the last fifty years? Do we still see married life and gender roles through predetermined rose-tinted glasses? Or have we started viewing them differently?

Television provides some interesting snapshots of how the depiction of married life has changed in India. The '70s saw the presentation of idealized role models for husband and wife through the long-running serial on Doordarshan, *Hum Log* followed by *Buniyaad*. Both were set in North India and had woven in stories of the freedom struggle, the ever-suffering wife and the wayward husband or son. Depictions of married life changed with the satellite television boom. The battle lines were drawn between the saas and the bahu, the mother-in-law and the daughter-in-law. The saga of saas-bahu battles ruled the roost almost for two decades. But over the last few years, we are seeing television channels exploring more nuanced roles for husband, wife and the ubiquitous mother-in-law. One of the bigger hits of 2012-13 was the serial *Bade Achhe Lagte Hain* (I Like You a Lot) where the husband-wife relationship was taken beyond the cardboard cut-out of working man and suffering wife. The actor playing the main protagonist in the serial, the perpetually overweight Ram Kapoor, became one of the most widely-loved actors, simply because he appeared more real to the viewers.

Bollywood, Kollywood – named after Kodambakkam in Chennai – and Tollywood or Telugu films too have started looking at relationships between couples a lot differently from how they were presented in the early years of Indian independence. *Mother India*, the famous Hindi classic to the more recent *Kahaani*, the roles assigned to the wife have dramatically changed. The concept of love marriage and elopement, a standard fare from the days of *Bobby* to the days of *Raja Hindustani*, too changed with the release of *Dilwale Dulhania Le Jayenge*.

Rachel Dwyer, professor of Indian Cultures and Cinema at SOAS, University of London, has observed that *Dilwale Dulhania Le Jayenge* was a watershed movie in Hindi cinema in many ways. It anointed Shah Rukh Khan as the biggest superstar of Bollywood, but at another level, it redefined the concept of marriage and love marriage. The hero of the film does not run away with his paramour, but seeks parental approval. And is willing to walk away, or literally take the train if there is no approval[1]. The movie completed an uninterrupted run of 1000 weeks at Mumbai's Maratha Mandir movie hall in December 2014.

In an ode to *DDLJ*, today's young men and women are looking for a combination of a love cum arranged marriage. While this may be a topic of a book in itself, it is suffice to say that compared to the generation forty years ago, who yearned for a love marriage but had no opportunity to find 'love' and so opted for an arranged marriage, the current generation of 2015 are opting for an arranged-love marriage, even though they have enough opportunities for a pristine pure love marriage. While newspapers report the prevalence of khap panchayats that rule against inter-caste marriage in many parts of rural India, we have found that in many villages, the panchayat approval can be obtained by paying a suitable 'fine'.

Demographers will inform us that there has been a steady growth of nuclear family homes, homes where it's just the mom, dad and kids. It is a myth that for centuries Indian homes were all 'Hindu Undivided Familes'. Sociologists tell us that for centuries, in most Indian societies, the eldest son stayed with the parents, while the younger sons and, of course, the daughters moved out – but for matrilineal societies as in Kerala. So we have had the concept of nuclear families in India for many centuries. But undoubtedly, the trend has gained speed with rapid urbanization and migration in search of work. According to the Indian Readership Survey, in the last twenty years, the share of nuclear homes in urban India, has gone up from 35 per cent to 45 per cent. The concept of nuclear families in itself changes some of the dynamics of the home. The absence of a mother-in-law gives a lot more power to the wife. The husband has a counterpoint to his power in the house. The ancient concept of the 'karta' or the head of the household is no longer prevalent in a large percentage of homes. All these are empowering the woman of the house to do a lot more than she has ever done, redefining her role in her own eyes as well as those of the society at large.

It is true that, unlike in the developed markets, the Indian woman is still playing the role of a homemaker. Rena Bartos, American demographics researcher, has through her research shown that the simplistic approach used by marketers of classifying women as non-working and working is flawed. Even among working women, she has shown that there are various shades of commitment to career and to family.

The role of the wife in India has now expanded beyond the home and the kitchen.

During the 2010s, we have seen several ads which have tried to present the man-woman relationship in a more edgy manner. Havells brand of juicers had an ad created by Lowe Lintas where the rather portly husband comes home after his morning walk with a buddy and somewhat patronizingly shouts out to his wife ('Babes') that she should quickly drum up a glass of fresh carrot juice and another of orange juice. The young woman brings him the new Havells juicer along with a carrot and an orange, and asks him to make it himself because she was stepping out for her morning run. Or in yet another ad, this time for the matrimonial website, Bharat Matrimony, the young man's parents suggest that since he got a promotion at work which allows them to live comfortably, perhaps his wife should stop working now. He – an antithesis of the Havells husband – responds that his wife is working because she likes to work and will continue to do so as long as she wants to. Shutting up the parents in the process.

Ariel, a laundry detergent brand from the global major Procter & Gamble, is running a major campaign called #ShareTheLoad, encouraging husbands to share the laundry load with their wives.

Are we seeing a revolution in the way marital relationships are evolving in modern India? The concept of marriage, the roles of the husband as provider, the wife as caregiver are as yet the most common paradigm in India. Ads have been able to capture this well and, as we saw, have started exploring the fringes of the stereotypical roles like in the Airtel advertisements. But I would submit that the Airtel ad was a depiction of a future, not the current reality. And in a sense, good advertising is an attempt to always stay one step ahead of the consumer.

Such a move, sometimes, results in accolades but sometimes it results in stone pelting, especially in our country where there are enough stones on the roads and enough idle minds and hands to throw them.

What may have caused this sea change? I think the transformation has been caused by a few distinct phenomena. Firstly, women in urban homes are a lot more educated than their mothers. So the big educational gap between the husband and the wife has narrowed dramatically in just twenty years. Given this education, the woman is a lot more vocal in expressing her desires. Advertising captures this eloquently. Secondly, couples are moving out of their home towns, more often than ever. This movement in itself has forced the couple to become more self-sufficient, putting more pressure on the man of the house, who now needs his wife's help and cooperation to carry his new burdens. Thirdly, growing financial needs have pressurized the woman to start working, with the support of her husband and often her in-laws. From being a thorn in the side of the 'bahu', the in-laws are slowly becoming a valuable source of help, at least in taking care of the children.

Once, we were doing research for a mosquito repellant brand in a mid-sized town in UP. Our planners and creative directors were speaking with consumers in a free and frank discussion, which we call 'Mind & Mood'. When we started probing the joint family system and the support a couple gets from their parents and vice versa, we came across a new phenomenon aided by the growing flat/apartment culture. The couples we spoke with said that they did not live with their parents, instead just close enough. Often they lived in the same apartment complex, or a short walk away. The lady made an interesting comment, '*Choola alag chalta hai, lekin hum saath khana khate hain*' (Our kitchens run separately but we dine together). This separate yet together is the new paradigm in urban India and this is having its own impact on couples and how they manage their work, life, children etc. It turns out that we did not discover something new. Social scientist Professor Shyama Charan Dube had also noted that a large extended Indian family may live together and may also jointly carry out some economic pursuits, but it is likely to have separate domestic arrangements for its nuclear units. They gradually come to have separate hearths (*chulhas*) and independent arrangements for cooking and dining[2].

Obviously, this helps increase the number of women who can join the workforce, at least till professional day-care centres come up – any venture capitalist reading this should examine investing in a day-care chain. Finally, the age of marriage is slowly but steadily increasing and as a result the wife is no longer a shy, coy teenager. One number is enough to bring this alive: as per the Census of India, the mean age of an Indian female at marriage has moved up from 18.3 in 2001 to 19.3 in 2011; the increase of one year in just a decade in demographic terms is a big jump, and if we were to take urban India, this number would be significantly higher[3].

The future will throw up newer issues and changes in relationships. For instance, live-in relationships are still scorned in most Indian societies. I was delighted to see the Tamil movie *O Kadhal Kanmani* by Mani Ratnam exploring this new dynamic. Chances are that we will see a lot of this happening in society leading to major issues for parents to tackle, which will also be reflected in Indian advertising. Fastrack has an ad where a young girl gets up from bed – she had spent the night with a guy in the boy's hostel – quietly slips out of the room, runs through the corridor, jumps over the gate and runs off into the street, all while putting on her clothes and shoes which were in her Fastrack bag. The brand asks its users to 'Move On'. Brooke Bond Red Label tea also has an ad which shows a live-in relationship. So brands are experimenting with the way man-woman dynamic is presented in advertising.

According to 'Meet the Modern Dad'[4], a February/March 2012 study by the Parenting Group in the US, fathers say the following tasks are mostly their responsibility: grocery shopping (49 per cent); cooking (43 per cent), driving kids to/from school, activities and appointments (39 per cent); getting kids ready for school or day care (36 per cent). I suspect these numbers will be similar for most parts of the developed world today. American retail marketing guru, Paco Underhill has noted that US women confess to devoting just around thirty minutes a day to food preparation. One expert has pointed out a connection between drop in home cooking and the United States' soaring obesity rate. This is why in the United Kingdom, where obesity rates are closing in on those of Americans', the British government recently passed a law mandating secondary-school students to attend cooking classes[5]. I wonder how this has panned out and if this is true, what an interesting way to get both boys and girls to learn about gender equality, healthy cooking and eating!

Indian couples are still negotiating the next phase of their duties but with women taking up successful careers and starting big and small businesses, we may see more stay-at-home husbands, who will be in charge of bringing up the child, attending PTA meets, visiting the family doctor, housekeeping and more. I am sure we will soon see ads that predict this future.

It is amusing to recall that in the '70s, the government of India used to run long commercials in cinema halls and on the television extolling the virtues of using a pressure cooker. In a boring monotonous voice, the ad explained to its viewers how a pressure cooker can save almost 30 per cent of fuel cost, since food cooks faster when cooked in a pressure cooker. I suspect the '*Jo biwi se kare pyaar*' tag line sold millions more cookers than the fuel-saving litany from our then socialist-leaning government.

Ab Main Bilkul Boodha Hoon, Goli Kha Ke Jeeta Hoon!

BAJAJ BULBS AD circa 1985 – *Jab main chota ladka tha, badi shararat karta tha, meri chori pakdi jaati, jab roshan hota Bajaj. Ab main bilkul boodha hoon, goli kha ke jeeta hoon, lekin aaj bhi ghar ke andar, roshni deta Bajaj.*'

('When I was a young kid, I was very mischievous, my mischief used to get discovered thanks to the light from Bajaj bulbs. Now I am an old old man, living on tablets, but even now, I get caught with lights from Bajaj bulbs.')

This jingle-based film written by ad veteran Mukul Upadyay still resonates in the collective consciousness of the country, at least with anyone who is over thirty years of age. The ad, shot in a style typical of the Doordarshan days, was almost a caricature of the old age lived by Indians. This simple ad for Bajaj bulbs showed a small kid trying to read comics under his blanket late at night with the light of a torch; but his parents would catch him because of the light from Bajaj bulbs. When the kid grows up to a ripe old age and has been living on medicines, he continues to be mischievous, trying to raid the fridge in the night for a slice of cake, only to get caught by his wife.

If you look at the societal coding of the ad, you would realize that in the '70s and '80s, old age was equated to a life of popping pills. And for those adventurous old men, beware, Bajaj bulb is just a click away.

Let us now move into the 2000s and see how the depiction of old age in advertising has changed.

The film shows an old man, well over seventy, wooing his over sixty-year-old wife. He shyly says that he has bought her something special for Valentine's day, and pulls out a small jewellery box. The old lady opens the small box and is shocked looking at the big diamond ring inside. The old lady says, *'Ab is umar mein kaha pehenungi heere?'* (Where will I wear diamonds at this age?). To which the loving old man replies with the killer line, *'Heere ko kya pata tumhari umar?'* (How would the diamond know your age?). The brand, SBI Life Insurance, and the writer of the ad, Piyush Pandey, managed to present a new dimension of old-age in modern India. Just because you are old and retired, you need not live a life of 'tablets and tonics'. If you buy a big enough policy from SBI Life Insurance, you can even afford to gift your wife a diamond ring.

Come 2010, the depiction of old age in Indian advertising has taken yet another step forward.

Here is an ad for another insurance brand, Max New York Life, showing the changing paradigm of old age in India. This old man is packing his travel suitcase. The old lady, his wife, is busy preparing a meal. She quizzes him about his packing, *'Ab kidhar jaa rahe ho? Abhi to wapas aye?'* (Where are you going now? You just came back!). The old man replies that he has an important wedding to attend in Kolkata. She asks, *'Kiski shaadi?'* (Whose wedding?). To which the old man replies, *'Arre, Deepak ko jaante ho na, mera morning-walking friend. Uski sister ki poti ka shaadi hai. Main kaise mana kar sakta hoon? Sirf paanch din.'* (You know Deepak, my morning walking friend? His sister's granddaughter is getting married. How can I say no to Deepak! So I am going, just for five days!).

The old man, obviously retired, has become an inveterate traveller. Thanks to the wise insurance or investment plans he had made when he was younger. The lady, probably used to his multiple trips, does her usual, 'Tsk, tsk' and continues shelling peas.

In yet another ad, this time by HDFC Standard Life, the retired old man, after teasing his wife about her cooking and cleaning skills since they could not pay for multiple maids now, finally tells her that they were going on a holiday to Singapore.

How come, you may ask, advertising has moved from depicting a life of 'pills and potions' for the old in India, to showing them as carefree folks, buying expensive gifts for each other and making a trip at the drop of a hat, or a card?

Advertising, as always, is playing up a stereotype to tell a story. I am sure both the brands advertised were not aiming at over-sixty men and women. The ads are probably aimed at men and women in their late or mid-30s. But instead of presenting a doomsday prophesy of 'if you don't plan for the future, you will live a life of misery', they are trying the approach of presenting a good life thanks to wise financial planning.

More importantly, advertising of multiple products have moved away from showing old age as a time of worry, to showing it as a time of relaxation and maybe even a bit of fun.

So, has old age in India really changed?

Fifty years ago, it was the norm in most Indian families that cousins and nephews who are in need should be looked after by the extended family. So in many homes, including my own, we have had my grandfather's or grandmother's elderly cousins staying with us for years. That has now changed, but as Professors Sudhir and Katharina Kakar observe, while there has certainly been a contraction of family obligations, they have not disappeared; one may not feel obliged to look after a distant aunt, but there is no question of not looking after the emotional, social and financial needs of an aged parent[1]. I wonder how long this will last, and fortunately, there is yet another countermovement helping the aged.

There has been a significant change in the economic status of a large number of middle-class Indians thanks to increasing salaries/pensions/savings of the employee class and the growing income of the business class. So instead of depending on their son or daughter to support them in their old age, many old couples are almost fully self-sufficient in managing their household affairs.

Secondly, there has been a significant increase in life expectancy over the last forty years. From around the fifty-year average that existed four decades ago, life expectancy across India, both urban and rural, has now jumped to over sixty-five. From 63.9 for males and 66.1 years for females in 2001-15, life expectancy is predicted to increase to 69.8 for males and 72.3 for females by the year 2021-25. If we were to look at urban middle-class India, life expectancy is now over seventy years. So the men of India have a full fifteen years to live after they technically retire, i.e., if they retire at sixty.

Thirdly, there is a growing sense that in old age you can have fun too. Research studies are showing, at least among the urban digitally literate old folks, there is a growing sense of not living a life of 'pills and potions'.

Economic Times, in its 8 August 2012 issue, reports that by 2013, India will have a population of 100 million in the age group of sixty-plus. In a country of 1.2 billion, with almost half the population below the age of twenty-five, 100 million, though small, is still a sizeable number – this is almost one-third the entire population of US and almost 40 million more than that of UK. Quoting an international study, the report says that while Indians seem quite old school in some aspects and are not yet ready to go under the knife for surgical procedures, however, they are willing to do 'anything and everything to stay youthful and younger' – approximately 33 per cent as compared to foreigners at 23 per cent[2].

Shiv Visvanathan, an eminent social scientist, observes that while catering to the aging consumer, brands have to be conscious that 'brand justice' is more important than 'brand equity'. He suggests that marketers need to figure out a way of targeting the aged consumer without explicitly denigrating them.

When Pfizer was getting ready to launch their impotency drug Viagra or sildenafil citrate, they realized that the topic was taboo and would provoke intense debate if the drug was presented as a cure for impotency. Which old man would admit he was impotent, went the argument. So the business and markeing strategist decided to work on what may have been termed the 'social justice' angle of presenting the problem. Since impotency was seen as an almost terminal disease that could not be cured, was there a way of repositioning it by a change in terminology?

A few years before Viagra was launched, the company started seeding media about a new problem facing American men, it was termed 'Erectile Dysfunction' or ED. I came across an article on ED in *Fortune* magazine a year or so before the official launch of Viagra. The company had managed to create a new disease which had an acronym that could be remembered by the lay consumer instead of the derogatory term in use till then, 'impotence'. When the drug, and the brand Viagra, was finally launched, it found ready acceptance and went on to become a billion dollar seller that created a whole new industry. Even US Presidential contender Bob Dole appeared in a television commercial for Viagra. Unlike in India, where prescription-only brands are not allowed to be advertised on television and print media, in the US, even politicians are game for starring in television commercials.

Viagra was not solving a life-threatening problem of old age like drugs for hypertension or cholesterol, cancer or osteoporosis. Viagra, launched in 1998, created a whole new class of drugs for ED and there are at least five big brands that offer this benefit to old men.

Viagra has had its share of abuse as well; it is taken by drug users to add to the effect of intoxicating drugs like ecstacy to reach an even higher level of tripping called 'sextacy'[3]. Yet another study found that adding 1 per cent solution of sildenafil citrate to the water in a vase makes the flowers stand erect for up to a week beyond their normal life span.

If Pfizer managed to take the stigma out of impotency by rebranding it as a clinical condition called ED, yet another industry managed to transform a closet product into a high-fashion accessory for the young and the old. Till two decades ago, hair dyes were used behind closed doors in India. With the opening up of the economy, global majors like L'Oreal realized what a potential market a country of 1 billion-plus people could be. They managed to give this product a new name; the poor old hair dye was reborn as hair colour. In addition to the many shades of black, the marketers also offered a wide variety of colours to attract the young. To help spread the hair colour culture, the company systematically trained hairdressers, both male and female, on hair colouring techniques. They even instituted awards to celebrate the most innovative hair stylist – again a rebranding of the plain old hairdresser.

The attitudinal shift, from 'I will suffer in silence' to 'I will fight old age as much as I can' is taking hold of the elderly Indian populace, at least in the bigger cities.

In yet another demographic shift, we are seeing a growing number of elderly, affluent empty nesters – empty nest is a demographic term to describe the status of a couple whose children have moved out – with their children comfortably ensconced in the luxuries of the West. In cities like Coimbatore, there are old-age gated communities rapidly filling up with these elderly couples. *Economic Times* in its *Big Story* (31 May - 6 June, 2015) speaks of how India's affluent middle class that's hurtling towards retirement faster than the previous generation is doing it in style by creating something that they can retire to. Speaking with my friend Ganapathy Subramanian, who was quoted in that article, I discovered that he plans to shift to a villa in Anandam, a senior citizen residential project by Aamoksh in Kodaikanal by 2016, write a book, teach and do some social work. As he says in the article, 'We wanted to travel and get rid of household chores. Anandam senior home was a good option.' Many more such communities are coming up fast and I would like to predict that the taboo attached to old age homes may not survive this generation. In cities like Mumbai, specialist services are being offered to such affluent NRI empty nesters. A doctor in our area, Prabhadevi in Mumbai, has offered a special NRI Parents Services Package. This package includes a weekly visit and health check up of the parents of the NRIs.

No wonder there has been a spate of products and services aimed at the affluent aged, from tourism packages to super luxury bikes and more.

My friend Balu and his wife, Sita, who live in Bay Area California decided to take an Alaskan cruise a few years ago. He opted for a cruise meant for slightly older travellers. When he had enquired about it, he was told that the cruise was not tiring and the average age in his cruise would be around sixty. Finally, when he boarded the ship, he discovered he, at the age of fifty-five, was by far the youngest, and he suspected that the average age of the cruise travellers was well over seventy.

The Economist, in an article dated 27 June 2015, spoke about the global boom for cruise holidays. Over 22 million took cruise holidays in 2014 with the fastest growing segment coming from Asia. The article also amusingly observed that from catering to just the 'newly-weds, over-feds and almost-deads', they are widening the net to get many other segments of travellers as well[4].

In India, we have had, for decades, the aged going on pilgrimages by bus. That is set to change in the coming years with the addition of luxury trips and cruises, rather than just bus journeys.

Juxtaposing the grandparent with the grandchild is an evergreen area for brands. Recently, we have seen new interpretations of this old plot. Airtel ran a television spot in 2000s showing a grandkid reuniting his estranged father with his grandfather. Google got a granddaughter to locate her grandfather's long-lost friend in Pakistan by using the search engine, literally searching for the friend. Another tear-jerker was run by the *Times of India* where the grandfather who was denied his slot in the Indian hockey team celebrates his grandson's success.

The affluent elderly has been a demographic that has been tapped by marketers in developed nations for over two decades. *The Economist*, in its article dated 5 August 2002 on marketing to the aged, quotes SeniorAgency International, a consulting company specializing in this field, to say that the over-fifty own three-quarters of all financial assets and over half the discretionary spending in the developed markets[5]. This is probably true of India as well.

To open your eyes to the ways elderly can be marketed to, let me end with another story from FCB Ulka's archives. We were approached by a large company specializing in knee replacement to do a television campaign with the full support of the Orthopaedic Association to popularize knee replacement surgery. The company was dismayed that as against the broad demographic trends we examined above, the number of knee replacement surgeries were not growing fast enough. They felt that a burst of TV advertising, without any brand mention could create a generic demand for knee replacement surgery and become a tipping point. Our team worked out a script that showed a family, kids, parents and an aged grandmother waiting to board a train. The grandmother is seated and as the train pulls into the station, she seems unable to get up from her seat. Research had shown that the biggest difficulty people with knee problem have is in getting up once they have been sitting for a long time. The grandkid comes running back, calling his Dadi to get up, and she says, 'You carry on, I can't go on'. At this juncture, her son too gets off the train and says that this cannot continue and they have to meet a specialist. The ad then asks the viewers to SMS 'Knee' to know more about Knee Replacement Surgery. The ad ends with the kid and his grandmother walking up a little hill, obviously the knee is now working fine.

The team at the agency had identified a veteran Marathi actress, Sulabha Deshpande, to play the role of the grandmother. When they met her to explain the script, they were delighted to find that she had already undergone knee replacement surgery on both her knees! So in this case, we truly had an aged consumer playing the real-life role.

Twacha Se Meri Umar Ka Pata Hi Nahi Chalta

WE HAD A crisis at hand. Our agency had done a great job on the soap brand Santoor after winning the account in 1988-89. The brand that had been launched as a sandal and turmeric soap had been repositioned as a skincare soap with a strong promise of 'Younger Looking Skin'. The films showed how the Santoor woman was mistaken to be very young till her daughter breaks the mirage by calling out 'Mummy'. The first few films showed her in a bookshop, at a wedding, in a bangle shop and then again at a wedding. The brand sales had responded very well to the new advertising that was clearly benefit-focused as against the advertising that was used in 1986-88 which was ingredient focused. Sales kept growing at a rapid pace right through 1989-1993. But then the brand hit a wall. Enter 1994, the brand growth had slowed to zero. What should the brand do?

One school of thought said that the advertising had to undergo major overhaul: the younger-looking skin promise is no longer valid; the 'Mummy' gimmick has run its course, etc. The other school of thought said that the promise and the 'Mummy' were all fine; we just had to relook at the way the stories were presented.

Indian women had started changing, if not in their day-to-day lives, at least in their desires and dreams. Our advertising was still shackled in the '80s thinking, went one argument. What if the Santoor woman started doing something that was different and in tune with the times? The copywriter at the agency wrote a script that showed the Santoor woman in an aerobics class and she is mistaken by one of her fellow participants to be a college student till the 'Mummy' happens. There were heated debates around this script. Will the middle-class woman understand the story? Will it alienate the core users of Santoor who were in love with its traditional ingredients? Will the story be credible?

The film was tested in the smaller towns of the core markets of Andhra Pradesh and Karnataka. To our delight, consumers gave a double thumbs up to the story. The film was made in 1994 and went on air in December that year. The brand sales once again started responding to advertising.

What were we doing wrong earlier? What did we do right this time?

Quite simply, we managed to capture the mood of the middle-class woman of the '90s and present it in a story that she could empathize with. No, millions of women were not going to aerobics classes, but they desired to look fit and young.

Santoor advertising right through the '90s, 2000s and 2010s has tried to reflect the mood of the changing Indian woman.

From being a pretty doll in a wedding admired by old ladies, the Santoor woman has gone on to learn aerobics, hula-hoop, play cricket, become a dress designer, fashion photographer, choreographer, television anchor and more. The promise of younger-looking skin has remained, so has the 'Mummy' gimmick. The brand has continued to grow and become the second largest soap brand in South/West India and the third largest soap brand in India, as we enter 2016.

AG Krishnamurthy, founder of Mudra, had this to say about the long-running Santoor campaign: 'When I do come across advertising like the Santoor campaign which stands out with grace over a long period of time, I think it deserves a round of applause. It is a very simple thought. It appeals to every human's desire to keep looking young ... it is special because with every new release they manage to add freshness and newness to the same old thought. I am sure that this courage to stay on the same course must be a collaborative effort of both client and agency'[1].

If Santoor managed to capture the changing Indian woman's aspirations, so have a few other brands.

Fair & Lovely from Hindustan Unilever had been launched in the mid-'80s as a fairness cream, and the promise was that a fair girl will attract a better husband. The early films even had the classic boy-meet-girl situations played out in millions of homes across India. This brand too decided that the format had run its course and now should start reflecting the changing aspirations of young women. Here is how they broke the shackles of marriage.

The father is upset that the family income is low because he has a daughter and not a son. Just then the daughter comes home from presumably yet another unsuccessful interview. She hears her father and is upset. She looks up the classifieds again where she chances upon an ad for an airhostess. She laments her dark complexion which she thinks will not let her land the job. Then she hears the ad for Fair and Lovely on television. The girl uses the brand and while the brand message is heard, she turns a few shades fairer. She lands the lucrative job. To celebrate the win she takes her parents for a cup of coffee to a five-star hotel. The father is thrilled and asks her if he can have a cup of coffee, addressing her as '*beta*' meaning 'son'. In some ways, this film that went on air in early 2000s changed the fortunes of this large successful brand. A product that 'got you fair to get married', became a brand that 'got you fair to get a job'. While there have been critics like Mouthshut.com who say that the ad is gender insensitive, the brand was reflecting a societal truth and cannot be blamed for that. In a sense, it helped move the debate in the right direction by taking the focus away from 'girls are only meant to get married' to 'girls can aspire for a job'. And one has to commend the brand and the agency, Lowe, for taking that stand. Could the film been better without the overt reference to the son? Maybe. But the use of the word, in my opinion, drove a knife into the heart of the society that tends to value a son over a daughter.

Let us move to yet another category, tea. Tata Tea was one of the most outstanding successes of its time. Launched in 1983, the brand got the nation singing its tune when it unleashed its *Anu Taazgi De De* film in 1996. The film, a copy of a famous song from an Amitabh Bachchan film, had Javed Jaffrey asking the model turned dancer Anuradha Aggarwal, '*Anu taazgi de de*' (Anu, give me freshness). The same brand decided to do a film where the woman protagonist had a bigger role than just to dance and sing paeans for Tata Tea. In the 2000s, the Tata Tea woman was ready to coach children to play better football, because her husband, the school coach, had a broken leg. And in 2010, the brand used its '*Jaago Re*' theme to show that the women of India are not ready to cow down to pressures. In one film, a young woman is at a government office and the smiling clerk is telling her that the job will get done if she gives him some *patte* – which means leaves and is also a colloquial term for currency notes. The young woman asks if 'small leaves' will do. To which the clerk says that small leaves are not very useful, some big leaves will be needed as well. To his surprise, she then takes out a pack of Tata Tea Premium tea leaves and places it on his table saying that the pack has a mix of well-selected small and big leaves.

Arvind Rajagopal, Professor of Media Studies at New York University, is a keen observer of societal trends as reflected through Indian media and advertising. He points out that the woman was always shown, in Indian advertising, as someone inside her house doing her duties, cooking, sewing and caring for the children and the in-laws. According to him, one of the earliest films that decided to show an upper-middle-class woman – short code: fair – woman actively engaging with the male market was the Surf Excel *Lalita ji* film made in 1984. The film shows a woman, played by Kavita Choudhary, actively arguing with the shopkeeper to get a better deal as she explains the virtues of her Surf detergent powder to an off-camera male. Alyque Padamsee, the adman behind the campaign, has said that the character, Lalita ji, was modelled after his own mother. He also goes on to say how Surf had to take on an emotional appeal to fight Nirma and this was possible only by presenting the Indian housewife as a hard-nosed bargain hunter who demanded value and not just a cheap price. Apparently, the film was almost rejected since it presented the Surf user as a 'rude and insulting woman'. But Alyque got Shunu Sen, the then marketing director of Hindustan Lever, to review the film once again and managed to sell the film to him, albeit adding a bit of humour and sarcasm. Maybe that helped to tone down the belligerence of Lalita ji. All said, the film did work for Surf and managed to help stem the wholesale migration of Surf users to Nirma. With Surf, the humble Indian housewife was finally given a voice to argue with a male character, even if only a lowly vegetable vendor[2]. It is interesting to compare the depiction of women in Indian advertising with what was happening in the UK, wonderfully captured by the BBC *Washes Whiter* commercials collection; even in the UK women were depicted in stereotypical roles of cooking and cleaning right though the post World War II period till around the '70s and '80s.

One of the earliest researchers who examined the presentation of women in advertising was Erving Goffman, often referred to as the 'most influential American Sociologist of the twentieth century'. He looked at the presentation of male and female characters through numerous lenses. How different are the scenes depicted in the advertisements versus real life and he concludes that one big trend was the presence of 'hyper-ritualization' wherein gender-defined roles are even more accentuated in advertisements, male appear more masculine, women more feminine in hyper-typical roles[3].

I was at a panel discussion in Mumbai in April 2015, where several panelists were discussing the role of a woman in Bollywood. Actress and producer, Nandita Das was at her vocal best explaining how dark skin was a big taboo in mainstream Bollywood movies even in the 2010s; and she pointed out how actresses turn fair as their career progresses. Anjum Rajabali, one of the most talented scriptwriters, also spoke about how mainstream Bollywood films were totally male centric. He explained that almost all the dialogues in most Hindi films, including his own, are spun around the male hero; if he is in the scene, he is speaking; if he is not in the scene, the female characters are speaking about him. He challenged the audience to go home and do this exercise. In fact, one of the divas of Indian films of the '70s and '80s, Sharmila Tagore has also mentioned that in her entire career, she played a working woman twice; as a singer in one film and a doctor in another. That was because she was the heroine. She adds that a working woman was always seen as a danger to society because she was a danger to the institution of marriage[4].

From the days of Anne French advertising hair removal in the 1950s in English language magazines, marketers have been trying to change their appeal to the Indian woman in many different ways.

When researching women in the '80s on their reasons for using cosmetics, Rediffusion unearthed a truth that will today sound obvious. Till then, the belief in advertising agencies, and in client organizations, was that women used cosmetics to look good and attract men. Well that was partly true, but women said that they also used cosmetics to feel good. This translated into a wonderful line for Lakme – the brand that had just moved to the agency – 'Looking good and feeling great with Lakme'. Cosmetic brands the world over have realized this truth and today tout many such promises such as 'You're worth it', 'Real beauty', 'Only the best will do', 'Beauty lies within' etc. Let us not for a minute think that all cosmetic brands have adopted the high ground of 'inner beauty', but all I was trying to present was that in advertising circles, there was much debate about understanding women a little better even as far back as 1980.

The opening up of the economy in the '90s saw the entry of global beauty brands that set out to redefine beauty. Sensing the opportunity, Pradeep Guha, then Director at Times Group decided to play up the Femina Miss India contest into a national celebration of beauty – and brains, if I may add. Not only were participants carefully selected from across the country with several regional rounds, Times also invested heavily in training them to make an impact on the global stage. Pradeep hit pay dirt in 1994 when two of his protégés, Sushmita Sen and Aishwarya Rai, won the two most prestigious beauty crowns, Miss Universe and Miss World. This double whammy did for the beauty pageant industry what Kapil Dev's World Cup victory did for one-day cricket. Young girls wanted to win beauty contests, beauty parlours started sprouting up across small town India and in came a slew of global cosmetic brands.

Gender stereotyping is an occupational hazard when it comes to brand marketing. For example, the Nirma advertising that gave Hindustan Lever sleepless nights in the '80s was but a portrayal of typical middle-class women who went by the names 'Hema, Rekha, Jaya and Sushma' – don't forget that the names were probably inspired by the ruling deities of that era: Hema Malini, Rekha and Jaya Bhaduri. All the washing was done by women; men and children just pranced around in that ad.

Ariel broke this stereotype in an ad, in the late '90s, where they showed a man washing clothes to avoid being scolded by his wife for spoiling the clothes she cares for. The brand has gone one step further in 2015, by unleashing the campaign #ShareTheLoad.

Whirlpool decided to gain favour with housewives by calling them 'homemakers'. The series of films done by the brand in the late '90s and 2000s showed how the woman of the house is in control while her husband creates chaos. The chant of the kids '*Mummy ka magic, chalega kya?*' became an anthem of sorts. Women across India even idolized the Whirlpool mom.

Come to 2005, when Hero was launching their scooter brand, Pleasure, they decided to position the brand for girls. Not only they did they avoid any reference to boy usage, they decided to cock a snook at boys saying, 'Why should boys have all the fun?'

As we have seen over the last few brand stories, Indian advertising has tried to capture the changing shades of the Indian woman. But please remember these are just exceptions that prove the rule. The average ad for a soap, toothpaste, shampoo, detergent, hair oil, tea, beverages, packaged foods, milk etc. still present Indian women in their classic gender-defined roles. To see if this is true, this author along with a team at FCB Ulka decided to pick about thirty television commercials, each of branded packaged goods, from 1987, 1997 and 2007. Of the thirty ads from each year studied, only three showed working women.

I would suspect the number would have increased in the last ten years, but here is a sobering thought: The rapid change of Indian women has also got Rama Bijapurkar to comment, 'Women in India have changed the most as a result of both social and economic changes of the past decade. They have changed far more than the men and more than "society" as a whole. Some of these changes are for the better [sic] and some have caused unimaginable backlashes, but overall women power has increased in the past two decades and we can expect it to keep rising in the future – it is now past the point of no return'[5].

Women have been the target audience for all household products as well as packaged foods and so they are also one of the most researched target segments. The joke in the market research industry is that in several cities of India there are prefixed 'focus-group women' who attend focus groups almost every day of the week. But that aside, companies and agencies have tried to understand the changing shades of Indian women for several decades.

FCB Ulka has done a series of studies to understand the changing Indian women. These studies called 'WomanMood' have been conducted every seven years. From 2001 to 2015, there have been three readings of urban Indian women – small town and big town. WomanMood I, done in 2001, showed that[6]:

- The woman sees herself as the 'Annapurna' – provider of the food in the house; but she is not too happy cooking
- The husband-wife gap has reduced but only on the surface
- Man is clearly the provider and the head of the household
- Kids are the focal point of the nuclear family
- Working women are aspirational, but they are evaluated by how good a homemaker they are
- Health largely meant cleanliness and family health

Now let us fast forward to 2015 and see what the new pillars are:
- The woman has become more assertive about her decisions for herself and the family
- She has converged roles and believes that all have to work together for the betterment of the family
- She believes that she has to work both for financial reasons as well as self-growth

- She needs her 'me' space and time with her friends
- Kids are to be given higher education to become independent

The changing dynamics of Indian women has also been reflected in the way the editorial content of women's magazines has changed. In FCB Ulka's study of Hindi magazines, it was found as against a predominance of articles on cooking, managing your husband, managing your in-laws in the last decade, today's Hindi magazines are reflecting the new aspirations of women – with extensive coverage about businesses you can start from home, courses you can do to improve yourself, basics of financial investments etc. It should be mentioned that the magazines are also covering hitherto forbidden topics like getting more pleasure out of lovemaking. Why not?

Television serials are also reflecting this new reality; saas-bahu serials are no longer occupying centre stage. Even serials about a woman trying to become an 'officer' have found acceptance. The stories are also reflecting the new reality of married life, with the husband trying to be a lot more understanding and accommodative than before.

In December 2014, the International Advertising Association in collaboration with Hansa Research released a study 'Changing Trends in Portrayal of Woman in Indian Advertising'. The researchers spoke to ninety-four professionals in marketing and advertising, and they concluded:

- Professionals endorsed that it is education and financial independence that is empowering women and giving them more decision-making powers
- Gender roles are less clearly defined today than what it was some years ago, but women still feel children are their responsibility
- Advertising today portrays women as more energetic, confident, multi-taskers than as 'homely'. Is there a new

stereotype of supermom emerging? In Asia, such moms got the nom de guerre of 'Tiger Moms'.
- Using women provocatively is seen as a way of grabbing attention now

There was still an overwhelming feeling that Indian advertising has not been able to portray the actual status of women in society. While there seems to be a change in the portrayal of women in advertising due to her newer roles, there still seems to be a lot of opportunity to explore various facets of women and showcase them in advertising.

> BEAUTIFUL HAIR: How come women in ads have such beautiful long hair? Well, that is the magic of – very expensive – computer graphics and what are known as 'hair extensions'.

Women of India are changing and the jury is unanimous in its verdict. And the general consensus is that the change has accelerated over the last twenty years. What has triggered this acceleration?

The first major driver would be the growing affluence and the consumption economy that has emerged in the last two decades. The desire to buy new things, provide better education to children, move into bigger homes, buy a bigger television set/car and take foreign vacations have all driven urban couples to re-examine the need for two earning members in the family. In addition, these have also redefined the role of the elder generation, who also want to partake in the largesse of a bigger family budget and are ready to play the role of a baby sitter.

The definition of a 'suitable girl' has changed and the Centre for Social Research, Delhi reports in *India Today*, 6 April 2015: 1960s meant pretty, virgin, accomplished; 1970s meant convent-educated, homely, smart, fair; 1980s meant tall, fair, slim and qualified; 1990s meant high earning, beautiful; 2000s meant compatible, working girl[7].

This in turn is creating new demographic seismic shifts. As mentioned in a previous chapter, the age of marriage is moving up steadily. According to 2001 census, about 24.9 per cent of girls in the age group fifteen to nineteen were married; the number dropped to 19.9 per cent in the 2011 census, a drop of a whopping 5.0 per cent in just one decade. In a similar vein, they are having children later, maybe trying their hand at working or getting better educated. *Livemint*, 18 March 2015, observes that these numbers vary across the states of India, depending on women's literacy and social customs[8].

If advertising is presenting women in new roles, Bollywood too seems to be waking up to this new India. From the days of *Mother India* where the mother was the ever suffering do-gooder, in the movie *Vicky Donor* she became a whisky-loving mom. An article in the *Sunday Guardian* dated 10 May 2015, lists the mother stereotypes as: righteous murderous ma; diving mother; hysterical mother; mistress mother; super-understanding mother; I-want-to-get-my-progeny-married mother; feminist ma; most ma imaginable; footloose ma; chief ma; kewl mom; step-mom; attention-seeking mom; reluctant mom; sad mom; hot mom etc[9].

The desire to do something on their own has driven women and mothers to enter new areas like start-ups. The new term 'Momtreprenuer' has been coined to describe them.

Is it that we have finally managed to give women their rightful place under the sun and vanquished the Manusmriti curse on women? Well, the numbers tell a different story. While women are 48.9 per cent of the population, they occupy only 11.4 per cent of the seats in the Lok Sabha, 10.8 per cent of the ministerial posts in the central government, 8.4 per cent of the supreme court and high court judges; 17.3 per cent of civil services; 5.8 per cent of the police; 10.3 per cent of small- and medium-enterprise owners; 2.7 per cent of CEOs/MDs. Thanks to government guidelines, around 42 per cent of gram panchayats are headed by women. Maybe the change that we are looking for will come from rural India (*Livemint*, 9 March 2015)[10].

The concept of 'Missing Women' was first used by Nobel Laureate Amartaya Sen. According to Sen, the ratio of men to women in developing countries like India and China were too low to be natural outcomes. He came up with a staggering statistic that more than a 100 million women were 'missing', many from India and China. The topic of gender discrimination in India is something that has been widely written about[11].

Now compare this with the developed world. Approximately, 70 per cent of all American females work outside the home. The comparative figure for India would be around 17 per cent. Women dominate higher education and in campuses across US and Canada, the ratio is 60:40 female[12].

The wheels of our nation need to turn fast and women can play a key role, as depicted by an ad by Taproot for the brand Nirma, released in the 2010s.

An ambulance is stuck in the mud. Its wheels keep turning throwing out dirt, but the ambulance does not move. All the car and auto owners are honking irritatedly, while bystanders look on. Then four women get out of their car, walk to the ambulance and push it out of the rut. Their clothes are now dirty, but the ambulance is on its way. As the women walk proudly to their cars, the Nirma jingle kicks in.

The moral of that story: our nation needs the powerful hands of women to get moving at a faster pace. And we need more advertising that celebrates those hands and minds.

Section Two
PRODUCTS

Only Vimal

It was the summer of 1973 and I was on a holiday break after a year at IIT Madras with its gruelling workshop sessions, two periodical tests per week and the stress of matching wits with really bright guys around me who seemed to know so much more than I did. It was now my time to shine and to show the Chennai Mylapore community that I had arrived. What better way than to walk into the citadel of Tam Bram society at Luz Mylapore, the Mylapore Club? I thought I should show off my new-found style quotient. In I walked wearing a pair of jeans and a kurta. I thought this was the latest thing that a cool chap – 'dude' was yet to be part of my lexicon – would wear on a lazy Saturday afternoon.

The older guys who were in the motorbike parking lot found my new attire rather odd. I heard some snide comments passed around: Where did this guy learn how to dress? It spoils the jeans … no, no, it spoils the kurta.

I learnt my lesson quickly. The next day, I walked in clad in a pair of jeans and a shirt – no comments were passed.

Interestingly, most top clubs across India have a 'no collar – no entry' rule for men. My kurta would have failed that rule, but I wonder if that rule will stay forever.

Wearing a pair of jeans in the '70s was a sign of style. A kurta on top and a pair of chappals to go with it was probably invented in the IITs as a statement of cool.

The ultimate style icon in the '70s was indeed Levi's jeans, and there was only one guy in IIT who owned a pair of genuine Levi's.

Joe Marie Swamy was my neighbour at IIT for four years; of which during the last three years, he was in room number 223 and I was in 224 at Godavari hostel. He had a huge drawing of the Mobius strip on his wall and we spent many hours staring at it wondering if it was two-dimensional or three-dimensional. Joe had a set of cousins in France and through them he got the album *Dark Side of the Moon* by the band Pink Floyd. The album released in March 1973 and found its way to Godavari hostel in July. For the next one year, it was played every evening, without fail for an ever-increasing breed of Pink Floyd fans. But Joe was also famous for another reason: he possessed a pair of genuine Levi's jeans! While the plebeians at IIT were stitching their own pair of jeans with locally available denim cloth, he had the real thing. I would imagine he wore his Levi's pretty much right through his stay at IIT. Joe went on to join BARC, Babha Atomic Research Centre, after completing his BTech. We lost him to cancer in the early '90s.

What is it with jeans and the young? In the US, blue jeans had initially stood for the Wild West and the adventurous spirit. In India, jeans used to connote a rich uncle in the US in addition to American culture, Coca-Cola and McDonalds.

No wonder the Hyderabad headquartered cigarette company, Vazir Sultan Tobacco, launched a cigarette in a package reminiscent of faded blue denims. They also decided to leverage the pulling power of their iconic cigarette brand, Charminar and rebrand it as, Charms. The company latched on to a popular phenomenon in colleges where students were reffering to Charminar as Charms, making it sound cool, unlike the auto-rickshawala's Charminar plain cigarettes. The new package became an instant success across the colleges of India.

Prof. Ramanuj Majumdar of IIMC has observed how the brand, which was launched in 1981-82, used its positioning and tag line – 'Charms is the spirit of freedom, Charms is the way you are!' – to become a brand success among the youth, possibly the biggest success in the cigarette market of that time[1]. The copywriter adman, Mohammad Khan, became a legend himself pretty much after that campaign!

Young Indian men were dressing differently and brands were latching on to this trend. If advertisers have it figured, can Bollywood be far behind?

Maine Pyar Kiya, the film which launched superstar Salman Khan's career in 1989 also had a role to play in the rise of the humble jeans. It was the first mainstream Hindi movie where the hero, Salman Khan, appeared almost throughout in a pair of blue jeans. Till then, jeans were a fringe phenomenon restricted to the EMT – English Medium Type: kids educated in English medium schools – youth in the big cities. With the endorsement of the hit Hindi film, jeans became a staple for every young Indian.

The American hat industry pretty much died in the late '60s. Between 1964 and 1970, the men's hat industry declined so rapidly that two of the leading hat manufacturers shut shop. According to the industry, it was a change in fashion precipitated by President John F Kennedy's hatless style[2]. Even the all American denim faced a challenge in the US after the release of the film *Rebel Without a Cause*, 1955, starring James Dean. Schools in some of the US states decided to ban jeans, fearing that their students too may start rebelling without a cause.

In India, around the time jeans were rising, the biggest male apparel brands to be advertised on television and cinema were Raymond, Bombay Dyeing, Gwalior, Dinesh and Digjam. Gwalior suitings had cricketer Mansoor Ali Khan, the Nawab of Pataudi, starring in their ads – his son, Saif Ali Khan, seems to have continued the Nawabi tradition by modelling for Siyaram in 2015. Dinesh had Sunil Gavaskar and Digjam for a period had actor-director Shekhar Kapur. Vimal from Reliance Industries entered the fray in the 1980s after the launch of Vimal sarees. Vimal suitings too used a whole gamut of stars including Ravi Shastri, Viv Richards etc. Vimal in many ways revolutionized fabric marketing not just with heavy decibel advertising. As AG Krishnamurthy recalls, Vimal took the concept of fashion shows to the length and breadth of India[3]. They opened large fabric showrooms and each showroom inauguration was with a huge fashion show, starring the top models of India. In 2014, this is being repeated by jewellery brands, many from Kerala, who are opening large showrooms and using Bollywood and Kerala film stars to gain attention during the inauguration. Not to be left behind, Bombay Dyeing too abandoned its long term model, Ardhendu Bose who had starred in the Bond-like magnum opus made in 1979, to use Karan Kapoor, film star Shashi Kapoor's son.

All the brands used to advertise suitings and showed models and stars in formal wear. While doing research for a suiting brand I was tasked to handle in the '80s – a brand called Caliber which is no more – I was piqued to know why brands touted 'suitings' when almost 80 per cent of the sale of fabric was to stitch trousers. Why not position a brand exclusively for 'trousers', even call it 'Trousering'. When speaking with consumers, it was found that a 'suit' was the pinnacle of good dressing. So if a brand was claiming it sold good suit material, it obviously

> GREEN SCREEN: Ever wondered how a film shows the hero in multiple locations, if all the time given by the actor is just eight hours. This is the magic of the green screen. Actors are shot against a green screen. The background scene, Goa or Kerala or Delhi, is then superimposed. All in a day's work, as they say.

included good trouser material. But the argument does not work the other way around. Something good enough for trousers may not cut the mustard or cloth, when it comes to a suit. So for decades, brands continued to spin the suitings story fully aware that consumers were only buying trouser length material.

In the '60s, '70s and '80s, men's suitings were a very large advertising category. They used to battle for the limited colour ads that magazines offered. Amidst all the suiting advertising, there were a few shirt brands too that were thriving.

Legend has it that the brand Zodiac was born because the company was stuck with surplus tie material that an importer in Europe did not take up. The founder's son, AY Noorani, had recounted how the business of launching silk neckties in a hot country like India was indeed serendipitious. The brand name Zodiac was selected from a set of computer-generated names simply because the name had so many possible linkages. What started as a necktie brand soon transformed into a shirt brand and, in fact, created its own long running brand mascot, in the form of the bearded Zodiac man. Kushwant Singh is said to have once observed that the Zodiac man is possibly the most recognized male model in India after the famous Air India Maharaja[4].

The Zodiac man was, in fact, the creative director at Ulka Kolkata, Dhanji Rana – the company had out of its graciousness provided Mr Rana with clothes and ties for his entire life.

In many ways, as veteran adman and market researcher Subhas Chakravarty observed, Zodiac created the tie culture in this hot and humid country.

Zodiac entered readymade shirts business soon after launching ties and they were joined by several other brands like Liberty, Park Avenue and, later, international brands like Van Heusen and Arrow. While many of the suiting brands have faded away, Raymond has continued to hold its sway on

Indian suiting consumers. From the legendary advertising done in the '70s which positioned Raymond as the 'Guide to the well-dressed man' written by Frank Simoes, the brand moved its positioning, along with the times in the '90s, to reflect the new ethos of the 'Complete Man'. Frank Simoes had a worthy rival in Kersy Katrak.

Mass Communication and Marketing, MCM for short, was a trailblazer agency. Set up in 1965 by Kersy Katrak and a team of professionals, it blew through the Indian advertising landscape like a tornado. The agency was a fountainhead of talent where many an Indian advertising star was born: Arun Kolatkar, Kiran Nagarkar, Mohammed Khan, Panna Jain, Ravi Gupta, Arun Nanda, Anil Kapoor, Ajit Balakrishnan, Arun Kale, Sudarshan Dheer, Avinash Godbole, Uma da Cunha to name a few. MCM created some landmark campaigns for clients including Swish Blades, WIMCO, IBM, Gold Spot, DCM, Ciba etc. Interestingly, one ad that they created gained notoriety even beyond the advertising world. This was an ad campaign done for DCM towels. The headline said, 'Towels so good you want to wear them'. The model was Maneka (Anand) Gandhi. Veteran journalist Vinod Mehta has observed that this was possibly Meneka Gandhi's first brush with fame: As an aspiring model, she had signed up with DCM to model for their entire campaign of towels that were launched in 1973. But her success on the modelling scene was short-lived. When she became engaged to Sanjay, MCM was summarily commanded to withdraw the campaign and clam up all possible remaining records of it[5]. The ad treated the big towel as a sari with great style.

In fact, sari advertising defined women dressing in the 'suitings' era. Legendary brands like Khatau got new wings with the growth of television in the '80s. Their advertising tag line, 'Some of the most beautiful moments in a woman's life are shared by Khatau', was well remembered though today it may be seen as not very popular. Vimal used a tag line which was also very popular, 'A woman expresses herself in many languages. Vimal is one of them' – again, written by the late Frank Simoes, one of the most respected admen of his time. While working on the Khatau campaign, the ad agency Rediffusion, which in those days was rather full of men, was at a loss to understand what could be 'beautiful moments' in a woman's life. Using qualitative research techniques, the research agency unearthed several moments recalled by women. One of them was immortalized into an ad; the ad showed a woman dressed in a bright yellow sari, heavily pregnant, relaxing in a rocking chair, bathed in the morning sunlight.

If Khatau, Vimal and Bombay Dyeing dominated the magazine and television advertising space, it was a relatively small brand from Surat that dominated the mind space of consumers. The brand Garden redefined saris by making it a fashion statement. The exquisite advertising, created by Arun Kale at Rediffusion, was the inspiration for many a sari campaign, including the ones by Vimal. To combat copycat brands, Garden changed its brand identity to Garden Vareli and the agency, Ambience and its creative director, Elsie Nanji, continued to create some memorable advertising in the 2000s.

The sari was what Indian women wore in advertisements right till the '90s. To prove or disprove this, I undertook an analysis of television advertising depicting women over the last thirty years.

For each decade, thirty consumer goods advertising was randomly selected. The ads covered a range of products such as soaps, detergents, milk food drinks, tea etc. Analysis revealed that in the mid-'80s and '90s, women were shown dressed in a sari more often than not, but the numbers dropped dramatically in the late 2000s – from over 65 per cent, the fall has been to 30 per cent. It is not as if Indian women are no longer wearing saris, just that advertising is no longer seeing a sari as an aspirational dressing style. As *Time* magazine reports in the article 'The Dying Art of the Sari', 25 June 2009: 'There is a general perception that you would consider a woman in Western formal wear more empowered than her more traditional counterparts'.[6] Even Shashi Tharoor, a most observant and articulate global citizen, has commented about the demise of the sari, 'Today's younger generation of Indian women seem to associate the garment with an earlier era, a more traditional time when women did not compete on equal terms in a man's world. Putting on pants, or a western woman's suit, or even desi leggings in the form of a salwar, strikes them as more modern. Freeing their legs to move more briskly than the sari permits is, it seems, a form of liberation; it removes a self-imposed handicap, releasing the wearer from all the cultural assumptions associated with the traditional attire'.[7]

There is possibly one other explanation behind why the sari has stopped occupying centre stage in advertising. In the '70s and '80s, sari was the one common form of dressing that cut across the whole country, north to south, east to west. The ways in which it was worn may have been somewhat different, but it was a sari all the same. But in the '90s and more so in the 2000s the salwar kameez has pushed the saree out of the ring and has become the dress the whole country wears. Go to any women's college anywhere in India, big to small town, you will rarely see a girl dressed in a sari. Even the 'half-sari' which used to be popular in some parts of South India has all but vanished and the salwar kameez has moved in. Interestingly, in some of the girls colleges in Tamil Nadu, students are advised to avoid jeans and T-shirt. I wonder how long that ban will last.

Advertising today celebrates the myriad styles in which men and women dress up. Suiting advertising is today restricted to a handful of brands like Raymond. The legendary brands like Bombay Dyeing, Binny, Vimal, Mafatlal, Digjam and Dinesh have all but disappeared. In their place have come readymade brands like Arrow, Zodiac – a true survivor if there is one – Louis Philippe, Peter England, Wills Lifestyle, John Player. All of them offer shirts, trousers and suits. In the casual wear space have come international brands like Lacoste, Benetton, Levis, Wrangler, Pepe etc. As you can see, there are really very few Indian brands in the list presented above.

While all companies were trying to ape the West, in came a brand that captured the imagination of the new-age male of India. A man who is western in outlook but Indian at heart. This brand, Manyavar, rode on the bandwagon of traditional wear for men, the sherwani and the kurta, to create a huge fan following. They took an industry which was retailer and tailor-driven, and made it into a branded game. Other brands like Raymond have followed but Manyawar has built a great momentum. So when you enter a formal party, you are bound to see men dressed in a formal suit, but you are also bound to see men dressed in a sherwani or a Nehru-style *bandhgala*. India's Prime Minister, Narendra Modi, too has set the style quotient high with his Modi kurtas, all reportedly custom-made exclusively by retailer Jade Blue in Ahmedabad. I won't be surprised if Jade Blue becomes a worthy rival to Manyavar pretty soon. Fabindia is yet another brand that seems to have been able to understand the ethos of the modern Indian man. Their range of cotton and silk kurtas can be seen at literature festivals and art shows as well as business school campuses around India.

So the Indian male has traversed the whole journey from the kurta-dhoti to the formal suit to the jeans and back to kurta; the Indian woman too has moved from the sari to the salwar kameez to trousers and jeans. Advertising has often captured this change and at times has facilitated the change.

Suitings and saris which were once very large advertisers are no longer such big spenders on television, though on print they do spend a significant amount. Even other categories of clothing, the jeans, shirts, etc are not big advertisers. So how do they build their brands?

The answer probably lies in how Raymond managed to survive, while others failed in the men's suitings business. Raymond's hidden weapon is its retail network. The Raymond Shop network started with a small corner shop in Ballard Estate, Mumbai around five decades ago. It has grown multifold with a dedicated team making it the largest retail store in the country having over 700 stores in prime locations, in over 200 cities in India. Their overseas network spans thirty-nine stores in fifteen-plus cities across the Middle East, Saudi Arabia, Sri Lanka and Bangladesh. The Raymond Shop retail chain occupies a space of more than 1.8 million square feet built-up area. None of the other suiting brands managed to build a retail network of the magnitude of Raymond. And this network became Raymond's captive media source, to attract and retain consumers.

With the rise of the department-store concept and shopping malls, apparel brands are spending enormous amounts of money building their presence in these locations. In a sense, what was spent on mass media advertising is now being spent on setting up and maintaining these high-street locations. It is true that even in the year 2014, more than 60 per cent of apparel sales come from small multi-brand outlets, but brands have realized that they need to invest in exclusive outlets as brand-building vehicles. International brands like Zara or Marks & Spencer do very little advertising; instead they use their stores as the medium of advertising.

Women across India have adopted the salwar kameez as their regular wear. In the years to come, the shirt-trouser ensemble too will grow in size and stature. It is, therefore, nice to see how in mid-2015 two women in Bangalore, Ahalya Mathan and Anju Maudgal Kadam, have launched the #100sareepact where they encourage women to wear saris for 100 days of the year and share the pictures on social media along with the hashtag and a note. The allure of easy-to-wear trousers is difficult to break, even with a buzzworthy sari pact, I think. In keeping with this trend, brands are becoming unisex. The biggest brands in men's ready-to-wear today also offer women's apparel. In addition, we are seeing the rise of designer brands such as Ritu Kumar and Anita Dongre who are going from prestige to masstige – a combination of mass appeal and prestige. These brands too are using retail presence to tom-tom their brand.

In the coming years, we will see the rise of more interesting types of apparel, both in design and appeal. For instance, Fabindia sells a quasi-ready-to-wear dhoti. There is a ready market for ready-to-wear sarees. Similarly, there are opportunities to unearth regional wear and take them national.

What women wear is changing rapidly across urban and even rural India. The humble churidar is giving way to leggings and jeans. The leggings and jeggings – jeans-like leggings – are giving way to palazzo pants and so on.

The superhit movie *Chennai Express* created a national phenomenon around the humble 'lungi' with its mega-hit song, 'Lungi Dance'. I am told that no wedding sangeet is complete without the bride party and bridegroom party doing the Lungi dance. I suppose there is an opportunity for a brand to launch ready-to-wear lungis, with a pre-stitched elastic top.

The humble lungi, which till a decade ago was the daily wear of peasants across India, may soon be on its way into tony clubs like the Delhi Gymkhana, as a lungi harem pant!

Bachche Toh Bachche, Baap Re Baap!

Dada was the name of a Dutch company that imported vanaspati ghee into India in the 1930s, as a cheap substitute to desi ghee or clarified butter. Ghee was an expensive food item in India and vanaspati, a type of vegetable shortening, was made by hydrogenating vegetable oil which made it mimic desi ghee in its characteristics. Lever Brothers, now Hindustan Unilever, has always been astute in its marketing ways. They set up a company called Hindustan Vanaspati Manufacturing Corporation in 1931. They bought the right to make Dada in India and they modified the name by adding 'L' from Lever Brothers to it, and thus in 1937, was born 'Dalda'.

Gerson da Cunha, the ad veteran who went on to become the CEO of Lintas – Levers International Advertising Services – which later became Lowe Lintas, recalls how Lever Brothers roped in Lintas to build the Dalda brand in the '50s and '60s. The brand had many battles to fight. First was the general perception that Dalda was an adulterated form of ghee, harmful for health. Second was the fear of the taste of food cooked in Dalda. Thirdly, there was the problem of non-availability of mass media. The company set up demonstration kitchens at grocery stores where consumers could see food being cooked with Dalda. Gerson recalls how Lintas was tasked to create print advertisements in over thirteen languages and each language version had to be created ground up, to reflect the cooking habits of that linguistic group. After many months of struggle it was Kersy Katrak who gave the breakthrough theme for Dalda – 'Mothers who care use Dalda'. Coming to Dalda, it went on to win the hearts and stomachs of Indians, till government regulation choked the profits from the brand and generic competition took over the category of vanaspati. Hindustan Lever then tried to transfer the brand equity of Dalda by launching refined groundnut oil under the same name – there was a rather cute ad for Dalda Refined Oil where the angry lady of the house admonishes her husband and son for eating samosas made for guests with the complaint *'Bachhe toh bachhe, baap re baap'*; the words continue to bring memories of delicious samosas – but HUL finally sold the brand to the American agri and food major, Bunge, in 2003 for reportedly ₹100 crores, says *Business Standard*, 5 March 2015[1].

In an article in the *Financial Express*, 9 June 2015, SL Rao, former Director-General NCAER, writes about the problems being faced by Maggi in mid-2015 and recounts that Dalda had many worse battles to face; Prakash Tandon, the first Indian Chairman of Hindustan Lever had mentioned to Dr Rao that *Harijan*, a paper founded by Mahatma Gandhi, had even written that you could go blind by eating food cooked with Dalda – based on a study done on mice[2].

Cooking mediums or cooking oils are the second-most expensive food item in the family food budget – the most expensive being milk, more on that later. And marketers from the days of Dalda in the '30s have been trying to change the cooking habits of Indians.

Saffola started the concept of healthy oil in 1960s and Sundrop joined the party in 1989. While Saffola was an expensive brand that used kardi oil and positioned the brand as the recommended choice for unhealthy heart patients, Sundrop which was launched as a refined sunflower oil brand was positioned as a 'Healthy Oil for Healthy People'.

Right through the '90s and 2000s, the battle was not so much between brands as between branded packaged oils and 'loose' oils. Given the price sensitivity of the Indian housewives, the branded players could not command a premium against the loose-oil sellers, to the extent that companies like ITC and HUL exited the cooking oil space. Marico's Saffola stayed the course of a more serious 'healthy' oil and is probably the most profitable cooking oil brand in India in the 2010s. Till date the brand continues to be positioned as *'Dil ka high science'* and their latest ad touts 'Not just 1 but 8-way care'. Adani Wilmar is the largest seller of cooking oils now, with their brand Fortune. In order to appeal to the bottom and middle of the pyramid, Fortune has focused on the cheapest oil, rice bran, and has built a national presence.

As Indian taste buds and health awareness evolve, we will see the growth of other types of oils. For example, olive oil has seen acceptance in the metro cities and imports of olive oil has grown at a compounded rate of 60 per cent over the period 2010 to 2013, to 11,916 tons according to *Economic Times*, 23 June 2012[3].

Here is a question? Which refined oil contains the least amount of cholesterol? We posed this question to a group of opinion-leader women in a focus group discussion we conducted in 1999. There was serious argument about the benefits of kardi oil vs groundnut oil vs sunflower oil. We then explained that all refined oils have zero cholesterol. The ladies refused to believe us. I suspect with the overload of food information, consumers, even today, have vague notions of what is healthy and what is not. And there is a new report every day that disproves something we held as true yesterday. Ghee is bad for you, no it is good for you. Olive oil is good for you, no there are a few things bad about it as well. And so on. Thanks to urbanization and the spread of mass media, I suspect, over the coming decade, we will see cooking oil purchase to fully transition to branded packaged forms. The loose oil merchant of yore will soon disappear. As household food budgets increase, the penny pinching by housewives with respect to cooking oils will also go away.

The story about converting Indian consumers from a commodity mindset to brand mindset is an ongoing saga. Interestingly, retail surveys differentiate between general merchants and grocers as follows: grocers sell grain out of open gunny bags; general merchants don't. The exception is organized retail players like Food Bazaar who too sell grains out of open bags. Moving from oil to grains.

It is late evening, the Tata Sierra mini truck screeches to a halt in front of what appears to be a beautiful farmhouse. The man storms inside, slamming the door shut and sits down at the dining table for his dinner. His wife, dressed in a golden yellow sari, is busy cooking in their open-plan kitchen. Their daughter is helping her mom. The man starts grumbling in Hindi that these Captain Cook atta company folks are making such heavy demands on us farmers. Selling wheat to that company is a herculean task. They want the grains to be of uniform size and shape. The grains should be so full of goodness that if you take the grains in your hand and shake it should sound perfect. So much trouble that it appears that they are not buying grain but gold. The smart wife responds, 'If they don't buy so carefully, how will the atta they make be great. And look at you, for the first time eating so many rotis!' The husband is shocked, 'Captain Cook! You too are using Captain Cook?' The wife and the daughter giggle. The husband has the last word when he adds, 'Give me one more roti!'

Captain Cook Atta, launched in the mid-'90s was the first attempt by a company to brand and advertise a food staple, atta or flour. The ad mentioned above, created by FCB Ulka and directed by Deven Khote, won hearts around India when it broke. But there were enough detractors as well. One ad critic wrote – How can they show a farmer's wife using packaged flour? Which country were they thinking they were in?

> FOOD STYLISTS: Food photography cannot start without a food stylist. It is the stylist who works with the cameraman or Director of Photography to create the magic. Adding a little fig, a mint leaf or an olive, they create poetry with food.

The idea of using a farmer's wife was intentional, since they would probably be the last to adopt a branded product. The critic was proven wrong, the brand was a success attracting competition from large corporates such as Unilever Annapurna and ITC Aashirvaad. And in the late '90s, the brand was sold by the original promoter, Nitish Jain of DCW Home Products, to Best Foods of USA.

Packaged flour has seen good growth in the 2010s, and ITC with its backward-integrated process has been able to build Aashirvaad into a mega brand. Interestingly, branded packaged atta has found ready acceptance in South India where atta is not the staple form of consumption. The North Indian consumer who is quite an expert in selecting the right grain and getting it ground at the nearby *chakki* is yet to fully give up her old habits.

Indian food habits are among the most difficult to change and marketers have over the last fifty-plus years been trying to chip away food habits and attitudes that have been deeply ingrained in the Indian psyche for the last two millennia.

Amul with a total turnover in excess of ₹20,000 crores is indeed the biggest food brand in India. India was a milk deficit country in the sixties and the government used to import milk powder from the developed world. But today, India is self-sufficient in milk, made possible thanks to the cooperative movement pioneered by the Gujarat Co-Operative Milk Marketing Federation and its brand Amul. The father of the White Revolution, Dr Verghese Kurien arrived in Anand in Gujarat in 1949 as a government employee to manage a dairy, but ended up helping farmers repair their machinery to revolutionize the Indian dairy sector by scripting Operation Flood, a cooperative movement that turned India into one of the world's largest producers of milk. The brand Amul was an acronym for Anand Milk Union Ltd but it also stood for the word 'amulya' meaning rare in Sanskrit. Not only was the choice of the brand name Indian, but Dr Kurien empowered his advertising partners to create advertising that broke through the clutter. Sylvester daCunha – and now his son Rahul daCunha – created the Amul girl dressed in a polka-dotted dress, and has continued to poke fun at the happenings in modern-day India. The agency FCB Ulka has worked with Amul to create the 'Taste of India' advertising campaigns as well as the 'Doodh doodh' milk campaign, all under the watchful eyes of Dr Kurien and now RS Sodhi.

Amul butter's outdoor campaign is a unique advertising experiment in many ways. The agency scans the daily news, picks a hot topic, creates the ad and puts its up as an outdoor ad. In fact, Amul's marketing team approves of the copy and design post facto. This was a tradition set up by Dr Kurien, who believed that ad agencies are but extended arms of the marketing company and should be fully empowered and trusted. It continues to be practised till date. I don't think there is any other brand anywhere in the world that has this level of trust with its marketing communication partners. From creating just one new creative every two weeks and putting it up across key cities, Rahul daCunha tells me that the first set of Amul hoarding designs were all rooted in the product promise of 'Utterly butterly delicious'. It was during the horse racing season in the 1960s that Rahul's father,

Sylvester daCunha had a brainwave of making the Amul butter hoardings topical. The first one showed the cute Amul girl riding a horse with the caption 'Thoroughbread', and thus was born the topical Amul butter hoardings. Today Rahul is attempting to put up two or even three new creatives a week; these are amplified through newspaper releases, making this campaign seem one of the biggest campaigns in corporate India. His books on old Amul hoardings are veritable treasure troves of how the brand has reflected the changing dynamics of the Indian society, the happiness of a nation, its sorrow, its crimes, its misdemeanors, and of course its foibles, all done with tongue firmly in cheek[4].

Thanks to the efforts of the cooperative movement, the price of milk did not shoot up. And thanks to smart marketing campaigns, Indians were encouraged to move from unbranded to branded packaged milk products. GCMMF managed to balance its role of helping milk farmers and the middle-class housewife, rather well, over the last four decades or more.

As a result of these efforts, milk consumption has moved up across the country and at the same time prices have not kept pace with inflation.

One well-documented fact is how Dr Kurien got his dairy technologists to try and make milk powder from buffalo milk, which global experts had said was not possible. Today a large portion of milk consumed by Indians, both powder and liquid is really derived from buffalo milk. A new report in *Business Standard*, 19 March 2015, said that Amul is now attempting to process camel milk; apparently camel milk is high in insulin content and hence is considered a healthy choice for diabetics[5]. Yet another report in *NewAge*, 18 March 2015 that quotes Agence France-Presse, said that a chewy cheese made by generations of yak breeders in Nepal has become an unexpected hit overseas, as a dog treat[6]. Known as churpi, the dried cheese made from churned yaks milk and cow's milk has long been a popular snack in Nepal.

Just as we saw in the case of cooking oils, I am sure in the coming years we will see the milk market get segmented with various types of milk. Already in Mumbai, there are brands that are offering organically produced cow's milk. Maybe they will offer camel and yak milk soon.

So have marketers managed to dramatically change the average Indian's food habits?

> SHOOTING ICE CREAM: How to shoot ice cream under powerful lights? Wouldn't it all melt away? Not if it is really mashed potatoes masquerading as ice cream. And the cream on top may even be shaving foam. So don't ever eat anything at a food photo or film shoot.

One of the most widely remembered ad that tried to change food habits was the National Egg Coordination Committee (NECC) campaign; Dr BV Rao founded Venkateshwara Hatcheries – now VH Group – in 1970 and went about revolutionizing the way eggs were produced. He was also a visionary who knew that food habits had to change to absorb the production of eggs. He roped in the ad agency Enterprise, founded by copywriter/creative director Mohammed Khan, to develop an egg promotion campaign, to be released under the aegis of NECC. This film, set to a wonderful tune, made eating an egg a day – *Roz khao ande* – fun and fashionable. '*Sunday ho ya Monday, roz khao ande*' (Sunday or Monday, have an egg everyday) went the hit anthem. Created by Enterprise and the strategic handiwork of Anand Halve, the egg campaign continues till date in a mutated form, but the '*Roz khao ande*' remains[7].

Consumer expert and social commentator, Santosh Desai has developed an interesting way of explaining the Indain food palate. He says that the thali is an interesting way to eat; the idea here is to eat the entire meal all at once; no waiting, no guessing about what lay ahead. Santosh observes that the thali is a wardrobe full of food; one gets to feast one's eyes and tongue on all that one eats simultaneously. He has observed that in food marketing, the thali is the key to the narrative. It is easiest to change habits with respect to the margins of the thali; so branded pickles and papads are easier to sell than say branded chappatis and sabjis[8].

Lijjat papad unlocked the 'edge of the thali' by going to mass media with its advertising during the Doordarshan days. Till date the funny hand puppet shouting 'Lijjat papad' is remembered by those of us who were brought up on *Chitrahaar* and *Chayageet*.

Market and consumer strategy expert, Rama Bijapurkar laments how no one has managed to offer the time-starved Indian upper middle-class housewife a ready-to-eat chapatti option[9]. Going by the 'thali theory', selling ready-to-heat-and-eat chapattis will be rather tough.

If we were to speak of one food item that is not strictly of Indian origin but can be found in every Indian home, we will have to speak of biscuits. Though biscuits came to India through the British and was popularized through the local bakeries, no other brand is synonymous to biscuits as Parle G. Parle Gluco was born in 1939, in the beginning of World War II. In fact, Parle was asked to manufacture military-grade biscuits for British soldiers but it ensured that it could manufacture nutritious biscuits for the masses as well. Parle Gluco came under attack in the '60s and '70s from numerous clones as well as the mighty Britannia Glucose – originally Glaxo Biscuits. Britannia even used Gabbar Singh from *Sholay* to endorse it. In a bold move, the brand Parle Gluco rebranded itself as Parle G with an illustration of a little girl, done by Everest Advertising. The company pioneered small packs to woo consumers away from loose biscuits sold in jars. The company invested in advertising on television and played on the new brand name Parle G and the Hindi suffix 'ji' – the common way to address a person respectfuly. The earliest ad was probably the one featuring two kids playing with their grandfather singing, '*Hum ko pata hai ji, Aap ko pata hai ji, Sab ko pata hai ji ... Swad bhare, shakti bhare, barso se,* Parle G' (We know it, you know it, everyone knows it ... Tasty, healthy Parle G). The advertisement not only established the new brand, but also made a strong social connect with the old and new generation enjoying a new brand of biscuits. Around the same time, Dabur Chyawanprash used a grandfather and a grandson playing badminton.

While biscuits went on to become a national favourite, breads continued to be niche product. Modern even used radio very effectively in the '60s and '70s with the 'Mummy Mummy Modern Bread' spot. Unfortunately, the government-owned company went into deep red and had to be sold to Hindustan Unilever. HUL on their part did try leverage the brand into biscuits and other products, but finally gave up.

Nestle did not succeed with its first Maggi product, Subhas Chakravarty, the ad and market research guru, once told me. In fact, Maggi soup cubes failed, but when they launched their brand of instant noodles 'Maggi 2-Minute Noodles' in 1982 and positioned it as a snack for the family – they hit pay dirt, making a product till then alien to the Indian palate an everyday meal and snack item. The most widely-remembered advertisement has two kids running home after school, shouting '*Bhook lagi hai, Mummy*'; the mother says 'Two minutes' and makes them a delicious plate of Maggi 2-minute noodles. The brand was positioned as 'Fast to cook, good to eat'. The brand, thanks to its powerful television advertising aimed at kids and moms, attractive pricing and simple instructions, went on to capture the imagination of a whole nation. Maggi noodles must have spurred the Indian chinese restaurant movement. But in mid-2015, Maggi became mired in a major controversy regarding its ingredients and package declaration leading to a nationwide withdrawal of the product. I am happy to report that as the year 2015 wound to a close, mothers and students around the country had reasons to rejoice as Maggi made a comeback.

If we look back at the thali theory, we will see how brands like Parle G and Maggi managed to sidestep the mighty thali and go for the snack-break market and with tremendous success.

Taking a leaf out of the Maggi story, marketers of oats have managed to build a ₹200-crore business in a few years leading up to 2015 by tailoring oats as a snack for the Indian palate. Saffola Masala Oats offers a snack that claims to be 'Hot, spicy and delicious. And it helps keep you in shape'. The brand even has a flash that says it is 'Ready in 3 minutes'.

In the 2000s, there has been yet another food revolution brewing in big city India. Driven by brands like Dominos, pizza is now becoming the most recognized foreign food item after noodles. Bollywood movie *3 Idiots* even makes a comment about how in our country a pizza promises delivery in thirty minutes, while an ambulance can take two hours to arrive. McDonalds has also created a burger mania among children. Modern-day shopping malls have become new dining destinations for middle-class India. Private equity firms are eyeing this space and are investing heavily in what is known as QSRs or quick-service restaurants. For example, Mumbai's humble vada pav has a national chain, Goli Vada Pav, that is now present in over forty cities.

Food habits will continue to evolve as we see more and more middle-class women enter the work force. Many myths will get dispelled. For example, there is this myth

> FOOD PHOTOGRAPHY: Shooting food calls for a lot of careful planning and execution. More importantly, food looks tasty when it is shot in extreme slow motion. As against twenty-four or twenty-five frames per second, food is often shot at 1000 frames per second. Add to this the extreme close-up shot and you will feel like licking the television screen.

that Indians are all vegetarian. But according to reports – *Outlook*, 10 December 2007 – 80 per cent of all South Indians are non-vegetarian and the number is 44 per cent for North Indians[10]. Are we going to become more and more non-vegetarian? Even hard-core vegetarians like the Birlas had to break out of the age-old custom of serving only vegetarian food at the company dining rooms when the group actively embraced globalization[11].

While Indians are changing, they are not changing fast enough for the ready-to-eat brands; they are yet to accept something that can be put into a microwave and plonked on the dining table in three minutes – at least not for a main meal – like dinner. Marketers are figuring how to break this barrier. What if you leave the last bit of cooking to the homemaker? What if you give ten options to garnish the dish? There are many more such ideas to be explored and advertised in the coming years. Television and digital media will play a big role in this transformation, both in the adoption of ready-to-eat foods as well as improving the image of cooking as a profession, art and science. The launch of cookery shows on general entertainment channels like Star Plus and cookery channels like Zee Khana Khazana are doing their bit to spread the joy of cooking and experimenting. At the Jaipur Literature Festival in 2015, I was amazed to see the hoard of young men and women chasing celebrity chef Vikas Khanna. *Economist*, 27 June 2015, reports that programmes like *Mr Paek's Home Cooking* is helping the relatively cooking-shy South Korean men to take up cooking[12]. I suspect, even in India there are many million young men and women who are trying their hand at cooking after seeing interesting cookery shows. My colleague's fourteen-year-old son can reportedly produce a three-course continental meal in less than an hour. And he likes doing it. I suspect he is going to be much in demand among the girls of his generation wherever he chooses to live.

Kraft's Macaroni & Cheese is the single-most popular packaged food item in the US, a staple in homes of working couples with kids, accounting for one dinner every week. We are yet to see a brand becoming a dinner staple in India. But the coming decade will see the emergence of packaged rotis and packaged veggie dishes among others. Farmers of India will be able to get a better price from more amenable new Captain Cook brands. And the mighty citadel, the centre of the thali, will finally fall.

Hamara Bajaj, Hamara Bajaj

The crown for the most popular advertising by an Indian automotive brand, car and two-wheeler, would undoubtedly go to the Bajaj scooter film *Hamara Bajaj*, created by Lintas. This was the year 1989. The country was heading towards a crisis and the government was trying its best to prop up the morale of the country. The famous 'Mile sur mera tumhara' song had been unveiled on Independence day, 1988. The time was indeed ripe for a brand to appropriate the national aspirations and desires. Which better brand than the brand that was the cynosure of every middle-class Indian, the Bajaj scooter.

During the '70s and '80s, a scooter was the most prized possession of every Indian. I remember my father buying a new Lambretta scooter and booking his next one the day he took delivery of the new one. There are stories about a young father of a three-year-old girl booking a Bajaj scooter for his to be son-in-law; planning ahead for more than a decade and a half. There were also schemes for NRIs to get a Bajaj Chetak scooter under a special dollar payment offer. My father got his first Bajaj Chetak scooter by cajoling my cousin who was returning to India from Malaysia!

In this milieu, it was appropriate for Bajaj to send out a message about the brand being in the heart of every Indian. The film, a montage of everyday use of the scooter, cutting across religious groups, regional differences, dress cultures, urban and rural etc., was a great hit with the masses. The jingle spoke about how the scooter was a part of India, today and tomorrow, a strong India's strong picture, our very own Bajaj. If you sit and counted the number of situations and people you will run out of fingers. I could spot a Parsi, a Muslim, a Sikh, a villager, an urban father, a running coach, a young lady and even a dog taking a ride on the Bajaj scooter.

Thanks to the spread of television and blockbuster programmes such as *Ramayana* and *Mahabharat*, the jingle was on everyone's lips. The company even managed to get a stay order from the court preventing a film production company in 2013 from using the title 'Hamara Bajaj'; almost twenty-five years after the film first aired. That was the power of the jingle and the film. In advertising parlance, this genre of advertising where a brand is shown being used across the country, in different situations is known as the 'Mera Brand Mahan – Hamara Bajaj' type film, immortalized by the ad agency Lowe Lintas.

Why was Bajaj prompted into advertising, if their scooters were still in waiting list?

For an answer, one has to drive from Pune, where Bajaj was being manufactured, to Delhi, the headquarters of the company that was set to dethrone Bajaj – Hero Honda.

RL Ravichandran, the then marketing head at Bajaj, made an interesting observation at the Pan IIT Conference at Delhi. He spoke about the challenges faced by Bajaj and how they were overcoming it. He mentioned that the day Hero Honda was launched, June 1984 to be precise, and started tom-toming fuel efficiency with its iconic campaign 'Fill it, shut it, forget it' – created by FCB Ulka Delhi, by the way – he realized that the scooter category's dominance may not last forever. He explained that scooters and motorcycles had co-existed in the Indian market for decades. In fact, motorcycles like Enfield Bullet even had iconic advertising

– '*Bullet meri jaan, manzilon ka nishan*' (The Bullet is my life, the aim of my destinations) made by film-maker Prahlad Kakkar for the agency Sistas (incidentally Prahlad used to ride a Bullet in the mid-'80s). The Bullet had also been featured in superhit movies like *Sholay* in the song 'Yeh dosti' featuring Dharmendra and Amitabh Bachchan. New-age Japanese motorcycles like Yamaha had also entered the market. But Bajaj scooters remained the all-time favourite. The reason: it made a sensible choice in terms of safety, fuel efficiency, maintenance etc. The motorcycle was always seen as a young man's vehicle, not meant for a family man.

Here comes Hero Honda with its model CD 100 claiming a fuel efficiency of eighty kilometres per litre as against other motorcycles and even scooters that offered 30 kmpl. In addition, the CD 100 shied away from any macho imagery, clearly signalling to the middle-class married man to get off his scooter and get on to a motorbike.

The story of motorbike vs scooter in the Indian market has many twists and turns and you could write a potboiler just by tracing the many characters and their moves, but suffice it to say that Bajaj decided to exit the scooter business after losing the fight to modern motorbikes. However, after the launch of Honda's gearless scooter Activa, scooters became the fastest-growing segment in the Indian two-wheeler market in the year 2013-14, rising to become almost one-third of the total market[1]. I am sure Bajaj is wondering that '*Hamara scooter, hamara na raha*' (Our scooter did not stay ours alone). In addition to Honda, all other players too have scooter offerings including Hero, Suzuki, TVS, Mahindra, Piagio; all except Bajaj.

The Indian's journey from the humble cycle to the scooter to the motorbike was, in fact, facilitated by the success of yet another category of two-wheelers, the moped. Kinetic launched its first moped in 1972 and even had iconic advertising '*Chal meri Luna*' in the mid-'80s. TVS too launched a moped, TVS 50. Bajaj had Bajaj Sunny. Enfield launched a 32cc mini-moped Mofa that did not require a driving license.

The rise of Bajaj and later of Hero Honda, rang a death knell of the moped. Except for Tamil Nadu, where TVS 50 continues to sell – and even had some wonderful advertising to support it with *'Namma ooru vandi, TVS 50'* (The vehicle of our land, TVS 50) – the moped category has virtually disappeared. So while cycles have continued to flourish, scooters have had a second coming; even the mighty Enfield, powered by some real smart marketing communication piloted by V Sunil of Wieden & Kennedy and RL Ravichandran – formerly with Bajaj – has risen from the ashes. Mahindra Group which bought Kinetic's scooter operations may be wondering if they should have bid for Enfield when it was a possible acquisition target. But before we lament the demise of the humble mopeds, don't be too surprised if a smart company is able to create an Indian 'frugally-engineered' moped that can deliver 150 kmpl efficiency or maybe an electrically-powered moped!

The single biggest event in the Indian auto sector was probably the rolling out of the first Maruti 800 on 14 December 1983, which would have been the thirty-seventh birthday of Sanjay Gandhi – Indira Gandhi's son who died in a plane crash before his dream of the 'people's car' was realized – from the Gurgaon factory. The first Maruti 800 was bought by an Air India employee, Harpal Singh. The car had an order backlog running for many years.

Maruti 800 dramatically changed the landscape of the Indian automotive industry. It was also the first public sector undertaking – albeit a joint venture with Suzuki Corporation of Japan – to sport a god's name, Maruti, the name of the mighty Hanuman. In the '70s, the total number of cars sold in India was around 32,000 units. The two marques that ruled the roost were the Ambassador from Hindustan Motors and Padmini from Premier Automobiles. These brands in a great year managed to hit a sales number of 37,000 – Padmini in 1987 – and 24,000 for the Ambassador in mid-'70s; but in just a few years, Maruti changed the dynamics of the Indian auto industry. When competition entered the market in the '90s, Maruti upped the ante with a great service network to dispel the notion that it is difficult to service a car that has Japanese genes.

> SYSTEM WORK: The computer has turned the fine art of a car shoot into a technical challenge. Gone are the days when cars were carted to distant locations to get fantastic still shots with the sun gleaming on the windscreen. Now the car is created on a system and superimposed on to the background.

The most famous Maruti ad featured two young men driving in the high mountains. They have no idea where they are when they spot a young lad. They call out to him, 'Kancha, is there any place where we can eat?' Kancha, meaning a young boy in Nepali, shakes his head. They then ask him, 'Is there any place where we stay the night?' The answer again is a 'No'. Then, against all odds, they ask him, 'Is there a Maruti service station here?' To their utter surprise, he nods 'Yes'. And the signboard says 'Zozilla Engineering Works – Maruti Service Station'. When I was discussing this film with Arun Malhotra, who used to be with Maruti, he had an interesting story to tell. The film had been made and everyone loved the film. But they had their Japanese bosses visiting who when shown the film, to their utter dismay, thought the film made a ridiculous over-claim. Winning their approval was a challenge. The bosses were soon at a dealer conference in Punjab, and Arun in his wisdom decided to show the dealers the 'Kancha' film, to see what they may say. To his delight, the dealers stood up as one and gave the film a standing ovation. The Japanese bosses were won over and the film soon went on air and won the hearts of millions of Indians. As an aside, Zozilla Engineering Works is a Maruti-authorized service station located in Kargil, a place which became famous many years later.

Maruti understood the psyche of the Indian auto consumer and has time and again reinforced the value-conscious Indian car buyer's belief that Maruti spells value-for-money. In a fitting rebuttal to the Hero Honda 'Fill it, shut it, forget it' claim, they came out with a film which has a young sardar boy playing with a toy Maruti car and he goes around the house continuously making a 'bhrrrrr' sound. His dad, a burly Sikh, finally gets irritated and tells him, *'Oye chote, bas kar yaar'* (Stop it, little one); to which the young kid replies, *'Papa ki kara, petrol khatam nahin hunda!'* (What to do, Dad, the petrol doesn't get over at all). Maruti time and again has managed to hit the fuel efficiency button with their advertising. In 2010, they came out with a series of ads that used the phrase *'Kitna deti hai'* (How much does it give?) meaning how many kilometres per litre does the vehicle allow. This term is used by all car buyers when considering fuel efficiency. The first in the series of films they rolled out has the value-conscious Indian consumer asking a space station director, *'Kitna deti hai?'* for the space shuttle on display. If we were to dive deeper into the origin of this exact turn of phrase, you may find that this is the exact phrase used between a buyer and a seller of a cow – 'how much milk does the cow give?' The highly focused value-for-money advertising by Rediffusion and then later carried on by Prasad Subramaniam of Capital Advertising helped build the Maruti citadel.

I was closely involved with the brand that first threatened Maruti's dominance of the Indian small car market. The brand, Tata Indica. The year 1999. After a round of highly-targeted print advertising – there was one which said, '50 CC Moped. 100 CC Motorbike. 800 CC Car. Time you can ask for more' – we were thrilled with the first ad film we had made for Tata Indica and were hoping that the client too would love it. But there was a twist in the tale and that taught me a useful lesson.

The film began with a young lady looking for a lift since her fancy car had broken down. She waves down a car, a brand new Tata Indica, driven by our young hero. She knocks on his window – air-conditioned car, you see. He lowers the window and she politely asks 'Lift?' The young man obliges, the pretty lady gets into the car, looks around and says, 'Nice car.' The man is pleased as a punch, smiles and starts driving as an English pop song starts. The film then runs like a fantasy dream of the young man. He is dating the pretty girl, takes out for a boat ride, a candle-lit dinner, throws a bouquet to her balcony (standing on top of the sturdy Indica), her father chases him with a gun, he escapes, then asks for her hand in marriage, they have a pretty church wedding, drive off in the Indica, they have their first child, a second one too is born, soon they have their two children, the mother-in-law and a big dog in the car, all singing loudly when he stops the car; he cannot take it anymore. At this stage, the film rapidly rewinds to the 'knock on the window' scene. The film ends with the car driving off and the tag line appears 'More dreams per car – Tata Indica'.

Did he give her a lift or did he not? The film-makers had shot two endings and wanted to have the car driving off with the girl on the road – the young man chickens out of a life of marital bliss and noise. The other ending just shows the car driving off; the viewer was left to figure out what really happened.

The agency team was keen that the film should have an open ending. The film-makers were keen that no young man will want marriage after hearing the cacophony of two kids, a dog and a loud mother-in-law.

While the agency has the final say in these matters, it was felt that the film-makers' views should also be presented to the client.

When the two films were shown to the client, he picked the agency version as his choice. And he explained that as the first Indian car, the brand has to present good values even in its advertising; the Indica owner will not leave a damsel in distress in the middle of nowhere without helping her.

The film went on to run for a few months and was widely appreciated.

> **Shooting Cars:** Car ad film shoots are a big affair. The innocent shot of the side of the car with the road showing may in fact require special rigs and fixtures. And the car has to be shot from an angle where it looks its sexiest. So it needs to sit well, hug the road when it moves. Cement bags inside the car help achieve some of that road hugging effect. The rest, the camera work has to take care of.

It is true that for many years Maruti 800 defined the automotive industry in India and this in turn created some exciting brand building opportunities. The Chennai-based tyre company MRF took tyre advertising to a new level by launching MRF Zigma tyres through a ninety-second film that was shot at enormous cost featuring a spaceship and special effects that were, pun intended, alien to the country then. Alyque Padamsee of Lintas is full of respect as he recalls the passion of the late Ravi Mammen in brand building and his vision for making MRF the most popular tyre brand in the country[2].

The success of Maruti in tapping the value mindset has also been its weakness – Indians do not consider Maruti as an aspirational badge – which it is successfully addressing in the 2010s with the launch of premium cars and even a premium dealership chain. In the Auto Mood studies done by FCB Ulka in the years 2000 and 2007, the car has undergone a significant image change in the minds of the auto buyer. A car is no longer just a transporter of human bodies but of egos. And badges like Honda are seen as more aspirational.

Cars and two-wheelers are among the most heavily advertised

categories around the world. In India, too they are emerging as big advertisers over the last fifteen years. In the car or four-wheeler category, new segments have emerged and are growing rapidly. Mahindra should be credited for seeing the opportunity that India offers for rugged SUVs. Their campaign for Scorpio, crafted by Interface Communication was a landmark for that segment. The first ad for the SUV took a shot at the sedan class with the tag line, 'Cars will now suffer from low self-esteem'. Remember Esteem was a very popular sedan from Maruti. By taking on the sedans, Mahindra changed the narrative on SUVs. Others have followed.

No discussion on great car advertising can conclude without an ode to the Volkswagen Beetle advertising from Doyle Dane Bernbach. Ad legend John Hegarty recalls how some fifteen years after the Nazis tried to exterminate the Jewish population of Europe in the Holocaust, it took a Jew – Bill Bernbach of the American agency Doyle Dane Bernbach – to help Germany re-establish its manufacturing credentials[3]. A little lesson there in humility and dangers of prejudice. Great advertising for cars has continued to roll and every year the American Super Bowl is full of dazzling new advertising. A few years ago, Volkswagen once again dazzled the world with its little Darth Vader film that soon went viral. Driving is a part of US culture, not so in India, till recently, thanks to our economic condition and, yes, poor roads.

I was invited to speak at a sales conference by an auto major about the changing Indian consumer. And I decided to pose a question to the audience: 'Who is the architect of the modern Indian road network?' I was pleased to hear the name Atal Bihari Vajpayee shouted across the room. I asked them: 'Who was the person who thought of a road network, before Vajpayee?' And Sher Shah Suri said a voice from the back. I said yes, then asked who came before Sher Shah Suri? A lone voice from the back said Chandra Gupta, rather timidly. But remember, the Gupta dynasty ruled more than 2000 years ago and Sher Shah Suri almost 500 years ago. It was only in the year 2001 that the Indian government proclaimed the need to link the nation through wide roads.

Indian road networks got a big boost with Prime Minister Vajpayee's dream of the Golden Quadrilateral. Road network jumped up from 2,447,000 kms in 2001 to 3,320,000 in 2011; an addition of almost 900,000 kms of roads, more than the entire road network the country had in 1971[4]. The growth of the road network in the United States of America after the Second World War spurred many industries, including the auto industry. In India, the growth of the road network is a sign of prosperity for millions of families who are touched by the roadways. *Economist* reports that if a village is a few kilometres from a highway, it has an instant impact on the GDP of the village. The villagers are able to reach hospitals and schools quicker. They can sell their produce in a town nearby, without losing time and effort. Their young can find employment in towns and commute home every weekend. And for the urban young men and women driving down highways, exploring new adventures is in itself a great pastime – as has been captured so well by the Mahindra film for its range of vehicles with the anthem-like song 'Live young, live free'.

If Indians are driving more, across the country, we are also seeing more women drivers. Of both two-wheelers and cars. In 2014, it was reported that almost one-third of scooter buyers were women. Hero Pleasure aptly captures this mood with its tag line, 'Why should boys have all the fun?' In many homes, the scooter is the vehicle for the entire family, while the motorbike is for the head of the household. I suspect, there is also a breed of young women who are getting on to a motorbike to ride across India. The actor-activist Gul Panag is their role model.

The number of cars sold in the country has risen from 32,000 a year in the 1970s to over 2.5 million in 2014. I feel that the Tata Motors Nano had the potential of pushing these numbers even higher. Many experts have opined about the challenges that Nano faced and I will not try and present my theories, but say that India will continue to be a market for value cars. For example, the sub-4 metre sedan pioneered by Tata Motors – Tata Indigo CS – is the perfect recipe for the Indian psyche: it is a sedan, has status value and can accommodate two large suitcases. It is compact to park and navigate; given its size, it is also very fuel efficient.

There is substantial head room for growth. Indian Readership Study (IRS) 2013 says that over twelve years, mobile phones have a penetration of 77 per cent across urban and rural India, two-wheelers are at 23 per cent and cars are at 4.7 per cent. The Socio Economic and Caste Census of India (SECC) 2011, released in August 2015, says that compared to 1.3 per cent of rural households with a four-wheeler in 2001, the number has jumped to 2.46 per cent in 2011; the comparable rural figures for two-wheelers are 6.7 per cent vs 17.4 per cent.

Urban dwellers are constantly complaining about traffic woes. Thus, the revival of scooters in the form of gearless versions has been attributed to their easy navigability through crowded city roads. There is also a growing shortage of chauffeurs. This has spurred governments to look at urban transport beyond two-wheelers and cars; metro rails, monorails, buses and even the humble tram is being thrown into the pot as a possible solution. A city planner once wrote about the US suburban phenomenon, that when a commute exceeds one hour either way, the commuter starts looking at other options. Maybe change of home, change of job or change of transport system.

Riding this mood for change, online taxi companies stormed the Indian market in the year 2014. Brands like Uber and Ola are trying not just to move consumers from the standard taxi to their better taxis, but I think their bigger game is to get people from owning cars at all. When my son was in Boston for a year in 2013-14, he was a strong votary of the 'no car, only Uber' bandwagon. I think this is bound to happen in India soon, if not already.

But a car plays many roles in a person's life. It is a status marker in addition to a pleasure-giving machine. The horse has been replaced by the modern car. So here is an amusing tale, purportedly a true story.

A Bollywood star, who also has his own film production company, was sitting with his production manager and cinematographer working out the budget of the next film he was planning. He told the production manager to budget ₹5 lakhs as the fee to be paid to the dialogue/screenplay writer. As they were doing this, through the window of the office they saw the dialogue/screenplay writer getting out of his chauffeur-driven Skoda Superb. The Bollywood star saw the car, turned around to the production manager and is reported to have said, 'No no, let us budget ₹10 lakhs for the dialogue/screenplay writer.'

And to end the story on scooters and two-wheelers – my neighbour's maid drives to work every morning on her own Honda Activa scooter.

Ghar Ghar Ki Raunaq Badhani Ho

In the late '70s, Jenson & Nicholson, a Kolkata-based company, stunned the country with its iconic outdoor campaign, 'Whenever you see colour, think of us'. This was probably one of the earliest examples of a corporate brand-building campaign done through the then primitive outdoor medium. Subhas Chakravarty, the then brand director of Rediffusion, Kolkata, explains how Aloke Kumar, the media manager, was tasked to rotate around forty designs through the 300-plus hoarding sites across key cities of India. Please remember, in those days, each hoarding had to be hand-painted and the hoarding contractor had to send proof of painting – often the day's newspaper or the weekly news magazine whose cover would be visible in the photographic proof attached to the bill. I remember hennaed hand, egg yolk, flame of a match, airline ticket etc. Created by Arun Kale – who incidentally won the Art Director of the Year Award at the Ad Club Annual Awards so many times that he stopped entering his work in that category; a bit like Lata Mangeshkar who did not want Filmfare to give her the best singer award after winning it many times – and his long-serving copy partner at Rediffusion, Kamlesh Pandey, the campaign not only won numerous awards, but also created a huge amount of word of mouth for the brand in the right circles.

Darshan Patel asked me a strange question, 'Why have you dropped the second line of the Nerolac jingle?' If Karsanbhai Patel taught Hindustan Lever some new lessons in marketing by launching India's and maybe the world's first economy washing powder, Darshanbhai created a storm in the self-medication market with a slew of launches in the late '90s. Brands like Moov, Krack and Itch Guard rolled out at regular intervals from his company – Paras Pharma – to take on the might of established Indian and multinational companies. I had decided to meet him to learn something about his magic and maybe ask for some business. So Darshanbhai's question was in a sense a compliment and a complaint.

Nerolac Paints is one of FCB Ulka's oldest accounts and the agency had created a very memorable jingle for the brand. The jingle went *'Jab ghar ki raunaq badhani ho, Deewaron ko jab sajana ho, Nerolac...'* (When you want to do up your house, when you want to decorate your walls, Nerolac). The new ad that had broken in 1999 had a group of painters singing the song, drumming on cans of paint as the house owner busts their party, and then joins them in the jiving. The jingle in the 1999 film took its inspiration from the jingle that was created in the early '90s but was set to a rap beat with a lot of interesting percussion arrangements. Darshanbhai had noticed that the original jingle's second line had been dropped. He even remembered the second line, *'Rangon ki duniya mein aao, Rangeen sapne sajao, Nerolac'* (Come to the world of colours, decorate your dreams with colours, Nerolac). I was amazed that he remembered the second line of a jingle that had been off air for almost seven years.

It is true that paints have been the single-most important home décor product that has been consistently been marketed for over forty years through some very powerful advertising.

Asian Paints created a revolution by establishing a supply chain that could handle thousands of stock-keeping units and built an IT system well before multinationals such as Hindustan Lever had automated their depot and distribution processes.

Asian Paints soon decided to challenge the dominance of brands like Jenson & Nicholson and ICI's Dulux by launching their own high decibel advertising. In 1990s, they caught the imagination of the country with an ad that featured a young man returning home as his mother is preparing food. The director of the film – Rajiv Menon – who later made some wonderful Tamil movies, used the Tamil festival Pongal to build a great look for the film. Ogilvy, the agency for Asian Paints, went on to create some iconic ads including one where a young couple are in Rajastan on a holiday; the lady spots a Rajastani man wearing a bright blue headgear, she loves the colour of the headgear and her husband chases him through the mela to buy it off him, because she wanted that particular shade of paint for her home. The series of *'Mera wala blue'* films went on to build a distinct identity of Asian Paints.

Almost as an answer to Nerolac, Asian Paints too did a beautiful film on how colours are a reflection of the people who live in the house with their *'Har ghar kuch kehta hai'* (Every home tells a story) ad; the ad was narrated by Piyush Pandey in his own characteristic voice. In the mid-2000s, Asian Paints launched its 'Home Solutions' where they started painting services through a dial-in facility. In 2014, they launched wallpapers under an endorsed brand name. Obviously, they are not resting on their laurels.

As paint brands were weaning away Indian consumers from the standard '*chuna* wash' or lime wash, which was the staple wall paint for many decades, cement brands too started touting their own strengths. In fact, traditional Indian homes, almost till the '50s were made with very little cement. But the '70s, saw cement brands entering the marketing fray. In a first, Birlas launched Birla White, India's first white cement, and boldly branded it Birla; the first product to carry the Birla name. Ambuja cement broke into the scene in 1989 with their muscleman advertising. The Ambuja campaigns created by the young agency of that time, Trikaya, made deep impact and helped Ambuja threaten the dominance of older players like ACC.

The floors of Indian homes also needed a makeover. From the traditional 'mosaic', there was a move towards different flooring materials. Spartek was the first flooring tile brand to use the power of mass media advertising. Lintas, their agency, used lifestyle imagery to help the brand reposition mosaic and traditional marble as old-fashioned. Unfortunately, the company could not recover from a wrong acquisition that they made in the early '90s and I suspect they got swallowed up by yet another player. The brand Spartek has virtually disappeared.

As walls and floors were changing, it is but natural that furniture too had to change. One company tapped into the furniture market by doing some iconic advertising for a simple product – glue. Fevicol from Pidilite Industries partnered with Ogilvy to build a huge business out of a simple white product called polyvinyl acetate. The earliest ads of Fevicol featured a thick board, which had been glued together using Fevicol. This board was being pulled from either side with the chant *'Dum laga ke haisha'* (Pull it with force). A man walks in, laughing at them because 'this board will not break since the joint was stuck together with Fevicol'. Fevicol was *'Furniture ka saathi'*. From there, the brand leaped up to show an overcrowded bus that is slowly going along a village road, with men sticking to every side of it. As the viewer is wondering what is happening, they are exposed to the back of the bus which carries the Fevicol brand name. Yet another one has a carpenter trying to break an egg but the egg does not break; we discover that the hen is feeding from a Fevicol container. The advertising of Fevicol has won international acclaim and I would submit there is probably no other glue brand anywhere in the world that has such a status among the advertising folks. Interestingly, the company does not stick with these ads alone. They have an elaborate carpenter training programme, and every year, they produce numerous carpentry and furniture books, all of which are widely used. Pidilite has expanded its product range to include children hobby gum, water proofing materials, instant glue etc. As long as there are carpenters making furniture in India, Fevicol will continue to dominate.

As Indians were getting more and more décor-conscious, even a bathroom fittings brand like Jaguar started advertising on television. The fact that a simple tap was being advertised was in itself a novelty that got them the enquiries. Jaguar, rated as a Superbrand in 2005, used some very bizzare ads to gain attention. One of their ads featured a gang of thieves who break into a classy home only to leave behind jewellery and steal their bathroom fittings. When the kid wakes up in the morning and finds the bathroom flooded, he says – 'Oh no, not again!' In another ad we have a young man forget his girlfriend when he sees the bathroom fittings in her house. Here too, the girl says, 'Oh no, not again' at the end.

Suddenly, material possessions were finding their pride of place in the living room. In the early '80s, refrigerators started arriving in bright colours like red, blue and green. Boring white and cream were no longer the flavours of the month. A red refrigerator became the central attraction in the living room. Around that time, the humble television too was becoming an object of desire and display. Onida entered the market with possibly the most outrageous advertising the country had ever seen. They actually showed a broken television set. The line 'Onida. Neighbour's envy. Owner's pride' created by the ad agency Advertising Avenues founded by Goutam Rakshit, captured the imagination of a nation that was waking up to colour television with the telecast of the Asian Games of 1982 held in Delhi. Suddenly, the boring black and white television gave way to colour television. And yet another material object started becoming the centre of attraction in every middle-class home. Right through the mid-'80s and early '90s, neighbours did come to watch colour TV especially on Saturdays and Sundays. The launch of *Ramayan* on Doordarshan (1986-1988) made the purchase of a colour television almost an act of faith, blessed by Lord Rama and later, Lord Krishna. Roads used to empty on Sunday mornings and media planners used to estimate that over 80 per cent of all television-owning homes were glued to their *Ramayan* telecast; religion no bar.

Washing machines, refrigerators and other household durables got a leg up when the government decided to reduce the excise duty from the 60 per cent levels to a modest 15 per cent during the wave of liberalization in the early '90s. It was reported that a Socialist party member stood up in the parliament to complain to the then PM, Narasimha Rao, that if washing machines became cheaper, thousands of poor women who were employed as domestic servants would lose their jobs. To which the erudite PM is reported to have replied, 'Do you want us to be a nation of maids?'

No washing machine ad defined the concept of a washing machine better than the original Videocon washing machine ad. Featuring the girl who had been made famous by Rasna, the film has her getting out to attend a kiddie party only to have her dress spoilt by the overfriendly dog. Her mom is nonplussed, takes her clothes and gets them washed in her Videocon washing machine. The song that went something like 'Videocon washing machine, it washes, rinses and even dries your clothes' sold the generic promise of a washing machine and went on to win consumer's hearts as well.

Indian homes were changing, dramatically. When I came to Mumbai, for the first time in 1975, I was fascinated by the flat culture of the city. In most cities of India, we lived in 'houses'. The poor lived in huts made of mud walls and a thatched roof.

The middle classes lived in rented houses, often a portion of a big house was rented out – the *barsaati* concept continues in New Delhi. The affluent lived in their own houses. Millions of Indian families in urban India never got to own a home. This has changed dramatically in the last forty years. The growth of the apartment culture has been spurred by nuclear families. As the size of an average Indian family has moved down from 5.5 in 1981 to 5.0 in 2011, and if you consider urban India, the decline may be a lot more. Marketing Whitebook 2010-11 quoting the Juxt Indian Urbanites study offers some clue on home ownerships in urban India[1]. The report says that almost 63 per cent of urban Indians own a house or an apartment or hutment, and 31 per cent live in homes that are over 500 sq. ft. The study says that among the higher socio-economic class, ownership is higher than 65 per cent. The growth in home ownerships has undoubtedly been driven by the growth of the apartment culture or condos as they are referred to in the US. The 2BHK has become a part of popular lexicon, across India, in just around two decades.

Along with the growth in ownership, there is also the trend towards better home aesthetics. From the days of having boring white or yellow walls, Indians are discovering the joy of colourful walls. From boring mosaic flooring, they are discovering the multiple options in flooring. Smaller towns now have a growing tribe of interior decorators. Even carpenters have moved up the value chain by calling themselves interior decorators.

The rapid growth of cable and satellite television – all delivered in glorious colour – has taken home décor aesthetics good and not-so-good, into all Indian homes. From watching Independence era soap operas, today families are glued to their television sets watching drama unfold in metro cities, often in homes that have been decorated in the most eye-catching manner.

For the more educated, the internet has been a great medium of education. Nerolac launched a website in 2005 to support their premium paints – Impressions. This website gave basic information on colour combinations as well as other interesting trivia about colour therapy, Vaastu (not trivia for many) and more. Asian Paints too has created a website with a lot of information for home decoration. I remember the magazine, *Inside Outside*, in the early '80s was an under-100 page magazine that was struggling to keep its head above water. Come to 2015, the same magazine often boasts of 100 pages of ads. Many other magazines have joined the interior decoration mania, including some international titles. So using a combination of websites and magazines, the collective décor IQ of middle-class Indians is growing by leaps and bounds.

In their own way, advertising agencies have a role in helping improve the art and décor IQ of the average Indian. While working on décor brands, they not only pore through the best of what the world has to offer, they also encourage art for art's sake within their four walls. In a sense, they are patrons of art by recruiting from leading art schools. From the days of Satyajit Ray, who was one of the founders of Clarion Advertising – an agency that was rated as one of India's top three in the mid-'70s – to present-day, agencies have been fertile ground for art, photography and film talent. American Cultural historian, TJ Jackson Lears speaks of how the agency Ayer ran its own art galleries in Philadelphia where art directors showcased the canvas's they painted on evenings and weekends. Interestingly, Indian agency Lowe Lintas too used to organize an annual exhibition in the '70s and '80s to showcase the artwork of its artists[2].

While art and crafts are slowly replacing the traditional calendars in middle-class homes, the year 2014 also saw the entry of yet another game-changing innovator group. Using easily available venture capital money, e-commerce sites have exploded in the furniture market. Brands like Urban Ladder are creating a new trend of ordering furniture on the net.

As Indian homes change, it is apt to recall a particular research project Ramesh Thadani once told me about. Ramesh Thadani was the CEO of IMRB, India's largest marketing research agency in the '90s and my long-term mentor – he passed away at a relatively young age in August 2000. I have spent many evenings at his feet learning about the intricacies of doing consumer research in a country as diverse as India[3]. We were once discussing homes and cleanliness of homes. Ramesh pointed out that Indians have a peculiar definition of dirt. There is dirt that is inside the house and there is dirt outside the house. The outside dirt is bad. So when you enter an Indian home you leave the footwear at the doorstep. Then there is dirt inside which is perfectly fine. Finally, there is this great disdain for what is not your own home, so an Indian housewife will be happy to dump her household garbage just outside her doorstep. How do you explain that? Is it that she is not bothered how dirty her outside environment is, as long as her home is clean inside? Or is it just ignorance that what is dumped outside indiscriminately can easily drift back inside?

Indian government launched the Clean India or 'Swaach Bharat' movement in 2015. Will Indians learn to clean up just because there is a nice slogan exhorting them to do so? Unfortunately, Ramesh passed away more than a decade ago, but I am sure he would have been able to give a theory and maybe a solution as well.

Jai Jawan! Jai Kisan!

A FARMER IS transplanting paddy crop and he has a young man helping him. The older farmer enquires of the young farmhand, 'Now that you are a father of a young girl, what are your plans? Are you planning to have one more child?' The young man replies, 'Yes, brother. Soon hopefully!' To which the older farmer replies, 'Just as we have to leave space between paddy saplings, so that they can grow better, we need to leave space between children, so that they can get the right amount of attention from their parents. So take my advice and space out your next child.' The short ad film to promote family planning and 'spacing' was aired in the government-owned television channel, Doordarshan during the mid to late '70s. I saw the film when I was not even contemplating a career in advertising. But all through the many years, the film has stayed fresh in my mind. I think it managed to build a vivid analogy on the need for 'spacing' by using something every farmer knows: when you are transplanting crop, you need to leave sufficient space between saplings.

While that piece of advertising was aimed at all men and women with a clear rural tilt, I think Indian media has seen a significant amount of advertising aimed at the rural consumer.

Professor Chitta Mitra used to teach marketing research and rural marketing at IIM Calcutta in the '70s. He had served at ITC in its marketing research department before entering the world of academics. His classes used to be full of war stories from ITC or Imperial Tobacco Company as it was known when he used to work there. One such story involved a cigarette brand called Red Lamp. Prof. Chitty Mitty – as he was fondly referred to by the students – spoke of an advertising tag line that was used by ITC to popularize Red Lamp in rural Punjab: '*Paani pump da. Cigarette lump da.*' A rough translation would be – for water think of a pump, for cigarette think of Lamp. Here again, you can see how the marketer used a simple analogy to build the brand connection. Some rhyming lines also helped. Prof. Mitra went on to set up a very successful marketing research company, C-MARC, that specializes in pharmaceutical research. A third innings, if I can call it that.

Who is a 'rural' consumer? Pradeep Kashyap, the guru of Indian rural marketing explains that there are many definitions of what may be termed 'rural', and it differs from source to source. A rural consumer lives in a social unit that is reasonably small but over a 5000 population where the primary source of income is agriculture; this definition from the Census seems to be the most popular. Studies have shown that by 2010, almost 60 per cent of the rural households got their livelihood from the non-farm sector; Pradeep Kashyap has predicted that this will grow to 70 per cent by 2020, thanks to urbanization, jobs in towns, better connectivity through roads and growing automation in the farm sector[1].

Indian marketers have been trying to communicate with rural consumers through several media. In the '50s and '60s, the general hypothesis was that any brand aimed at the rural consumer, primarily farm inputs, had to have clear graphic codes that can be communicated through primitive modes of advertising, like wall painting. So ICI has 'Chand Chhap' urea; Zuari had 'Horseman' urea and FACT has 'Two elephants' as its logo.

While working on the fertilizer campaign for FACT in the late '80s, I got an exposure to some of the nuances of farm inputs marketing and advertising. We were planning to make ad films for FACT Urea and were warned that the films have to run in all the then four southern states. When the pre-production meeting was taking place, the FACT team had their agricultural expert, the agronomist, sitting in. As we explained the need to shoot versions in two languages to handle the lip-sync problem – it was a dialogue-heavy film – the agronomist warned us that we need to be sensitive to the 'dhoti issue'. I was a little confused and looked at the film-maker, who had made several rural input films. He nodded wisely and said he had planned for the 'dhoti issue'. After the meeting, I cornered the film-maker to understand the dhoti issue. He explained that farmers in Kerala and Tamil Nadu wore the dhoti in one way, whereas farmers in Andhra and Karnataka wore it very differently. For those of you who are getting confused, in Kerala and Tamil Nadu, men wear the white dhoti in the 'lungi' style, as popularized by the famous 'Lungi Dance' song.

It dawned on me what a challenge it must have been to sell modern farming methods conceptualized by educated experts to Indian farmers, who were largely illiterate in post-independence India. So farm inputs were marketed through word of mouth and opinion leader's forum. Advertising used to have simple codes such as animals, gods and nature-based analogies.

One of the major modes of communication for farm inputs was through 'test demonstration plots' where farm input companies demonstrated the efficacy of their fertilizers, pesticides, hybrid seeds etc. by getting an innovative farmer to participate in the study.

Farm input advertising had to reach the corners of India with very little media coverage. So All India Radio and wall paintings were the only recourse, however difficult or limited in reach they may have been. Communication codes had to be simple and easy-to-translate into various media. Rural advertising experts, like RV

Rajan, have had a tough time educating Indian marketers about the challenges of reaching their message to the rural consumers[2].

As rural prosperity increased, other product and service marketers too wanted a share of this pie. Brands got tailored to suit the rural wallet. As Pradeep Kashyap explains, brands had to overcome four hurdles to reach rural consumers. First was affordability; average rural consumers had smaller wallets compared to urban consumers, so brands had to tailor packs that were affordable; sachet packs gave a big fillip to brands' rural plans. The second is the challenge of availability; brands had to reach rural consumers in a cost-effective manner; village weekly 'haats', farmer's markets or fairs became the most cost-effective way of reaching a large number of affluent villagers at a reasonable cost of distribution. Hindustan Unilever created its own network of women sales agents called Shakti Ammas. The third challenge is that of awareness; till the growth of low power transmitters and television, the reach of conventional media was very poor even if we include radio; in the 2000s, television had managed to enter a large number of rural homes and it is predicted that by 2030, or even earlier, all rural homes will have television sets. In 2010, almost 40 per cent of all rural homes had a television set; the growth of mobile phones has also unleashed a new way of reaching rural consumers. The fourth challenge is that of acceptability; there was a mistaken impression that rural consumers will settle for feature-poor cheap products and this has been proven wrong time after time; rural consumers want products that are value for money, but not feature-poor or under-designed[3].

Brands like Nirma opened up the world of washing powders to rural consumers. So did Colgate tooth powder and Chik shampoo sachets in the '80s and '90s.

There is one big question that begs being answered. Is the rural consumer that different from his urban cousin?

Let me answer it by sharing a story about a fundamental marketing tenet that rose from research with farmers. In all marketing courses, students are taught the concept of 'Diffusion of Innovation'. This theory says that in every product category, not all consumers will try and accept the product with equal enthusiasm. There are various categories of consumers who will come into the product's fold at various stages. The first to try the product would be those who are called 'Innovators'; they are a small minority. Then come the 'Early Adopters' followed by the 'Late Adopters'. These two groups are fairly large in number. Then come 'Early Majority' and 'Late Majority'. Finally, there are the 'Laggards'. The empirical research to prove this theory was done by Professor Everett Rogers with farmers in the US mid-west on their adoption of Monsanto's hybrid seeds[4].

If we are using theories developed among farmers to explain the adoption of all products including hi-tech gadgets, I don't think we should see farmers or the average rural consumer as any less sophisticated shoppers than urban consumers.

The government of India too has had to struggle with the challenge of disseminating their messages to rural consumers. Campaigns like the small pox and polio vaccination drives used a mixture of media, including mass media as well as wall paintings and even puppet shows at village fairs. Thanks to the tireless efforts of thousands of field workers, and some smart advertising in mass media, we have been able to eradicate small pox and polio from India. But the journey towards healthcare for all is yet to be completed.

As the Indian economy has grown, rural consumers have embraced products including toothpaste (56 per cent), biscuits (76 per cent), washing powder (90 per cent), pressure cooker (25 per cent), two-wheelers (11 per cent), LPG stoves (20 per cent) as per the Indian Readership Survey 2010 – RK Swamy & Hansa Research India market report[5]. The numbers are continuing to climb up, thanks to growing affluence and aggressive marketing by brands who find rural markets less cluttered hunting grounds.

The growth of mobile phones in rural India has opened up a great new medium, as proven by the Hindustan Unilever's '*Kan Khajura Tesan*' campaign. This campaign created a new way of engaging with rural consumers; they were asked to make a missed call to a number to receive some free entertainment call on their phones. The free entertainment could be jokes, songs or anything else. The entertainment module also included a few ads for HUL brands. This campaign, running in primarily media-dark north Indian markets, is reported to have generated over 12 million users with over 50,000 missed calls a day. Conceptualized and executed by the creative agency Lowe Lintas and the media agency Omnicom's PHD, this is a breakthrough in rural market communication, where a marketer, by roping in a mobile partner, managed to create a new medium to deliver their sales message. The missed call/call back mode was also used very successfully by political parties during the 2014 parliamentary elections.

The rural consumer is changing and the evidence of that can be seen in the modern farm inputs advertising. In an ad written by Robby Mathew of Interface Advertising for Mahindra Arjun tractors, the star is the tractor, but the person using the tractor is the Andhra superstar, Mahesh Babu. He does not demonstrate the tractor, instead uses it to beat up the goons by literally drowning them in mud and slush.

Broadcast Audience Research Council (BARC) has for the first time in the country embarked on measuring the television ratings in rural India. On 22 October 2015, BARC published the rural ratings of television programs, a first. Starting October 2015, every week, BARC will put out rural viewership data and this should further emphasize the growing importance of rural consumers to marketers. This move is coupled with the change in the way marketers are analysing socio-economic groups.

Till 2013, the Socio Economic Classifications (SEC) were fundamentally different for urban and rural India. For urban India, it was based on the education and occupation of the Chief Wage Earner (CWE); and for rural India, it was based on education of the CWE and type of house the family lives in. With the adoption of NCCS (New Consumer Classification System) by the marketing community in 2013, SEC classification across both rural and urban India has become standardized and will depend on the education of the CWE and the number of durables owned by the household. This is the beginning of our journey towards seeing all consumers through the same lens, rather than tinted 'urban' and 'rural' lenses.

The rural transformation that is happening is being driven by several factors. Economists report that an increase of 10 per cent in tele-density or mobile penetration helps the GDP by at least 1 per cent. Similarly, it is said that if a village is less than 10 kms from a highway, its economy gets a 10 per cent boost. With the growth of mobiles and road networks we are seeing prosperity reaching the furthest corners of rural India. Better connectivity will allow greater access to education, healthcare and jobs. This coupled with the Unique Identification System (UID), universal banking and direct money transfer, we should see subsidies reaching deserving rural households, pulling them out of poverty and bringing them into the consumption cycle. The slogan coined by our late Prime Minister Lal Bahadur Shastri in 1965 to enthuse the soldiers and farmers of India, 'Jai Jawan, Jai Kissan', will finally ring true.

Har Ek Friend Zaroori Hota Hai

IT WAS THE year 2000. Our agency, FCB Ulka, had been invited by one of the new mobile service operators to pitch for their business. We realized that this was a big opportunity for the agency. We had bagged some fabulous advertising accounts in the late '90s and the American major, Foote, Cone & Belding (FCB) had become a majority shareholder of the agency which was erstwhile known as Ulka Advertising. We knew nothing about how to drive subscribers to a new telecom brand. Mobile was the preserve of the affluent then. So in order to help us plan for the pitch we reached out to the FCB head office in New York. Fortunately for us, FCB had a long and illustrious history in telephone service advertising in the US. They had handled the AT&T long distance advertising for many years and had created some landmark campaigns for products like 'One Rate Plan'. We had seen all this work and were quite excited to invite the global experts to help us plan the pitch.

As we were working through the mechanics of the presentation, we got talking about the players who had already entered the market. There was Airtel in Delhi. MaxTouch and BPL in Mumbai. Just as in the US, mobile service operators were selling a bundled plan to their buyers; the per-minute pulse rate was around ₹16; you had to commit to a plan that would cost you anything between ₹2000 to ₹2500 per month; your phone came bundled as a part of the plan. You had to give a deposit to the service provider and pay your bill promptly at the end of the month. In January 1999, Airtel had launched their prepaid card called 'Magic' in Delhi. We were intrigued by this new offering. So we sought the wisdom of our American colleagues to understand what pre-paid was all about. The answer we got, which we did not fully agree with, was indeed shocking. Our friends from the USA asked us, 'Why would anyone buy a prepaid mobile card? In the US, only drug dealers use prepaid cards. We don't think it makes much sense for your new client to even consider it!'

How wrong they were!

Prepaid cards transformed the Indian mobile services market by unlocking the mobile phone device, the complicated billing and collection system, and made mobile phone recharge cards something a small retailer could stock and sell!

I believe that prepaid cards revolutionized the Indian telecom industry pretty much like the shampoo sachet revolutionized the shampoo category. Prof. Venkat Ramaswamy of University of Michigan coined the term 'Productization of Services and Servicization of Products'. It is becoming increasingly difficult to separate a product from a service. A car company makes more revenue from its service pack. And now a telecom service company retails its service through a refill card from a neighbourhood shop. And no example demonstrates this better than the way mobile operators like Airtel spread their reach. In 2014, over 90 per cent of all mobile subscriptions are prepaid. While I have a postpaid connection for my mobile phone, I only have a prepaid 3G connection for my iPad.

No other service has captured the imagination of the country like mobile phones, and advertising has had a big role in the growth of mobile services.

It all began in August 1995, when the then Chief Minister of West Bengal, Jyoti Basu made India's first mobile phone call to the Union Telecom Minister Sukh Ram. By May 2012,

India had over 900 million mobile subscribers. If we take out all the 'dead' numbers and dual-SIM ownerships, we are told that almost 77 per cent of over-twelve-year-olds in urban India have a mobile phone, according the Indian Readership Survey 2013. The number in reality may be a bit lower, but still, mobile phones are one of the most well-penetrated categories in the country. Bureaucrat and author Pavan Verma traces the growth thus: in 1948, India had a total of 80,000 telephone lines; when STD services were launched in 1961, there were one million lines; when economic reforms were initiated in 1991, there were 5 million; this grew to 37 million total connections (landline and mobile) in 2001; then the rocket fired to 350 million in 2009 to 950 million connections in 2012[1].

Airtel was the first operator to use the star power of Shah Rukh Khan to drive mobile consumption. In one of their early ads created by Rediffusion for prepaid mobile phones, they even used a paan shop as a location. A young couple is at a paan shop. We hear the phone ringing. The customer pulls out his phone from his pocket. No, it is not ringing. The lady asks him to check her phone which is also in his pocket. It too is silent. The paan shop owner pulls out his phone from the drawer but his phone too is silent. Then we hear the shop assistant, who is sitting beneath the elevated shop front sorting betel leaves, talking loudly into his mobile phone. I think in my mind that advertisement communicated succinctly how everyone can now own a mobile phone. You don't have to be an affluent customer or a shopkeeper, even a shopkeeper's assistant can have a mobile phone.

Mobile service in the country got a fillip when Reliance Mobile was launched through a very disruptive rate plan on 28 December 2002, the birth date of Reliance Group founder, Dhirubhai Ambani. AG Krishnamurthy, founder of Mudra, recalls how the launch of Reliance Mobile was a fulfilment of Dhirubhai Ambani's dream of giving every Indian the power of mobile telephony[2]. The print ads proclaimed '*Roti, kapda, makaan aur mobile*' meaning food, clothing, shelter and mobile, while the television films offered Reliance Mobile as '*Kar lo duniya mutthi mein*' (Take the world in your hand). The brand also featured cricket star Virendra Sehwag as a symbol with the *Sehwag Ki Ma* film where Sehwag, the swashbuckling Indian batsman, gets a message from his mother wishing him luck. The deep-pocketed operator decided to give incoming calls for free. This quickly moved all other operators to make incoming calls free, and call rates were dropped as well. So though the trend of not picking up an incoming call due to the fear of being charged for it faded away; the concept of the 'missed call' continues as Indians have figured out something that is even lower than the lowest call rate offered in the world – which is that 'missed calls' are free. Launched in December 2002, Reliance Mobile offered a phenomenal deal to poor users by offering a bundled phone for as low as a few hundred rupees a month. It spurred all other operators to review their own rates and that led to further reduction in tariffs.

With the launch of Magic from Airtel, and others quickly followed, the mobile instrument was delinked from the tariff plan. So from the days when you had to pay a fixed amount every month, you could pay for your incoming calls and outgoing calls, Indian mobile users were free to pick the mobile phone they wanted, spend exactly what they wanted to spend and get incoming calls for free.

This setting was further disrupted by the launch of Tata Docomo in the year 2008. Being the eighth entrant to join the game, the operator chose to innovate with its tariff plans and offer a 'per second billing plan'. Till then, Indian users of mobile phones were paying for a full minute even if they used just 20 or 30 or 40 seconds. The advertising for Tata Docomo shows a man sitting in an aircraft, in the middle seat. An elderly gentleman approaches with presumably his daughter, who sits down next to the young man. He is happy but the father returns requesting him to exchange his seat as he wanted to sit with his daughter. Our young hero is a little crestfallen, moves out and goes looking for his new seat. And lady luck smiles. He is seated between two beautiful girls, dressed in skimpy clothes. He smiles as the voiceover says, 'When life can change in seconds, why pay in minutes?' The campaign managed to drive Tata Docomo to the top spot in acquisition in every single market. The market leaders reacted and the entire industry started talking of 'pay per second' plans.

As rate wars erupted, three operators managed to create their own identity in the market. Idea cellular, owned by Aditya Birla, decided to stick with socially-conscious messaging about using the mobile phone to achieve social good. Their brand ambassador, Abhishek Bachchan, offers the Idea brand to solve many problems, including internecine battles in villages, marital discord, the literacy problem and more with a catchy line, 'What an Idea, Sirji!' Interestingly, a similar term was often used by the famous comedian of Bollywood, Johnny Walker, in the film *Aar Paar*: 'What is your idea?'

Airtel too has had its share of great advertising that cut across barriers. One of its brand ads – that did not tout a rate or a pack – was the famous 'Football' ad. A little boy is having his food when he sees a football bounce outside his window. He goes out to find another boy standing on the other side of a heavy barbed-wire fence, in what looks like the border between two warring countries. The owner of the football cajoles the kid across the barrier to kick the ball back. They further cement their friendship by getting into the no-man's land and playing football. The kids speak a language which no one in India would have understood. The voiceover at the end explains, 'There is no wall, no barrier that can keep us apart, if only we talk to each other.'

The Airtel musical signature created by AR Rahman takes over as the kids play on, laughing and talking. Created by Chax (KS Chakravarty), then at Rediffusion, it continues to be one of the all-time great mobile service ads.

In 2012, Airtel unleashed the '*Har ek friend zaroori hota hai*' campaign where the jingle explains that every young Indian has a unique bunch of friends: those who help; those who seek help; those who borrow; those who lend etc. Set to a very hummable tune, the ad was a great hit. In the process, making Airtel appear cool and young to its users. Agnello Dias of Taproot was the master creative director behind this ad which helped launch his agency into the big league.

If Airtel has played the young kid card, Hutch, now rebranded as Vodafone, too has tugged at the heartstrings of viewers. In the 2005 period, they introduced to India a new breed of dogs. The ad has a little boy being followed right through the day by a pug. The message said, 'Wherever you go, our network follows.' A couple of years later, they changed the boy to a girl but the pug remained. Animal activist Menaka Gandhi at an award function in 2014 singled out this ad for criticism saying that it created an artificial demand for pugs who are by nature not suited for Indian climate. Further, she pointed out that pugs are so small-limbed and fragile that they can rarely have a natural birth process. Though this is probably true, the film created by Ogilvy & Mather was a big hit with viewers.

Vodafone followed the pug with yet another interesting character called the ZooZoo in 2009. Using these Martian-like characters, Vodafone wooed the Indian Premier League cricket fans with a new ad a day for the entire second season in 2009. The ZooZoos, created by Rajiv Rao of Ogilvy & Mather, could be called the biggest ad icon of this decade. In fact, PETA or People for Ethical Treatment of Animals awarded the brand for replacing the pug with a more humane alternative, the ZooZoos.

Consumers seem to be enticed by children and childlike characters says Mary Bourdeau. In a *Mind of Market* study, it was found that in judging sincerity, both consumers and creative staff unconsciously use criteria related to 'neoteny' which means the retention of juvenile features in the adult animal. This is directly related to people's fascination with infants and baby animals. Neotenous characteristics include large, round eyes and high foreheads that remind us of infancy, innocence and naivete. People perceive message transmitted by a baby-faced person as more sincere because they see babies as innocent and honest, says Professor Gerald Zaltman[3].

As mobile service providers continued their advertising barrage, mobile handsets, once unlocked, also started wooing customers. Interestingly, the first ever Indian ad to win the prestigious Cannes Lion for television was an ad credited to the agency Nexus Equity for Ericsson mobile phones in 1996. Made to demonstrate how tiny the phone was, it showed a lady speaking to someone on the phone while an elderly gentleman across the table thinks she is talking to him: 'Hello!' '*Hi!*' 'What are you doing tonight?' '*Me?*' 'Join me for dinner?' *Sure!* The man gets up and walks across to the lady's table as she finishes her call – he sees her mobile phone only then. She and mistakes him for the steward of the restaurant and asks him for 'One black coffee, please'. The film co-written and directed by Prasoon Pandey, with Piyush Pandey, was widely seen as the first significant winner from India at the Cannes ad awards festival.

Nokia innovated with mobile phones for India providing torchlight-enabled phones, rugged phones and more. Nokia phones were known for their almost-indestructible quality.

Indian brands jumped in and companies like Micromax,

Karbonn and Lava have risen in the years 2010 to 2015. Samsung has emerged as the leader with a market share of over 15 per cent. Nokia, after a fall from 40 per cent market share, is rising once again to 10 per cent. There are so many new brands entering the market that the leader board is bound to change every few years. While the top three positions may stay constant, all other spots are up for grabs.

What has driven this mobile phone mania?

In the early 1980s, it took many years to get a landline phone. The shortage was so acute that the government set up a special commission to accelerate the usage of phones. The first move entailed setting up phone booths across the country. Pioneered by Sam Pitroda, these yellow colour-coded public phone centres offered STD and ISD facilities, and got the lower classes used to the concept of a phone call. So when the mobile phone revolution started in the late 1990s, the country was waiting for it, almost. By September 2004, the number of mobile phone connections overtook the number of fixed landline connections and there was no looking back.

> DIGITAL VIDEOS: Brands are discovering the joy of long format storytelling with the opening up of the digital medium. Interestingly, the first to use this in a big way was the auto major BMW with its 'Hire' series of films, done even before the birth of YouTube. Match that for innovation.

When fishermen in Kerala made calls from their mobile phones from the high seas to decide which seaside town to head towards to get the best price for their catch, you know something major is afoot. Every plumber, carpenter, service provider in India today has a mobile phone, just as PK Dubey of the movie *Monsoon Wedding*. The *Economist* speaks about how a 10 per cent increase in mobile phone penetration can increase a nation's GDP by 1 per cent[4].

In 2008, I had spent a day at EMRI, the emergency services NGO in Andhra Pradesh. Set up by the much-maligned Satyam's Ramalinga Raju, it was run by Venkat Changavalli, a veteran from the corporate world. While speaking with him, I discovered that over 80 per cent of the emergency calls they were getting were from mobile phones.

Using the power of the phone, young entrepreneur VSS Mani set up Justdial services to give you instant answers to your problems. His service too gets almost all its calls from mobile phones.

In a strange jump of faith, Indians moved from a situation of standing in a queue outside an STD booth to having a phone in their pocket. While the penetration level of mobile phones is reported at 77 per cent, chances are that in over half of those homes there would be no landline. If 1995 was a stellar year for mobile phones, in a strange bit of serendipity, it was also the year VSNL launched Internet services in India. In a sense, Internet entered India a lot quicker than mobile services and both together are changing and will change the country in the coming years.

Today there are more users of Internet on mobile phones than those who access the Net from a computer or a laptop. In mid-2015, there were over 700 million mobile phone users, of which over 100 million are smartphone users and their numbers are jumping up every month. No wonder global experts such as Chris Houghton, head of India region for Swedish telecom equipment major Ericsson – they sold their handset business to Sony – says that Indians spend three hours daily on their phones and 25 per cent check their phones 100 times a day; *Times of India*, 6 April 2015[5]. This compares well with the global and US studies where it is shown that an average mobile phone user looks at his phone 150 times a day; 60 per cent don't go a waking hour without looking at their mobile phone; 40 per cent even admit to checking their mobile phones while in the toilet[6].

Social media sites like Facebook, Twitter and LinkedIn are seeing a large part of their traffic coming from mobile phones. Websites are today designed for mobile phones and the term RWD, or responsive web design, is a common currency. Google too has been doing its bit to spread the word about the Internet. E-commerce vendors are driving up Internet usage and some of them have totally abandoned all other forms except mobile. They too, like mobile service providers, have gone in for a payment system that reduces the buyer risk, by their 'payment on delivery' model.

> TWITTER STORM: Brands are today waking up to tracking what social media is saying. And are gearing up to respond quickly and responsibly. Many a Twitter storm has been created thanks to some immature response to a customer complaint. So the Twitter handle of a brand better be in the hands of someone responsible and responsive.

The coming years will see further innovation in the mobile Internet space. Banks are already advertising mobile bank accounts. The government is speaking of mobile cash transfer. Service providers are also advertising to spread the message.

The year 2015 has seen a lot of debate on net neutrality and hopefully the dust will settle on this issue soon so that there is a fair way through which service providers, consumers, digital content creators, e-commerce vendors, social media platforms can all help each other.

A lot has happened in India in the last fifteen years. Indian mobile brands have shown a way of overcoming hurdles posed by our financial legal systems to drive consumers to the new service. A lot should happen in the coming years to help Indians benefit from the dumb instrument in their pocket. Imagine a service that offers tuition classes on the mobile phone? Or an English tutor who uses his cellphone to conduct daily quizzes?

Sanjeev Aga, former CEO of Idea Cellular, observes that just as the famous inventor Michael Faraday quipped, 'What is the use of a newborn baby?' when asked, 'What is the possible use of the new electric motor?', the power of telephony has just been unleashed in India and he believes that telephony is merely the first newborn application of an underlying technology which is far deeper and even more game-changing[7].

As mobile service providers and application providers develop newer and newer services, Indian advertising agencies will be called to woo the consumer and spread the message. Chances are they will not be flying anyone in from their New York office for expert advice. Or maybe they will.

Section Three
SERVICES

Baraatiyon Ka Swagat

WEDDING CELEBRATIONS HAVE always had a unique place in Indian advertising. For those of us brought up on a steady diet of Doordarshan, one ad stands out as a stellar example of how social norms relating to weddings were presented in the advertising of the '70s and '80s.

The home is all decked up for a wedding. The father and the mother of the bride welcome the bridegroom's parents. The father of the bride, played by the thespian Bollywood actor Ashok Kumar, is at his cloying best. The father of the bridegroom, played by Shammi Kapoor, another superstar of his time, says in a somewhat authoritative voice, 'The baraat will reach at 8 p.m. sharp', and as the music builds up, he adds 'But we forgot one thing.' The music becomes foreboding. 'Don't worry, we don't want anything. We only wish that *aap baraatiyon ka swagat, Pan Parag se kijiye*' (the bridegroom's party should be welcomed with Pan Parag – the pan masala brand). The bride's side is always worried about last-minute demands from the groom's side in all Indian weddings, it could be the latest car, a tola of gold or more; but on hearing the brand name Pan Parag, old man Ashok Kumar's face lights up. He pulls out the distinctive blue Pan Parag tin from his kurta pocket and says, '*Hume kya malum aap bhi Pan Parag ke shaukeen hai!*' (We did not know you too are a fan of Pan Parag). The tension is fully diffused and the two old men enjoy their Pan Parag. This was yet another hit ad produced by Everest Advertising, Delhi, for their Kanpur-based client Pan Parag. This particular ad aired in 1982 and it is reported that during the period 1983 to 1987, Pan Parag was the single biggest brand on Indian television.

Those were the days when pan masalas were allowed to be advertised on government-owned television channels. This story narrated to a teenager of the 2010s will sound like fiction and reminiscent of the *Mad Men* television serial on American television where a cigarette brand's advertising was the topic of one episode.

Numerous brands used the wedding theme to sell themselves. And if we were to dissect the ad narrative, we can see how brands managed to delve into age-old customs and practices. If the Pan Parag ad subtly played up the dowry menace and the usual last-minute demand from the groom's side for extra dowry or other such favours, we can observe many such rituals played out in numerous ads across the years. Some of them may sound anathema in the 2010s.

One of the memorable ads made by FCB Ulka during the mid-'80s was for Godrej Storwel, showing a new bride entering her new home. Here the brand played on the fact how a Godrej Storwel was practically a part of the trousseau. The same could be said of the next two examples: the Samsonite ad which showed a bride packing her clothes in her new suitcase; the Titan watch ad which had the father of the bride gifting his daughter a lovely watch on her wedding day.

It is not just the wedding, but also the other smaller symbols of marriage that have been used successfully in advertising. For example, in a 2015 ad for Tata Docomo, we see a young man admiring a young woman driving the car next to him at the traffic signal. The girl too smiles when she realizes that she has attracted yet another fan. Then to break the young man's heart, she raises her hand to move a lock of hair behind her ears. On her hennaed hand, she also sports the *choora*, the special red and white bangles worn by a Punjabi bride when she is married. Nothing more is needed to explain the story. Interestingly, the concept of the choora is typically North Indian, though today the ad may work across India, since Hindi television and cinema have used chooras often enough. I wouldn't be surprised if choora becomes a national phenomenon in the coming years.

If traditional weddings have been a part of Indian ads for many decades, we are seeing new interpretations of weddings in the 2010s.

A solemn Hindu wedding is in progress. The bride and the bridegroom are walking around the holy fire as prescribed by the scriptures. The bride is dark-complexioned and beautiful in all her wedding finery. An elderly couple, obviously her parents, look on smiling. On the bride's mother's lap is a little girl, who smiles at the bride signalling, 'Me too'. The bride is surprised and happy as her partner stoops to pick up the little girl and they complete the circumambulation ritual. The penny drops for the audience as they realize that the little girl is the daughter of the bride. Obviously, it is not just another Hindu wedding. The brand Tanishq and its ad agency, Lowe, got a lot of positive buzz for this ad, for the boldness with which they depicted the new marriages of our times. Interestingly, they did not depict a court wedding, but a typical Hindu wedding. They did not resort to dialogues or tearful farewells. Without using any words, they managed to communicate what Tanishq is all about – joyful celebrations. Arun Iyer of Lowe Lintas is full of praise for the senior client at Tanishq, who took the bold decision to run the ad though many in the room had their doubts.

Jewellers and weddings are inseparable in India to the extent that Malabar Jewellers of Kerala – now found across India and the Gulf – has come out with a coffee-table book called *Brides of India* featuring typical wedding jewellery of each community of India.

Let us now switch to yet another wedding.

This looks like a destination Christian wedding in Goa. The setting is just as it is in any Hollywood film. The suited gentry are waiting for the bridegroom and his party to arrive. Just when we wonder what is going to happen, typical Indian bhangra music breaks out and the bridegroom arrives with his gang of friends, all dressed in Indian attire, colourful sherwanis and bejewelled kurtas. The gang starts dancing and the assembled crowd joins in, but the father of the bride is not amused. It was supposed to be a solemn wedding and the bridegroom was late. But then he too breaks into a dance move, to the delight of the bride and her groom.

Manyawar, the brand that made this ad has been a sensation of sorts. It has managed to build a business in excess of ₹500 crores in double quick time by riding the growing boom for Indian formals for weddings. The ad is typical in many ways. You would have expected the groom and his friends to arrive dressed in formal western suits for the Christian wedding depicted in the ad. Instead, they appear in Manyawar sherwanis. The wedding is also an indication of the growing inter-religious weddings we are seeing.

For many decades, Indian brands have used numerous religious celebrations to connect with consumers. Diwali is a top festival when it comes to advertising. From Indian brands like Amul to global brands like Cadbury, Diwali is a constant favourite. Cadbury has even tried to convert Indian consumers

> **SOAP OPERA:** How did soap operas get their name? Well the original radio plays in the US were sponsored by soap manufacturers like Procter & Gamble. These then moved to the television medium and the name stayed.

from traditional Indian sweets to chocolates by targeting Diwali gifting.

We don't need to feel guilty that we are alone in making a religious festival a festival of consumption. Michael Schudson says that in the USA too, Christmas is a 'festival of consumption' – but it is equally a festival of reunion, of restating and renewing ties of kinship and friendship. During the Christmas season, department stores in the US sell more than 40 per cent of their toys, 28 per cent of their candy, 25 per cent or more of cosmetics, books and art[1].

Nothing brings alive this marriage of Christmas and commerce than the story of Coca-Cola and Santa Claus. In the 1920s, Coca-Cola was having difficulty selling its soft drinks in the winter. They hit pay dirt when they started showing Santa Claus enjoying a Coke after a long day of delivering gifts. They also showed Santa dressed in a 'Coke red' outfit, which was the first time Santa was shown in a red dress. And as they say, the rest is history[2].

As India becomes more and more prosperous, we have seen brands unearthing old festivals to sell new products.

For example, the American car major Chevrolet used Karva Chauth to communicate how their cars can play a role in helping marriages blossom. Karva Chauth is the day when North Indian wives observe a fast from sunrise to moonrise for the safety and longevity of their husbands. In this particular film, the husband drives home where his wife is waiting, but the moon is not out yet. He takes her out in his car to the moonlit beach where they use the sunroof feature of the car to complete the ritual. Again, Karva Chauth is not a well-known festival in South India, but the brand did run this film nationally.

Valentine's Day too has become a big festival for marketers, irrespective of the protests from hardcore right wingers. I am told restaurants are also full of couples in their '40s and '50s on that day, not just teenaged love birds.

Even festivals specific to individual states are being showcased in national advertising. Asian Paints used the Tamil festival 'Pongal' to sell paints. Philips has used Durga Puja to sell television in the years gone by. Numerous brands, including mobile players, have used the Ganpati festival of Maharashtra to connect with consumers.

Is this obsession with festivals and celebrations a new affliction?

Not really, if you look at the old advertisements. From soaps to cycles, brands in India have used religious calendars to sell their wares. These mass produced, colour-saturated images of gods and national figures have been used very successfully in Indian advertising for decades[3]. Interestingly, the calendars live on, well after their utility, as wall hangings. While the god picture was probably inspired by the works of famous painters of yore like Raja Ravi Verma, the brand logo often finds itself at the foot of the god. Even if the date section is eliminated when the picture gets framed, the brand can continue to live on as a part of the wall hanging. These calendar art forms, printed in lithographic style, are today collector's items sold for thousands of rupees.

Overt use of religious symbols in advertising did take a back seat soon after Independence, thanks to the socialist-leaning Nehru government and the growth of atheistic Dravidian parties and Communists in some states of India. But the late '80s has taken all these restrictions off. Though calendar art has virtually died, thanks to the decline of wall-hanging calendars, we are seeing new avatars of these in the form of desk-top calendars.

The growing affluence of Indians has led to an increasing desire to celebrate all possible occasions. In fact, Big Bazaar, India's most aggressive organized retail player, has started mining local insights to create new occasions to celebrate and obviously shop at Big Bazaar. Each Big Bazaar outlet has been encouraged to engage with the local population to find out the typical festivals of that state, district, postal code, and create new offers to celebrate these. It is interesting that in a way Walmart too does this in the US; each Walmart store in the US has its own Facebook page and they use this device to engage with their regular shoppers. But I suppose as against Big Bazaar, Walmart has no-religious themed celebrations.

Festivals give the upwardly-mobile Indian consumer a legitimate reason to celebrate and consume. Nothing comes close to the gold-buying frenzy that has been unleashed by Akshaya Tritya. In 2015, Akshya Tritya fell on 21 April. Kalyan Jewellers of Kerala created the biggest advertising blitz ever to usher in Akshya Tritya in Chennai. The jeweller took over all the available outdoor advertising sites for a month. They occupied every page of all the newspapers: *Hindu*, *Times of India*, *Daily Tanthi* etc. On that day, they flew down all the big star brand ambassadors to open the biggest ever jewellery store in Chennai. The city took a full week to recover from the gold fever unleashed by Kalyan Jewellers. If the famous villain in the James Bond film, *Goldfinger*, painted women in gold, Kalyan Jewellers almost painted the city of Chennai in gold.

The rise of festival shopping has also managed to get new converts. Even the big e-commerce brands like Flipkart and Amazon are 'shaukeen' of festival shopping. For Diwali 2014, both brands went wild with full-page ads in all the leading dailies. Snapdeal, yet another e-commerce brand decided to create a series of thirty ads featuring television personalities and stars, each explaining their plans to do Diwali shopping on Snapdeal. com. I wouldn't be surprised if all these players decide to outdo Kalyan next year for Akshaya Tritya.

Is it just increasing affluence that is driving this festival shopping bonanza?

I suspect there are several other social phenomena helping the trend. In urban households, with husband and wife working, there is a paucity of time to sit back and relax. Fortunately, there are numerous festivals for the typical urban couple to celebrate through consumption; to get out and shop, and show that they care for each other and their kids.

Sunil Khilnani, an eminent academic researcher, has observed that rising consumerism and the extension of the market during the 1980s did not fuel an individualistic hedonism nor breed liberal individuals. Rather, it was experienced as an opportunity to sample the pleasures of modernity within collective units like the family. The author quite aptly describes the Bollywood hit film released in the mid 1990s, *Hum Aap Ke Hain Koun*, as a four-hour celebration of singing, dining and wedding festivities [4].

Celebration and spending on celebrations is taking on new dimensions as India becomes more and more affluent. For example, weddings were the single biggest occasion for any family to splurge on clothes, jewels, sweets etc. Now you can add many other occasions to that, such as engagement parties, often held a few months or a year before the real wedding. Then after the wedding is the Indian version of baby shower or *godh bharai*. Then the first birthday of the child. We get invited to at least one silver wedding anniversary party every month; add to this the fortieth birthday, fiftieth birthday, sixtieth birthday celebrations.

Increasing affluence has also encouraged consumers to use other occasions to shop. As if there is a shortage of festivals in India, we are now seeing the growing popularity of Valentine's Day, Mother's Day and Father's Day.

In addition to celebrating their own festivals, we are seeing communities and religious groups crossing the boundary and celebrating the festivals of others. For example, there are Ganpati pandals put up by Muslim communities in many cities of India. Christmas has been celebrated by clubs where most of the members are Hindus.

Unlike the West, in India, religiosity is very much alive and kicking – for more read my book, *For God's Sake*. Marketing, which was till the '80s fighting shy of embracing religion, is now doing it with a vengeance. Festivals that were little known till a decade ago have become national phenomena. This trend will continue and I am sure advertising agencies will continue to mine new ideas from the rich festival calendars of India. And I am sure in their own way these ads will contribute to what is unique about our country: multitude of colours, celebrations and contrasts.

Tan Ki Shakti, Man Ki Shakti

MY FIRST JOB was at a then relatively unknown advertising agency called Rediffusion Advertising, started by Arun Nanda – he topped his batch at IIM-A; the first batch – and Ajit Balakrishnan – IIM-C alumnus who went on to set up India's first online portal, Rediff.com. I was excited to meet my new colleagues and one of them was Rajiv Agarwal, an IIM-A graduate. He too had chosen the perceivably more risky option of advertising after saying 'no' to marketing. During the 1979 Diwali break, my brother, who is quite curious about everything, wanted to know more about my life in advertising. I was the first person in our family to have taken up employment instead of opting for business. The first question he asked was, 'Who else joined your company from the IIMs?' I threw in Rajiv's name and the fact that he was a top-ranking student from IIM-A. My brother was not to give up easily, and continued his probe: 'Where did he study before IIM-A?' Fortunately, I had done some homework, so I replied that Rajiv was from Delhi had studied at St. Stephen's College and had done his schooling at St. Columba's. When I mentioned St. Columba's, my brother jumped up: 'Is he the guy who won the first ever *Bournvita Quiz Contest*?' Now, I did not know the answer to that.

But truth be told, Rajiv Agarwal was indeed the first winner of the *Bournvita Quiz Contest*. He and a classmate of his won the contest the first time it was broadcasted on Vividh Bharati, in 1973!

It would seem rather strange that someone would remember the name of the winner of a radio quiz contest, some seven years later. But that was the power of the radio medium in the '70s, and of India's first branded quiz show.

Do remember that the quiz was in English and was broadcast on the government-run Vividh Bharati network of All India Radio. But it had a great following, at least among the big city, English-medium kids across India.

Cadbury India as the sponsor was quite pleased to see the mass following of the programme, but after a decade, they too were not sure if the programme gave any commercial benefits to the brand Bournvita. But since it did have such a large following, they continued it on radio for nearly twenty years, hosted by brothers Hamid Sayani and Ameen Sayani at various points in time. It transitioned into a television programme on Zee TV and ran uninterrupted from 1992 to 2001. Then it had a checkered story on Sony and later Colors television channels. The country also got to meet a new quizmaster when it broke on TV and Derek O'Brien, the star quizmaster was born – he became a West Bengal Trinamool Congress spokesperson in his later avatar and a Member of Parliament; I wonder when he will conduct a quiz programme at the Indian Parliament. Incidentally, his father Neil O'Brien was a great quizmaster and used to host the intercollegiate and inter-corporate quiz contests in Kolkata in the '70's and '80's.

In 2014, *Bournvita Quiz Contest* (*BQC*) moved to the digital medium and is hosted on Google's YouTube channel. Chances are it will keep changing with the times but will continue to build stars like Rajiv Agarwal! Incidentally, Rajiv Agarwal with Arun Kale went on to start the ad agency, Nexus Advertising, which went on to do some great work for brands like Raymond.

You have to remember that *BQC* was an elitist programme in some sense. It was in English and though there were many winners during its thirty-year history from smaller cities, the quiz was very much an affluent affliction, if you could call it that.

This changed in the year 2000 when *Kaun Banega Crorepati* (*KBC*) shot up like a rocket, creating a movement the likes of which we had not seen before.

Was *KBC* a programme that was inspired by *BQC*? Or was it based on an international format? How did it capture the imagination of the masses?

KBC was based on an international format of big-prize-money-quizzing called *Who Wants to Be a Millionaire?* In fact, the programme is licensed from the original owners of the franchise. Star TV had been launched in India as an English channel and it could not match the allure of Zee TV which was offering a great bouquet of Hindi programming. Star TV realized that they too needed to move to Hindi but wanted to have a killer program that could be the Trojan horse that will help them enter Indian homes.

Mastermind from BBC, hosted by Magnus Magnusson from 1972 to 1977 was the first taste many of us got to television quizzing during the days of black-and-white Doordarshan broadcasts; Magnus' catchphrase 'I've started so I'll finish' became part of common language in London. But it was *Who Wants to Be a Millionaire?* that married simplified quizzing with big money. It had worked its magic in UK and later in USA, helping the channels they were aired on to rise to the top. So Star management realized that it could be their magic bullet. The program combined quizzing with big money. Would that be enough to break through viewer inertia? Or would it become elitist like the *BQC*?

It was young Sameer Nair, then programming head at Star TV, who suggested that the programme needed something more than just a simple yet interesting quiz and big money. He suggested that Star TV rope in a big celebrity, and why not

The Rasna girl's 'I love you Rasna' was heard all over the country in the early days of television, creating a new drinking habit across India. [Courtesy: DDB Mudra]

The Liril girl cavorting under a waterfall was a welcome relief in the hot, humid cinema halls of India, making her an all-time favourite. [Courtesy: MullenLowe Lintas]

This award-winning 'Thanda matlab Coca-Cola' poster and outdoor design saw the beverage giant appropriating the Hindi word for 'cool', even roping in superstar Aamir Khan for the television commercials. [Courtesy: McCann © The Coca-Cola Company]

Pepsi's 'Nothing official about it' campaign cocked a snook at Coca-Cola's designation as the official sponsor for the 1996 Cricket World Cup, redefining the way the religion of cricket was practised in the country. [Courtesy: JWT]

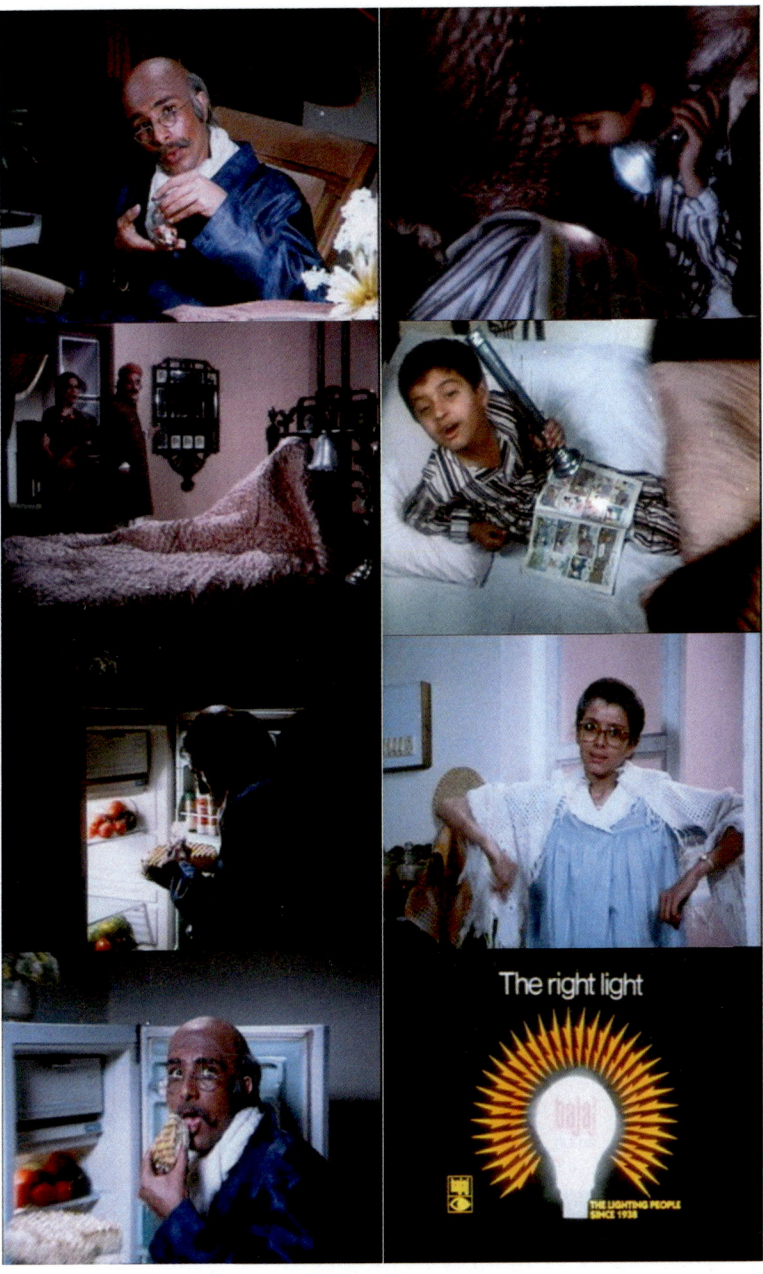

'Ab mein bilkul boodha hoon' but I am still up to mischief: The endearing story of an old man remembering his childhood captured the hearts of the entire nation. [Courtesy: Bajaj Electricals]

Since 1982, Maggi 2-Minute Noodles, 'fast-to-cook, good-to-eat', has been an all-time family favourite. [For reference purpose only. Courtesy: Copyright holder and JWT]

The new voice of middle-class Indian women was never articulated better than with the Surf 'Lalita ji' campaign. [Courtesy: MullenLowe Lintas]

The first time Amul hoardings became 'topicals' was to celebrate the Bombay Derby Races many decades ago; hundreds of 'topicals' have followed this one. [Courtesy: DaCunha Advertising]

As girls started riding more and more scooters, Hero launched its women-only Pleasure with the tag line: 'Why should boys have all the fun?' [Courtesy: FCB Ulka]

The Fevicol campaign was proof that scintillating creative advertising can happen for even a humble adhesive. [Courtesy: Ogilvy & Mather]

(*Left*) The Asian Paints campaign made paints a social talking point and 'Mera wala blue' a household phrase. [Courtesy: Ogilvy & Mather]
(*Right*) Jenson & Nicholson's outdoor campaign was an iconic first in corporate brand-building. [Courtesy: Rediffusion Advertising]

(*Left*) Indian tourism soared new heights with their Incredible India campaign, releasing some terrific advertising in the international markets. [Courtesy: Amitabh Kant and Ogilvy & Mather]
(*Right*) The Air India Maharaja is one of the most widely recognized advertising icons for many decades, taking Indians to exotic destinations around the world. [Courtesy: JWT]

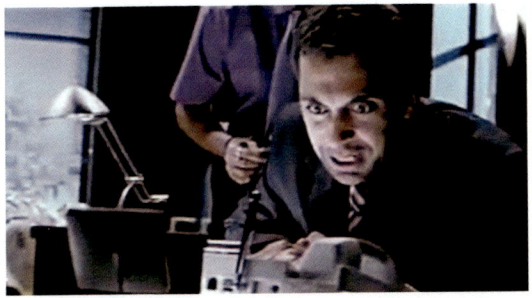

'Hitler. Arrogant. Rascal. Idiot…' The name-calling of an obnoxious boss in the Naukri ad set a new boss–subordinate relationship trend in the country. [Courtesy: FCB Ulka]

Cadbury's beloved Dairy Milk dancing girl–cricket ad continues to tempt millions of adults to bite into a chocolate bar. [Courtesy: Ogilvy & Mather]

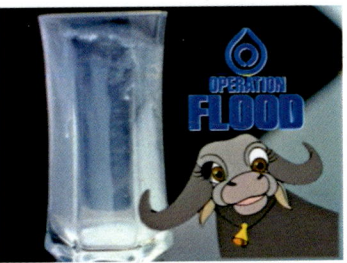

NDDB's Operation Flood was the world's biggest dairy development programme. The signature campaign used 'doodh' musically to make milk sound cool and aspirational. [Courtesy: FCB Ulka]

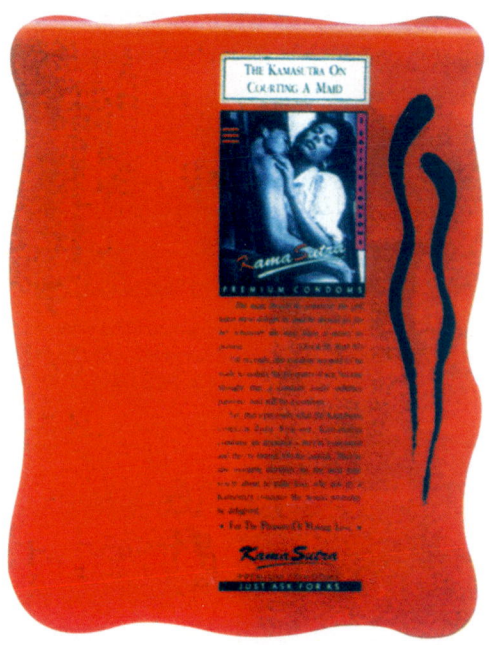

Kamasutra (or KS) made condom-wearing appealing and attractive.
[Courtesy: MullenLowe Lintas]

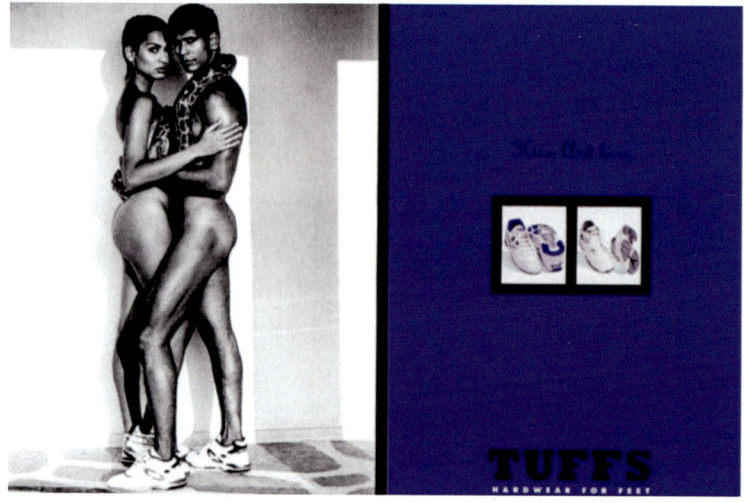

The ads featuring two nude models ended up creating history as one of the longest-running advertising cases in Mumbai law courts. [Courtesy: Ashok Kurien]

Amitabh Bachchan, he asked in their internal strategy meeting. Incidentally, the Big B, as he is known now, was not too busy then. He was coming out of some financial issues relating to his company ABCL (Amitabh Bachchan Corporation Ltd.), but he needed convincing, which Sameer and the team managed to do.

The first episode of *KBC* went on air in mid-2000 and it changed the fortunes of Star TV Network. On the back of *KBC*, Star Plus launched a host of serials including the famous saas-bahu ones featuring the eternal conflicts between the mother-in-law and daughter-in-law. Big B played his role to perfection, that of a gentle quizmaster, engaging with his participants and viewers alike, the angry young man of the '70s and '80s was reborn as the caring uncle of the 2000s. The success of *KBC* also ended up becoming a great launch vehicle for Amitabh Bachchan version 2, and Big B was born!

Interestingly, Star Plus hosted Season I and went on to launch *KBC II* with Amitabh Bachchan as host in 2005-6 after a five-year hiatus. Unfortunately, with Big B falling ill, they had to abandon the second season midway. Star Plus tried *KBC* once again in 2007, this time with a new quizmaster, superstar Shah Rukh Khan.

In 2010, the *KBC* franchise moved to Sony TV and Big B came back to play the tough yet gentle quizmaster once again and the channel has continued to offer a new season every year.

What is interesting is that Sony TV managed to position the programme as not just a big prize money contest. The advertising theme lines used over the years 2012 and 2013 are clearly insightful of the changing attitudes of the Indian masses: '*Sirf gyaan hi aapko aapka haq dilata hai*' (Only knowledge will get you what is rightfully yours) and '*Seekhna bandh toh jeetna bandh*' (If you stop learning, you stop winning)! It may be apt to remember a quote from Mahatma Gandhi: Live as if you were to die tomorrow, learn as if you were to live forever.

The success of *BQC* and *KBC* have had a beneficial effect on quizzing in the country. The Times Group of publications launched the *Economic Times* Brand Equity Quiz in the 1990s as India's first corporate quizzing event. Tata Group launched the Tata Crucible – The Business Quiz in the 2000s in two formats, the Campus Quiz and the Corporate Quiz. Tata Consultancy Services took the route of IT quizzes in schools and now conducts this tough quiz in hundreds of schools around the country. And the list of brand sponsored quizzes is rather long, all serving the cause of knowledge development.

From the days of *Bournvita Quiz Contest* to the days of *Kaun Banega Crorepati*, there has been a sea change in the way the masses have started seeing the role of knowledge and education in their lives. *KBC's* new theme lines so aptly capture the desire, the hunger of the masses and the middle-classes to seek education.

> ELEVATOR PITCH: Can you explain your idea in less than thirty-five words before the elevator reaches the floor at which the client is going to step out? Be ready with an elevator pitch at every pitch meeting.

Much has been written about Indian society and how it has been, for millennia, driven by class and caste delineations. Knowledge was the preserve of the upper classes, especially the Brahmins. It was Swami Vivekananda who observed – 'The only way to bring about the levelling of caste is to appropriate the culture, the education which is the strength of the higher castes'. The country had a paltry 30 per cent adult literacy rate when the country gained its Independence. In the last sixty years, literacy rates in India have moved to the 70 per cent league. But it is not just literacy that has changed, but the role of education in modern Indian society that has dramatically altered. What the founding fathers decided to do in terms of affirmative action, or reservation, is now finally changing the landscape and more importantly the attitude of parents to education.

What could be other factors that are driving the growth of the education sector in the country? In the '60s and '70s, there was only one way of becoming rich: you start a business, cheat on taxes, bribe the right people to get clearances, and you became rich. In the 2000s, a new way of becoming rich or wealthy has been unearthed and in some sense *KBC* may have triggered this one. The common man today knows that if you have the right education, you can get a job and legitimately become rich.

Some of us who have had the benefit of IIT/IIM education, often lament the excessive news coverage given to starting salaries of fresh graduates. The crore rupee salaries that get written about in the front page of newspapers make us cringe. But in reality, these very same reports are bringing about the attitude change in people towards education. Everyone knows that though the crore salary is not for all, there is hope that a ten-lakh salary is possibly within grasp, with the right education.

The importance of education keeps coming up in any discussion you have with consumers, anywhere in India. In early 2013, I was in Ranchi to deliver a TEDx talk at IIM Ranchi and the taxi driver who was assigned to take care of me turned out to be a great conversationalist. He proudly told me that the biggest tourist attraction in Ranchi was Dhoni's house! But that aside, he had lost his father at a young age and was driving a taxi to ensure that his sister and brother get the best education possible. It is rumoured that while many of the professors of IIM Calcutta fail to get their wards into IIM-C, one of the institute vehicle drivers actually managed the miracle!

Consumers keep speaking about the importance of education and the need to create a nest egg to enable their children to get the right education. This desire is true across the world and President Barack Obama has written about a research done by

Elizabeth Warren and Amelia Tyagi, which says that the primary reason a woman takes up employment, even in the USA, is to fund the education of her children[1]. In a survey published in the *Economic Times Wealth* supplement, 23 February – 1 March 2015, 54 per cent of the Indians surveyed said that they were satisfied with their levels of saving. And no prizes for guessing the top financial priorities: the number one priority is children's education at 64 per cent, the next is buying a house at 57 per cent. It likely that if the same survey had been done twenty or thirty years ago, things like children's marriage (now at 45 per cent) and planning a retirement (now at 38 per cent) may have ranked higher than children's education. It is to be noted that cost of education, especially higher education has shot up over the last twenty years, but be that as it may, there is a growing movement toward educating children, both boys and girls. It is also true that in many areas, the public education system has failed to meet the growing educational aspirations of Indians. Annual Status of Education Report warns us about the ticking time bomb: in 2006, 53 per cent of children in Class 5 could read a Class 2 text; in 2014, this has dropped to 48 per cent; *Livemint*, 23 February 2014. So if the subsidized public system is failing to deliver, there is no option but for lay public to spend on their children's education in a never before scale.

Education or *gyan* is going to become an even more important topic in Indian society. Government of India's reservation system is bound to get further refreshed. Cost of higher education will continue to rise. Dileep Ranjekar of Azim Premji Foundation, which focuses on school education, is a vocal advocate of Teacher Education Reform. He says that every teacher education institution should be situated in a multidisciplinary university that provides the benefit of inputs from experts in the disciplines of sociology, philosophy, psychology, anthropology, technology, basic sciences etc[2].

Given the education mania sweeping through the country, there has been a boom in the number of engineering and business schools across the country and Chetan Bhagat's book, *Revolution 2020*, captures the ugly underbelly of the Indian education system. But there is no gainsaying that the education explosion is going to continue for the next five decades. Millions of Indians need to be educated and skilled, and there will be innumerable opportunities for education ventures, from kindergarten to schools to professional colleges to technical institutes.

AG Krishnamurthy, the founder of Mudra Communications, would probably go down in history as the first person from the world of advertising to have conceived a business school totally dedicated to advertising and marketing. The institute that is his brain child, MICA, is today ranked as one of the top business schools in India, at least for kids interested in a career in marketing.

Indian television advertising has used the classroom to sell products for over three decades. From the days when Raju won the cup because his school uniform dazzled the brightest, to the naughty kid who smuggled Hajmola into the school dorm, to friends fighting over the lunch box, we have seen the classroom and school ambience used to great effect in advertising various products. Of late, we have also started seeing classrooms featuring in humorous settings as well.

A student runs down the corridor. He is late for his class which is being taken by a rather stern professor. As he tries to sneak in, he gets caught by the professor who shouts, 'Get out'. Cut to the kid running down the corridor again. He once again tries entering the class, but this time by walking backwards. The professor spots him and assumes that he is trying to leave the class. He shouts, 'Sit down.' The brand message flashes, 'Mentos, *Dimag ki batti jala de*' (Mentos, lights up your brain).

In yet another humourous take, the class is seated and the professor announces that they will be discussing the rural development bill. He makes a key announcement, 'I want proper parliamentary behaviour' at which stage total pandemonium breaks out, reminiscent of some of the worst days at the Indian parliament. The brand message flashes saying, 'Behave yourself, India, the youth are watching … *The Hindu*'. Written by the veteran ad man, Piyush Pandey of Ogilvy, the ad is an ugly reflection of our parliamentarians.

It is not as if advertising has only lampooned the classroom and student behaviour. In one of the most popular advertisements done by Raymond in the mid-2000s, set in a boarding school ambience, the students give a warm send off to their favourite teacher by gifting him suitings material from Raymond, which he discovers when he gets into his car to drive off. As an ode to that film, Raymond did a second part in the 2010s, where the student, now a grown man, invites the teacher to his wedding. Once again, presenting the special bond between student and teacher.

The computer was once seen as an evil machine that could destroy jobs. Some public sector companies, especially the bank employees' unions, went on strike opposing bank computerization in the '80s. But one company saw an opportunity in this chaos. NIIT became the provider of affordable computer education across the country. They even roped in chess grandmaster Viswanathan Anand as their brand ambassador. I wonder if a chess grandmaster has been used as a brand endorser anywhere else in the world. Today, computers are there in all schools and NIIT has had to change its business model. They have partnered with institutes of higher learning, like IIM Calcutta, to provide satellite-aided diploma programmes. They have also launched national-level skill assessment tests called NITAT or National Industry Targeted

Aptitude Test, and grandmaster Viswanathan Anand continues to play the role of their brand ambassador.

What role will advertising play in the growth of education in twenty-first century India?

Indian print medium has been the big beneficiary of the education ad boom. It is probably difficult to believe, but educational institutions are one of the biggest category of advertisers. What started as the advertising medium for coaching classes like Brilliant Tutorials – which at one time ran front-page ads in all leading newspapers of India 365 days a year – has now become the preferred advertising medium for respectable universities. The new-age digital medium has been a big beneficiary as well. Lovely University of Punjab was the single biggest advertiser in the digital medium in the year 2013.

With the growth of the Internet and smartphones with wi-fi/data access, the education sector in India is set to undergo further change. The growth of MOOCs, Massive Open Online Courses, across the western world is already upon us. The role of the physical classroom will drastically change and, as Swami Vivekanda observed, the barrier put up by the old interest groups will come down rapidly.

Ajit Balakrishnan, an IIM Calcutta alumus and Chairman of the Board of Governors of IIM-C, is emphatic as he quotes French sociologist Pierre Bourdieu to say that education has a larger role of creating 'Cultural Capital'; an asset that an individual possesses which can give continuous financial returns just like Financial Capital[3].

What was once a preserve of the upper-class elite, to be protected from the lower classes, is today becoming a mass movement! There are many ugly stories behind the growth of the education sector and the obsession with higher education for purposes as low as 'better dowry'. Testing services are worried that over 50 per cent of the students in Class 5 across both rural and urban India cannot do the Math tests meant for Class 2. IT companies lament the poor quality of Indian engineers to the extent that experts like Narayana Murthy have gone on record to say that over half the engineers produced by the engineering colleges of India cannot be called engineers; which reminds me of a cartoon in our IIT Madras magazine, *Campastimes*, in the '70s and I quote (sic): 'Six Munths Agao I Cuddn't Evun Spull Engunier. Now I are One.' Amen.

Zindagi Ke Saath Bhi, Zindagi Ke Baad Bhi!

'Aap ka agency ka capacity kya hai?' (What is the capacity of your agency?)

The question floored us. This was the mid-1990s, the stock market was boiling hot. All agencies had set up specialist IPO or financial services arms. Trikaya had Trikaya Options. Agencies like Pressman, Ad Factors, Clea and Concept were growing by leaps and bounds. FCB Ulka set up FCB Ulka Futures and Basudev Biswas was picked to run the division. He managed to locate some potential clients and one such client was in our conference room. And the MD of this company, Vatsa Corporation, asked us this question. We did not understand the import of this question. We told him we have a lot of experience across numerous categories like foods, cosmetics, personal care products and he was thrilled that we had so much experience. So he asked again, 'Kya capacity hai?' We requested him to explain. He said, 'If I ask you to spend ₹10 crores on a launch campaign for a new product, can you do it?' We replied, 'Yes, of course.' He asked again, 'What if I want

> **PITCH FEES:** Clients sometimes offer to pay a 'Pitch Fees' when inviting agencies to pitch for their account. The sting in the tail could be that by paying the fees, they can claim ownership of the idea. So watch out, the generous client may not actually be that generous.

₹50 crores to be spent, do you have the capacity?' It then dawned on us that he wanted us to take the financial risk by spending the money and then wait for him to pay. I immediately told him that as per our guidelines we insist on advance payment till we establish a credit system with a new client. They quickly left the conference room. We realized how vulnerable an agency could be in the go-go days of IPO boom. I suppose they visited many agencies and we did see a full-page ad in a daily newspaper a few days later. I am sure the agency concerned which had the 'capacity' would have written them off as bad debt. Financial advertising, especially IPO advertising, has often given the ad industry a bad name, and no wonder SEBI developed such stringent guidelines that in the later years, IPO advertising came to be known as 'Tombstone' ads in the business. Unfortunately, in the late 2000s and 2010s, the IPO market became so dormant that it has probably hurt growth plans of many small- and medium-sized companies.

While equity culture in India is growing in fits and starts, one financial product seems to have got universal recognition and acceptance: life insurance.

What has Bollywood got to do with life insurance in India? The parliament of India passed the Life Insurance Corporation Act on 19 June 1956 creating the Life Insurance Corporation of India, which started operating in September of that year. It consolidated the life insurance business of 245 private life insurers and other entities offering life insurance services; this consisted of 154 life insurance companies, sixteen foreign companies and seventy-five provident companies. Life Insurance Corporation celebrated its fiftieth anniversary in 2006 and adopted a new, more modern, identity of LIC, in rich gold and blue. LIC is synonymous to life insurance in the country. Their promise is captured in their long-running slogan, '*Zindagi ke saath bhi, zindagi ke baad bhi*' (During life and after life).

Stories of the work done by LIC agents is legendary and LIC has managed to maintain a strong network of agents. At one time, it was reported that the famous Hindi actor, director and producer Raj Kapoor's daughter, Ritu Nanda nee Kapoor was the number one LIC agent in India. More than mass media advertising, LIC managed to create a band of loyal agents who were its advertising media. The company used various perks, like creating a 'Chairman's Club' for elite agents, giving them special privileges like extra commissions, special training and the use of specific titles on their visiting cards – all that adds to building status for the agent.

With Mrs Indira Gandhi's government nationalizing the fourteen major private banks in 1969, and another six in 1980, the major lenders to Indian industry became government-owned. Marketing and advertising was used by banks only to tom-tom government schemes and loan melas, as they were known. In all their life, none of the government-owned banks used any film star in their advertising. In fact, they abhorred advertising of all kind and saw it as a necessary evil to be used only when in dire need, like a 1000th branch inauguration by the chief minister of the state. Only then an ad happened.

ICICI, or Industrial Credit and Investment Corporation of India, was set up as an industrial investment corporation in 1955. ICICI set up a bank in 1994, and later the parent company merged with ICICI Bank. It was ICICI Bank, under the leadership of KV Kamath, that started tapping the potential of mass media advertising to build a financial services brand aimed at the middle-class market in India. One of the boldest things that ICICI Bank did was rope in Amitabh Bachchan as their brand ambassador in 2001. The bank claimed that Mr Bachchan's universal appeal would help them communicate their brand message – that customers would find it safer, simpler, smarter to transact with ICICI Bank – to a large diverse customer base encompassing people from all sections and life stages. The ads featuring Amitabh Bachchan were soon followed by a powerful campaign with the tag line, *'Hum hai na'* (We are there for you). The bank also moved to a more modern identity in 1998, featuring the 'I man', as the logo is referred to. By adopting a strong marketing and advertising stance, and using the power of technology, they innovated across the spectrum including Internet banking and mobile banking, ICICI Bank became the fastest growing bank in India. If you had said in 1990 that a bank would use a film star to build its brand image, you would probably have been scoffed at, but in the India of the 2000s that strategy has worked so well that today several banks, both privately-owned and those with significant government holdings use assorted stars to build their brand equity.

Financial products and brands have used advertising to connect with Indian consumers in many different ways. Often, advertising attempted to simplify the complexities of financial instruments and processes.

For instance, when the Hongkong and Shanghai Banking Corporation (HSBC) bank was launching India's first automated teller machine, it had to explain the concept of the ATM to a bank customer who till had been used to going to the physical bank for his money. So the word ATM was converted into a new acronym: Any Time Money. The Any Time Money concept caught on dramatically. From India's first ATM in mid-'80s, today there are thousands of ATM machines around the country. I know of some bank customers who don't visit the physical bank premises at all.

Or take the simple fixed deposit. The common misconception is that once you put your money in an FD (fixed deposit), you cannot pull it out without incurring significant loss of interest. Again in the mid-'80s, Citi Bank decided to create the concept of an 'Unfixed Deposit'[1]. Simply put, the bank converted every deposit into sub-units of a smaller quantity. So if you have a big deposit and you need to withdraw a small amount, you can still do that by breaking one part of your unfixed deposit. The campaign created and run by JWT, then HTA, the long-time agency of Citibank, was a big success.

In conservative Tamil Nadu, fixed deposits ruled the roost and it was rumoured that an ad in the *Hindu* was worth its weight in gold, literally. The *Hindu* management was also particular to preserve its heritage and rejected ads from unscrupulous companies. Reputed finance companies like Sundaram Finance had queues forming outside their offices on 1 January by customers who came to claim their wall calendar, as it was seen as a good luck charm.

Taking a loan for anything except for business was still seen as taboo. If a loan was taken for a wedding, it was taken behind closed doors.

One company changed the dynamics of home loans in the country – HDFC or Housing Development Finance Corporation. HDFC was set up in 1977 as a housing mortgage company and slowly spread its wings. It did not use much mass media advertising, except for some print advertisements. But they used other means of building credibility. For example, builders were encouraged to put up signages saying that the building had been 'cleared' by HDFC. I remember when I bought my first apartment in 1987, I had taken a home loan for ₹1 lakh. One of my neighbours wanted to see my loan agreement and requested for a copy of the same. When I enquired why, he explained that if you can get a loan from HDFC, it is likely a guarantee that the builder had adhered to all building and city norms.

The aversion to taking loans for furthering one's lifestyle is changing. *Times of India*, 2 December 2014, reported that 22 per cent of urban families have loans to repay, and of these loans, 82 per cent were loans taken to finance housing, education and marriage[2]. In fact, the average urban debt has moved up from ₹11,771 to ₹84,625, from 2001 to 2012, says the same report. So it looks as if the floodgates have opened, slowly but steadily. Automobile companies report that over 70 per cent of all cars are bought through finance schemes. Even mobile handsets are being sold with attractive EMIs. The breed of products and services that are being sold through EMIs include holidays, television sets, jewellery and more.

If advertising has had a role to play in the growth of banking, insurance, home loans and mutual funds, should the stock market be far behind?

The first company to tap the power of advertising to build a stock market culture in the country was probably Reliance Industries. As Mukesh Ambani, Chairman of Reliance Industries Ltd. told his shareholders in June 2012, ₹1000 invested in the IPO (initial public offering) of Reliance Industries in 1977 would be worth ₹7.78 lakhs in 2012, a compounded annual growth rate of 21.6 per cent'[3]. Well, if the stock market has been such a good performer, why is it that most Indians still park their money in gold and fixed deposits in banks?

The answer probably lies in the unscrupulous ways in which the stock market and the IPO system was manipulated by operators like Harshad Mehta. Using loopholes in the Indian banking system, operators played the market till the hand of law caught up with them in November 1992. Playing the market for a period of ten years, Harshad Mehta had corrupted the system and destroyed the credibility of the stock market. The overhang of the IPO scams still continues to smell bad. It is unfortunate that even though the stock market may give better returns, Indians continue to park their savings in fixed deposits, real estate and gold. For instance, *Hindustan Times,* 22 April 2015, showed that over a period of five years – January 2010 to January 2015 – NSE Nifty Sensex went up by 10 per cent, real estate by 9.7 per cent, gold by 5.8 per cent, bank fixed deposits by 9.3 per cent and post-office deposits by 8.8 per cent – this is the pre-tax compounded annual growth rate. If you apply tax to this, the returns from stocks would be significantly higher[4].

Credit cards have had a slow start in India, though thanks to the spread of ATMs, debit cards have had a booming time. Even e-commerce merchants have figured out that getting Indians to use their cards is a problem and have deployed the cash-on-delivery model. But as we move forward, they will have to move to electronic payment systems. There are sufficient examples of pure credit/debit card plays. For instance, BookMyShow sells 10 million tickets a month purely through cards. And I believe that is the way to go.

MasterCard is one of the global majors in credit cards and they measure their market share as the 'share of personal consumption expenditure' of the whole economy. In markets like Korea, they reportedly got the government to levy a cash surcharge. This works as a win-win across all players, except the people operating in the grey economy. Handling electronic cash is so much cheaper and every single dollar is traceable. In India, we have often seen the opposite. Many merchants will give you a cash discount if you brandish a card at them. MasterCard also has a global advertising campaign named 'Priceless', which has been running from the year 1997. When FCB New York was handling Citibank, it had an iconic tag line 'The CITI never sleeps' which ran around the world. In one of our global meetings, we were introduced to the concept of 'Lifestage Marketing' which was the buzzword at that time. Research had shown that a bank customer is a bank customer for life, unless he is faced with a lifestage change. So the time to get a customer to switch is when they get married, or when they change their job or when they shift home or city. Citibank successfully leveraged this learning and today a number of Indian banks too are adopting these strategies powered by data analytics. For instance, some banks can predict, based on your credit card usage, if you are going to default or if you are going to shift to another brand of card etc. The banking industry is probably at the cutting edge of using data in advertising and marketing. Some of these banks are running well over 100 different email campaigns every month to tap the right customer at the right time.

The Indian income pyramid is changing. Of the total 240 million households in India, the deprived (below ₹1.5 lakhs a year) is still a huge 135 million, but the aspirers (₹1.5 to ₹3.4 lakhs) has grown to 71 million, with the middle class at 31 million (₹3.4 to ₹17 lakhs) and the rich at 3 million (above ₹17 lakhs), according to the NCAER CMCR 2010 report. According to Kotak Wealth Management's 'Top of the Pyramid Report 2015', there are 1,37,000 ultra high net-worth individuals in India, each with a net surplus capital of ₹25 crores[5].

As the JWT *Campaign India* magazine report on Changing India, dated 7 October 2011, says, on the face of it, the Indian investor has not abandoned his traditional conservative ways when it comes to his personal investment philosophy, but there is a clear sense of an increased aspiration that is fuelling rapid changes in the financial landscape in the shape of acceptance of expertise and technology. There is a growing desire to use expert advice – often on an online portal. Over the last twenty years, financial brands have grown in stature and recognition. Personal finance is today powered by technology; frequent trips to the bank have reduced; online payment of bills is becoming more and more common. The young have embraced technology rapidly with mobile banking becoming a big driver. The woman of the house has transformed from housewife to home manager to home finance manager. Growing awareness is leading to more focused financial planning for key life events. Banks across the world have discovered the truth behind what is known as

'Lifestage Marketing'; target consumers who are moving from one life stage to another, from student to working person, from single working person to a couple, from a couple to a couple with kids and so on. In India, till recently, each of these segments were small from a big brand perspective. But that is rapidly changing and each segment is now becoming a large, juicy piece.

Advertising is also reflecting this growing trend. For example, a recent advertisement for HDFC Life, a life insurance company, was about a father and his young child who had a physical disability; the father saves wisely so that his daughter's dream of becoming a dancer, in spite of her disability, comes true.

Even humour has become a staple for financial services ads. In an ad for a mutual fund, a middle-aged man is shown reading the newspaper in a small Irani café. The waiter comes to his table, places a hot cup of tea, but then he stoops to take a sip from the cup before moving on. The customer is shell-shocked, as the voiceover rolls in with 'Is your mutual fund taking away what is truly yours?' The company promises to be transparent with the way they treat their customers – no hidden fees, no hidden charges.

Advertising is, as yet, not a powerful force in financial marketing, the way it has been in other product categories like telecom/mobile or automobiles. I suspect it is because public sector operators are still a major force in Indian banking and they are shy of using advertising. Secondly, the public issue market in India has had a rather roller-coaster ride thanks to unscrupulous operators. I also believe that the prevalence of huge amounts of unaccounted cash in the grey economy hinders the purposeful use of capital. Even today, in most parts of the country, purchase of gold and real estate is through cash. And cash purchases do not need the push of advertising. Therein lies the rub.

For the country to grow and achieve its rightful place in the galaxy of developed nations, it is important that financial inclusion and financial literacy become the mantra. On 9 May 2015, Prime Minister Narendra Modi launched innovative group insurance schemes and group medical insurance schemes. Money transfer from the government to the poor is going to go the electronic route. All these spell good news for the legitimization of capital. Hopefully, this will lead to greater transparency and accountability. Then we can see advertising step in to take consumer adoption to the next level.

God's Own Country

How to sell airline travel to Indians in a post-Mughal, post-British Raj, independent India? Make them feel like a maharaja of course.

The Air India Maharaja was the brainchild of the puckish, irreverent Bobby Kooka, who headed the airline's advertising function from the 1930s to the 1970s. Anvar Alikhan, the advertising industry veteran who has written extensively on the growth of Indian advertising and advertising icons, has a special place in his book for the Air India Maharaja and Bobby Kooka: the little Maharaja was not born suddenly, as people imagine, but, rather, he evolved serendipitously over a series of many avatars. The very first one was in 1939, on a poster that showed a turbaned character being carried aloft by four eagles – a take-off on an old Persian legend. There was an immediate outcry from Bombay's Parsi community, who protested to JRD Tata that it insulted a much revered Zoroastrian figure. In 1946, the Air India Maharaja first took the form in which we recognize him today. By 1950, the Maharaja had acquired all the elements of his final form: the stripped turban, the twirled mustache, and most importantly the mischievous sense of humour flawlessly executed by the long-running agency partner of Air India, HTA (now JWT). As Bobby Kooka is reported to have said, the Maharaja '…would make the point that needed to be made, but he'd do it differently: with wit, with charm, with style.

He'd poke fun at everybody, and everything, in sight (most of all himself). He could be anything in fact, except boring.' Undoubtedly, the Air India Maharaja was the most popular advertising icon of its time. In the 1980s, he lost some of his charm and wit. Though the Maharaja was dismissed from his services for some time in the '90s, in the 2010s, he has been brought back; but somehow he lacks the wit that Bobby Kooka had so carefully nurtured[1].

So air travel was for the maharajas, right! Then something happened.

Captain GR Gopinath launched India's first low-cost airline, Air Deccan, on 23 August 2003 with the first flight from Bangalore to Hubli. The airline with its tag line 'Simplifly' offered never before deals on air tickets. The airline commissioned Leo Burnett/Orchard Advertising to create a poignant ad for the airline. The film depicts an elderly carpenter in a small village getting a letter from his son. The postman who opens the letter for the illiterate old man announces that it is an air ticket from his son, to fly to Delhi, where the son is probably working. The film then, through well-composed vignettes, takes the viewer through the dreams of the little boy, the carpenter's son, to fly and how the carpenter makes him a wooden plane to play with. The film culminates with the old man making his first air journey with a simple bag, which incidentally contains the aforesaid wooden plane. The film went on to win the hearts and minds of middle-class Indians and took away the fear of flying from many of them. Air Deccan opened the gates for many other low-cost carriers to enter the market. Unfortunately, Air Deccan hit several air pockets prompting a merger with Kingfisher Airlines in December 2009. And that turned out to be a sad story.

Fortunately, for first-time and economy-minded air travellers in India, other low-cost airlines moved into this space and IndiGo seems to have made a lasting impact with its no-nonsense pricing, no business class, no frequent-flier programme and no hot beverages (on short haul flights). IndiGo, set up in 2006, has managed to build for itself an interesting brand personality with smart airhostesses (who may be wearing wigs), nuts sold in reusable tins, and some interesting song and dance advertising, very artfully created by Wieden & Kennedy, Delhi.

The Indian tourism industry has tried many tricks to get the middle class to travel for leisure. Traditionally, all travel has been for family reunion purposes or for religious reasons. In fact, till recently, religious tourism accounted for anything between 40 to 70 per cent of all domestic travel – excluding travel for work or family events. National Council of Applied Economic Research estimated that in 2012, around 50 per cent of all packaged tours were religious tours, while leisure accounted for 28 per cent[2].

Indian government has tried to build domestic tourism traffic. One of the most successful domestic tourism campaigns was the one orchestrated by Amitabh Kant when he was the Tourism Secretary of Kerala. He put Kerala on the map of all domestic tourism-minded Indians with his 'Kerala – God's Own Country' campaign. The captivating films, the print ads and the brochures showed the North Indians – who were the least aware and thought that everyone from the south of the Vindhyas was a 'Madrasi' – a different South India, with great beaches, backwaters and festivals featuring thirty-plus elephants.

Taj Hotels has probably done more for Goan tourism than any other body. During the mid-'80s, Taj, which had set up two excellent properties in Goa, ran a cinema film campaign touting the virtues of Goa during the rains. The then marketing director of Taj Hotels, the irrepressible Camellia Punjabi and her advertising agency partner Frank Simoes made a great team. It is said that during one such meeting as Camelia began on one of her long discourses – and these could last an hour or more – Frank slipped out of her office with no one the wiser.

But the campaign and the magic they created together resulted in the hotels in Goa experiencing a significant uptick during the monsoons, which till then was seen as a very very lean season. Camellia and her sister, Namita, went on to create the upmarket Indian restaurant Chutney Mary in UK. Frank retired some years later to live a life of peace in Goa – where else!

Advertising and marketing has the power to change perceptions and drive traffic to ostensibly the poorest of poor holiday destinations. Advertising legend David Ogilvy narrates a little story about tourism advertising: 'I once found myself conspiring with a British cabinet minister as to how we might persuade Her Majesty's Treasury to cough up more money for British travel advertising in America. Said he, "Why does any American in his senses spend his vacation in this cold damp of an English summer when he could equally well bask under the Italian skies? I can only suppose that your advertising is the answer"'[3].

Mary Wells Lawrence who broke the glass ceiling for women in advertising recalls how Milton Glaser, who was the most respected designer of his time, was asked to create posters for New York because the state had nothing to help its tourist programs, no poster, no maps at railway stations, no bumper stickers for taxis and no money to make such things. She says it was love of New York which took Milton Glaser to her office with a batch of posters. While they were 'oohing' and 'aahing' over them, he pulled a piece of paper out of his pocket and said, 'I like this, what do you think?'; it was the 'I love New York' logo with a heart in the place of the word love. Bang, 'I ♥ New York' was born. Possibly the most imitated of all tourism logos[4].

One of the most memorable print campaigns was the one done by Trikaya for Mauritius Tourism in the early '90s. With copy by Alok Nanda and art by Vikas Gaitonde, it would rank among some of the best print advertising produced in

India. The ads had evocative headlines like 'We have no branches', 'Shaken. Not Stirred'. Great photography by Prabhudda Dasgupta added to the look of the campaign. One fascinating feature of the campaign was the typography choice; the headlines had interesting

> FONT CREATION: Advertising has had some great font creators. RK Joshi created the unique Ulka font that used features of Devnagari for Roman characters. Vikas Gaitonde created a special font for the Mauritius tourism campaign. Ravi Deshpande created a special font for AAAI's Goafest.

long extensions for the letters 'l', 'g', 'h' etc. Vikas Gaitonde explained in an interview that he had created that particular English font to reflect the spirit of Mauritius, where no man-made structure is allowed to stand taller than a fully-grown coconut tree. Hence, the taller 'l' and 'h'. Those were the glory days of Indian print advertising where copy and art made a great combination to woo the affluent audience. As an aside, you would be fascinated to know that in the city of Athens, no structure can rise over the ancient Parthenon temple that sits atop the Acropolis; similarly, in Paris no structure can be taller than the Eiffel Tower.

Time share resorts too started emerging in India during the late '80s. The pioneer Sterling Resorts grew too rapidly and as a result could not service the demand it created. Club Mahindra followed but has been able to build a significant national presence. They created a product that was more personal than a hotel holiday with special facilities and activities for children.

The '90s saw a dramatic change in the way Indians booked their train tickets. IRCTC set up a great online booking system that took a lot of the toil out of train booking – though the website is a bit slow and unresponsive due to heavy traffic, something that should be of concern to the authorities. Redbus has done the same for bus travel in the 2010s. Interestingly, a lot of bookings for train and bus still happen through agents, but now the agent does the booking from his office. In a sense, Indians have developed a hybrid model for managing the transition from standing in a queue at the railway reservation counter to using the Internet to book on the computer.

The late '90s saw average Indians starting to travel abroad. One big driver of international travel is Bollywood films. Yash Chopra shot so many of his films in Switzerland that the country accorded special status to him; in fact, his favourite shooting spot, the lake Alpenrausch was rechristened the Chopra Lake. The idea of using Bollywood to help international travel has been adopted by several other countries as well, such as Spain in *Zindagi Na Milegi Dobara*, Germany in *Don 2* etc. So instead of running short ad films, countries have used Bollywood to run full length country ads.

In spite of the rapid strides made by the tourism industry, for a 2 trillion dollar economy, travel and tourism contributes only $80 million (2011). The flip side is that tourism employs almost 37 million people. So the potential to create more employment and jobs through tourism is indeed tremendous.

No wonder the government of India roped in Amitabh Kant to pilot the India tourism campaign in the 2000s. His campaign 'Incredible India' has been seen in many parts of the world. In a first, the campaign used many innovative media to build awareness in the high potential market of New York. The whole city got a taste of India through a range of activities including India Parade, buses with full wraparound of the 'Incredible India' message, Times Square display and more. Amitabh Kant, who had cut his teeth as Tourism Secretary of Kerala from 1997 to 2001 when his campaigns made Kerala the number one tourism hotspot in the country, played a stellar role as the government of India's Joint Secretary Tourism (2001-07). It was a time when tourism was hardest hit. After the 2001 attack in

New York, air travel gained a notoriety of its own. Atal Bihari Vajpayee, the then PM of India speaking at a chief ministers' conference, spoke eloquently about the need to build tourism to combat terrorism. Amitabh Kant and his agency team, Ogilvy & Mather's V Sunil and Satbir Singh, along with a host of other agency partners managed to make an impact on the global stage with their 'Incredible India' campaign. During the campaign period, tourist arrivals in India went up from 2.38 million in 2002 to 5.48 million in 2008. A remarkable feat[5].

While we could be happy with the increase of tourist inflow to India, a tiny country like Thailand gets more international tourists with 26 million vs our 6.7 million in 2013. Not only are we not attracting enough tourists, we have more Indians travelling overseas than tourist arrivals in India, 16 million vs 6.7 million in 2013; and over 1100 million domestic travel were recorded in 2013. So obviously, as far as tourism is concerned, we seem to be a 'consumption'-driven nation and are yet to fully tap the international potential offered by the many wonderful destinations we have dotted around the country.

Tourism, which was meant for the rich maharajas of India, is no longer restricted to the rich. The growth of low-cost airlines, the ability to book train and bus tickets from home, the falling cost of international travel (and ease of travel) are some of the contributory factors that have helped Indians adopt a leisure travel habit. I don't think the surface has been scratched as yet. The potential is really sky-high.

What gives me this confidence and why am I sure it will happen?

JWT's Changing India Report published in *Campaign India* magazine, 7 October 2011, points to ten broad travel trends. Snacking travel: holidays are now extending beyond Diwali and summer; a long weekend is a time to take a break, travel to Kerala or even Singapore; Informed Traveller: access to information has taken some of the surprises out of tourism travel, websites like Tripadvisor are seen as more reliable than the report from a travel agency; Technology changing travel: mobile and Internet are changing the way travel is being planned and enjoyed; Social capital of travel: social media has created bragging rights out of travel – photographs, food and more are crowding social media sites, so you travel to share on your Facebook page, Twitter etc; Staycation: people are trying out home vacations, coupled with visits to the local spa, shopping mall, entertainment destinations; Sports Tourism: local and international sporting events are spurring new travel destinations; Couch Travel: the growth of travel and Discovery television channels has created a new market for travel – from your couch. Add to this the travel magazines, and you can stay at home and vicariously travel around the globe; Active seniors: today there are special packaged tours aimed at senior, sixty-plus citizens, specially curated for their needs and pace[6].

Taking off from that report, I can speak of five clear pointers that can be spotted on the horizon. The first is the increasing affluence of middle-class Indians, who are tasting the first signs of prosperity. One way of enjoying that prosperity is to travel for leisure, not for family or religious purposes. The second reason is the growing levels of stress in urban cities. This stress is not just with white-collar workers but is also present with blue-collar workers – for the last five years, even the chauffeurs who work for the senior executives of Mumbai business world plan a four-week holiday, almost collectively. The third reason is the relative ease of planning and organizing travel, thanks to the Internet, online reviews, bargain shopping etc. The fourth reason is the varied segmentation of tourism travel. It is not just families with kids who travel or young adults, we are seeing young girls travelling in groups, senior citizens travelling in groups, even kids going on international tours. Many events are being packaged around interesting places, for example, Goafest, the annual advertising festival and the Jaipur Literature Festival to just name two. I can go on with more reasons, but the fifth reason could be the great social capital that tourism gives, and this was brought alive to me almost twenty years ago. A friend from the US who was in Chennai on holiday decided to go to the Cholamandalam Art Village to pick up some works of art, paintings, sculpture etc. When I asked, he mentioned that after each of his trips, he invites friends home for dinner and the art he picks up on each trip becomes the topic of conversation. In today's world, Facebook has become everyone's bragging ground after even a short trip, whether it is to Dubai or to Fort Kochi.

Tourism advertising is also keeping pace with this thirst for adventure. The digital medium is creating many nano-segmentation opportunities. For instance, you are searching for a hotel in Goa and you get a sponsored message from a tour operator. For MakeMyTrip, FCB Ulka created some very interesting long-format ads that created waves on social media. One film featured a little sardarji boy named Khushmeet Singh Gill. He is a lover of the sea, which he has never seen for real, and claims that his name defines him, as he has 'Gill' in it. He wears blue all the time, even goes to sleep in his flipper-slippers. He is now looking forward to going to Goa with his parents, but lo and behold, a cyclone strikes Goa the day they are set to leave for his long-desired beach holiday. He is heartbroken, but his dad gets a call from MakeMyTrip and the agent tells him that he can 'Uncancel' the trip; he can take the same trip on a later date with no extra charge. Little Gill finally makes his trip to the sea.

As the Indian economy continues to grow, we will see growth happen in the tourism industry across many dimensions. The top end will continue to grow and exotic international destinations will be unearthed every year. If it was Machu Pichu in Peru last year, this year it may be an Art Tour in Florence, Italy. The ultra-rich are also discovering exclusive destinations in India. The hotel chain Oberoi has built brand new heritage properties across India under the 'Vilas' umbrella. The middle class is discovering the joy of international travel. From Singapore, Dubai and Bangkok, the list has expanded to London, Paris and New York. Now, the list is growing even faster with the addition of countries like South Africa, Turkey and Australia. From holidays being lumped during school holidays, we are seeing an openingup of other months for leisure holiday travel. This will continue to grow as young married and unmarried couples start travelling on short breaks. Also, the elder travel groups are quite time-independent.

There is a lot of potential to be unlocked in the tourism and travel industry as Ashwini Kakkar of Mercury Travel expounds, 'The more you travel, the more you realize how little you have travelled'. So banks are planning to tie-up with travel agencies and package tour operators to design unique finance schemes: Why not go to London instead of Jaipur, for just ₹3000 EMI for twelve months? You can expect more action on this front in the next decade.

At one time, international travel was equated to shopping. I have a suspicion that this will continue as long as we see shopping as a pleasurable pastime, but the main reason for travel may soon become experiencing the new. If so, 'God's Own Country' will be ready to shower its blessings on many million more tourists.

Naukri: H for Hitler, A for Arrogant

THE DOOR SLAMS open. The angry husband is back home. He yells at his wife, *'Mujhe phir yeh job nahin mila. Eise pile kameez pehenke jayenge to decent job kaise milega'* (I did not get the job. Who will give me a job if I go dressed in such unwashed-looking yellow shirts). The perplexed wife exclaims, *'Main to washing powder se hi kapde dhulati hoon'* (I get them washed with washing powder). The husband shouts, *'Kuch to karo'* (Do something) and flings the shirt at her.

At this, the voice of god – in advertising parlance, this is an omniscient voice makes a dramatic impact on the structure of the film narrative with the characters reacting to the voice directly – says, 'Presenting the new Wheel detergent washing powder with the power of lime, to make your clothes sparkling white'. The pack of Wheel magically appears in the scene. After the mandatory product demonstration, the story ends with the husband coming home after landing a job, and doing a waltz with his devoted wife.

The brand Wheel was launched in 1987 by Hindustan Unilever to take on Nirma, and the ad mentioned above, created by Lintas, was a big hit. It managed to tap into the angst of the youth who were not getting jobs. Remember, the Indian economy was going through a meltdown around that time and was saved by the wave of liberalization that was unleashed by the Narasimha Rao government in 1991.

Well, companies have used the platform of getting jobs and doing well in jobs to sell their brands for over fifty years. Old Indian print advertisements collected and presented by Arun Chaudhuri provide some interesting vignettes highlighting the way society has changed. Take the case of the malted beverage brand Horlicks. The ad, purportedly run in newspapers like the *Hindu* in the 1950s, presents a compelling argument for the brand in a comic strip format. The story titled *Typist Promoted to Secretary* has the boss pulling up his assistant, 'This report is full of mistakes, Mani. I don't know what's come over you lately. You were one of our best typists.' Mani's colleague also adds, 'How could you make these mistakes, Mani? The draft is perfectly legible!' To which Mani responds, 'I don't know. I can't seem to concentrate … feel so tired all the time.' At home, his mom advises him – remember, it was the '50s, so it is the mother, not his wife – 'Your tiredness doesn't seem natural, son. Why don't you see a doctor?' The doctor recommends Horlicks to our tired hero. Mani takes Horlicks every day, learns shorthand and gets promoted from typist to secretary[1].

The story may sound quaint in its own way to today's young executives who may have no clue of what 'shorthand' means. But the story vividly portrayed how a brand can help you save your job and maybe even get a promotion.

In the late '80s, Ponds Dreamflower Fragrant Talc (DFT) broke the traditional mold of talc advertising to get into the territory of jobs and interviews. The film, created by JWT and produced by White Light, starts with a young female fashion designer, played by the gorgeous model Colleen Khan, getting ready for an interview. She is nervous and practices her presentation in front of the mirror. Dressed in a pink saree – remember the other rule of advertising, the main protagonist should be dressed in brand colours – she looks confident, and after gulping at the first question, she gets her stride back to answer the questions confidently and present her designs. Shots of Ponds DFT are interspersed in the film to communicate that applying this talc will give you the confidence to face the toughest interview. As she walks out of the building, there is a man, presumably her husband, waiting outside. She gives an 'All Okay' sign to her husband who rejoices in her achievement. Till then, Ponds DFT used to be family centric in its advertising approach, showing women and family, all applying Ponds and going out to the beach or wherever. For the first time, the brand went out of its comfort zone to connect with the new young Indian women, who were just about getting ready to start doing white-collar jobs. Till date, that ad of DFT starring Colleen Khan is remembered in advertising circles very fondly.

If Ponds did the interview advertisement in the '80s, it was Fair & Lovely's turn in the '90s. The brand which stood for 'get fair get married' changed track to present a girl getting a job as an airhostess because of her fair skin thanks to Fair and Lovely. Getting a job, any job, was the call of that decade. But if you cut to the 2000s, the narrative takes a different turn. A whole new breed of young people were joining the workforce and they are not just looking for any job at any company for any salary.

No ad captured this new generation better than the following one.

The boss is in a bad mood. Two young male executives are standing around his table. One is stirring his tea while the other is presenting reports which the boss flings away. Then his secretary peeps in to say, 'Sir, hotel reservations on Line 2.' The boss puts the phone on loudspeaker and says, 'Yes, I need to book a table for two ... Poolside.' When the hotel clerk asks for his name, he says very gruffly, 'Hari Sadu'. The clerk is unable to understand and asks him to repeat. At which stage, the executive, whose report the boss had been throwing away, offers to spell out his name to the hotel reservation clerk, and the condescending boss hands over the phone to the subordinate who rattles out cheekily: 'Just write down Hari Sadu. H for Hitler, A for arrogant, R for rascal, I for Idiot.' The boss is shocked. The super comes on saying 'Guess who's just heard from us?' The brand Naukri.com flashes with the tag line 'India's No.1 Job Site'. The film has the second executive, who was stirring the boss' tea, hold up a spoon and say 'S for Shameless'.

The ad for Naukri.com was created by FCB Ulka and brilliantly directed by Rajesh Krishnan. It went on to be rated one of the best ads of the decade. It also helped Naukri.com become by far the biggest jobsite in India, withstanding powerful international competition.

More than the humour embedded in the story, the ad touched upon a key concern of highly qualified young executives as they start working. Research done by the agency had revealed that when quizzed on why an executive is keen on changing his or her job, many reasons are thrown up – salary, working hours, title, job description, company etc.; but the unsaid reason is that the executive does not like working with his or her immediate superior. If you hate your boss, you will change your job (and boss), even at a lower salary. And if you love your boss, you will stay on even if you can get a better paying job elsewhere.

Times of India, 10 March 2015, speaks of a study done by the Global Dale Carnegie Consulting organization and it says that a large section of the Indian workforce is only partially engaged (44 per cent), and many are actively disengaged (10 per cent). A full 13 per cent of Indian executives rated their immediate supervisor poorly and another 45 per cent were neutral. Employee engagement is affected by what managers do, how they behave, what they say and, more importantly, how they say it. Employees who are unhappy and dissatisfied with their immediate supervisor are less likely to identify with the organization's vision and more likely to be absent or resign. The problem of being disengaged is not just an Indian problem. The organization reports that while 46 per cent of Indians were gainfully engaged (54 per cent are not engaged), it compares favourably with Asia Pacific where 35 per cent are engaged and the rest of the world at 34 per cent[2].

Management thinker and author, Daniel Pink speaks of the Type I employee and Type X employee. He explains that research has shown that today, a large section of white collar employees need to be motivated through 'Intrinsic' means rather than through money and other such 'eXtrinsic' tools. Quoting a Gallup study, he says that more than 50 per cent of employees in the US are not engaged at work and nearly 20 per cent are disengaged[3].

Look at the contrasts: there is a significant level of unemployment in India across all levels, but those who are employed in white-collar jobs are not fully engaged.

The growth in white-collar jobs in India is a phenomenon that got its wings post-1991, or after the country got rid of its fear of computers.

We know that India was one of the last countries to embrace technology and the power of the computer. In the mid-'80s, a computer was close to god in all companies. It was kept in an air-conditioned computer centre and, just as in a temple, you had to take off your shoes when you entered the holy portals of the computer. Companies had to wait for years to import a computer. Padma Bhushan S Ramadorai, former MD of Tata Consultancy Services, has written about the trials and tribulations faced by the IT services pioneer in the late '70s and '80s. Bank employees protested against the introduction of computers. Even in large multinational corporations, it was not something that was easily accessible; it was always revered and worshipped. In the early '80s, India was immune to the PC revolution that was sweeping the world[4].

IBM launched its IBM PC on 12 August 1981 in the US. Using the character of Charlie Chaplin's Tramp in its advertising, the brand presented for the first time a friendly face for the computer, a human face that the common man could relate to.

If IBM was making waves of one kind, it took Apple to shatter the glass ceiling or the glass wall. All advertising pundits would agree that the most or one of the most iconic advertising ever produced was the Apple Macintosh commercial created by Chiat/Day. The film *1984* was a take on George Orwell's famous book of the same name. Directed by Ridley Scott – who had directed *Aliens* and *Blade Runner* – the ad cost $1.6 million to produce; media investment behind the commercial amounted to just $500,000 for a single insertion in the 1984 Super Bowl. It changed the discourse on personal computers. Author and clinical psychologist, Professor Carol Moog describes the *1984* ad eloquently thus: '*1984* is a sixty-second epic movie in which a vacant-eyed crowd, clothed in Spartan sameness, sits mesmerized before the image of the Orwellian Big Brother on a huge screen. Suddenly, a stunning powerful female athlete wearing a Macintosh logo runs toward the screen and smashes it to pieces with the force of her sledgehammer. We, the people are set free. We, the people, bought lots of Apple computers'[5]. To know more about the drama before the ad went on air read Steve Jobs' biography by Walter Issacson[6].

We in India were quite immune to the charms of the Tramp and the perils of *1984*. Even if we were charmed or scared, we could not afford the PC, let alone the charming Apple Macintosh, given the import duties and red tape.

I was a group product manager at Boots Company in the mid-'80s and, as is my wont, I was piqued by an ad from Ador Consulting. This company was offering training for executives on their IBM PC machines. Thanks to the support of my boss, and without the knowledge of the EDP manager of the company who may have blown a fuse, I enrolled for the three-day programme. I learnt the magic of spreadsheets and was spellbound by VisiCalc on that machine. I also learnt that Ador was open to doing data analysis on their IBM PC for companies. The next month happened to be the annual budget-setting month at Boots. The regional sales managers descended on Mumbai, worked hard bargaining for their respective regions and were anxious to take their worksheets home. The marketing department at Boots consisted of a team of analysis clerks who used to track the sales numbers, marketing expenditure, medical representatives' expense claims etc. It was the usual practice in the company, once the overall and regional budget numbers were agreed upon by the RSMs, to call a statistician who used to work out the month-wise, brand-wise, pack-wise budgets for each region, each state using an ancient adding machine. The machine helped work out the break-ups and the process took a fornight and more for checking and validation. I offered to get the same job done through a PC, via Ador, in two days. The head of the analysis department was shocked. The RSMs were incredulous, but thrilled that they would be able to take back their worksheets when they left Mumbai at the end of that week. The first year the company decided to run the process parallelly, only to discover the power of the PC spreadsheet program and abandon the ancient adding machine method.

No thanks to my VisiCalc adventure, Boots – which became Knoll, and again later Abbott – was one of the first pharmaceutical companies to fully computerize its depot operations and was quick to adopt the PC culture.

Affordable computer training from companies like NIIT, Aptech and others transformed the computer which was seen as a job destroyer, into a job creator and as they say, the rest is history. In most of the daily newspapers, ads from NIIT and Aptech appeared in the front page or page three, at regular intervals right through the '90s and 2000s.

The twenty-first century has aggravated the problem of skills and employment now that there is widespread awareness of the opportunities offered by a good job. On the one hand, there are high levels of unemployment, with thousands of applicants for jobs as mundane as a security watchman. When Mumbai police started hiring policemen, there was a virtual stampede. Yet at the other end, there is disengagement in work. On the one hand, there is a demand for semi-skilled workers in various sectors, but there are not enough trained workers.

> PORTFOLIO: This is the big folder a young aspiring copywriter or art director lugs along to all the interviews he or she attends. With the growth of digital media, the more savvy creative folks have their portfolio on the Net and can take a prospective employer through all their work by clicking the right buttons.

The job dilemma is to be seen in the context of the larger problem of skill development. In almost all big cities, modern retail stores are looking for staff. But they are not able to find any. Similarly, companies are looking for quality executives and are finding it a problem to get the right talent.

Talented men and women are also leaving the workforce unable to balance life and work. The stress faced by mid-level managers was captured in an ad done for the life insurance company, ICICI Prudential. Offering 'retirement solutions', the ad shows a relatively young man who says he does not want to retire from his desires, his family commitments, his passions and his adamant nature. If at all he retires, he will retire from work, not from his life. He then refuses to take a call from his 'Office' on his mobile phone.

This is the other India, which is now ensconced in a well-paying but stressful job. Brands are trying to connect with their new attitude of finding the elusive 'Work-Life Balance'.

There is the larger India which is now under-employed, which needs to be trained so that they can get well-paying jobs. The thrust of the government of India in the 2010s is to push sectors that can provide jobs to the lower-middle-class and lower-class citizens. Unlike the IT and the organized service sector, the other major sector that can give them jobs is the manufacturing sector. A report in the *Times of India*, 17 March 2015, quotes a study done by the government department, DIPP, analysing investment and job creation from August 1991 to March 2014. It says that for every one crore rupees investment, different sectors yield different levels of employment potential: Industrial Instruments can create 103.2 jobs, whereas Fuels create only 0.5 jobs per crore invested. However, there are areas like Leather & Leather Goods (42.0) and Commercial & Household Equipment (25.0) which yield good employment potential. I presume areas like media, apparel, software and tourism can create a lot more jobs per crore invested[7].

There was a telling report in the *Hindu Business Line*, 5 May 2015, which quoted Labour Bureau statistics to say that in one of our southern states there were as many as 13.5 per cent postgraduates who were unemployed. So the question is not just about education and skills, but relevant useful skills.

While there are issues facing the manufacturing sector relating to land, power, water, air, etc., one big issue is also the non-availability of trained workers. The government of India is hard at work encouraging skill development initiatives and we hope all these efforts yield results.

The government has also been trying to advertise to the youth of the country to get skills that will help them gain respect in society. The campaign *'Hunar hai to kadar hai'* (You will be respected if you have a skill) was all about young boys and girls getting skilled to get a job and rescue their family from poverty.

Jobs will continue to be a hot topic in India for many many more years to come, as millions of young men and women wait to join the workforce. Brands will continue to target them and, more importantly, we will hopefully see a flood of skill development agencies and institutions using the power of advertising to build their businesses. We are seeing some signs of this around the country. For instance, there is an English-training institute called Veta that has grown dramatically in the last decade. If we have to skill millions of youth, we need a hundred more Vetas and NIITs. And I am sure they will be able to use the power of advertising to speed up the skill-development process. The narrative around jobs in advertising will definitely shift from the colour of the shirt and skin to skills and abilities.

Kyaa Haal Bana Rakha Hai!

ANIL KAPOOR, THE marketing manager of the OTC brands of Boots Company India, had a problem. While Strepsils, a brand under his care, was doing well, his other child, Coldarin was anemic, even five years after its launch. It was the late '70s. Television was yet to spread across the country and legacy brands in healthcare were ruling the roost. Coldarin was created as a tablet specially formulated for colds; it contained a strong dose of analgesic aspirin, a decongestant and stimulant caffeine. The brand name Coldarin was derived from its formulation 'Cold Asprin'. How to help the brand grow was the challenge facing the company.

Advertising historians point out that advertising possibly got a bad name thanks to the various remedies they sold promising miracle cures. These products, broadly classified as 'Patent Medicines', at one time accounted for as much as 50 per cent of all advertising in the USA. Professor James Twitchell has pointed out that the outrageous claims of many of today's over-the-counter nostrums (fast, fast, FAST) may have had their inspirations in the early free-for-all unregulated promise-the-moon advertising of patent medicines[1].

Yet another American Professor of Media Studies, Michael Schudson confirms the dominance of patent medicine advertising in US newspapers; his analysis was that they occupied 25 per cent of all ad space, second only to department-store advertising[2].

In India, too, we did see a number of those kinds of products touted through the print media. Brands like Scott's Emulsion – 'Each spoonful leads to health', Vites – 'Grows hair', Andrew's Liver Salt – 'Hot weather fitness', Ephazone – 'Relieves asthma attacks', Angiers' Emulsion – 'Recovery after Malaria', Sirolin – 'Stops cough', Glycodin Terp Vasaka – 'Remedy for coughs' etc were regularly advertising in the daily newspapers in the '50s and '60s[3]. My granduncle, PS Iyer had an eponymous agency and had the account of a brand called Jeevamurtham for whom he placed small-sized ads in the daily Tamil newspaper. These ads continued till he reached the age of ninety-nine when he finally shut his agency.

But unlike in the US, these patent medicines did not end up making people like my granduncle very rich because they never became a big phenomenon in India, since the reach of mass media was limited and these remedies had to fight the home-remedy habit which was ingrained in Indian minds.

The Indian consumer was very careful of what medicines to take and who to consult. In fact, the British pharmaceutical company ICI ran a series of advertorial ads in the late '50s, building the reputation of the allopathic doctor. One such ad run in the *Reader's Digest*, 1957, says, 'Your doctor is a man with a cause. Having chosen his profession, he has dedicated his life to fighting disease and to bringing relief and succour to the ailing and the sick'[4].

Coming back to our Coldarin story. The brand was facing the might of the triumvirate headache pills: Saridon, Anacin and Aspro. Saridon was promising 'Relieves pain and refreshes you', and had a catchy jingle, '*Sirf ek, sirf ek, Saridon*' (Just one Saridon). Aspro spoke of its 'Microfined Formulation' that promised fast action. And Anacin had a 'Four-way action formula' that worked for headaches, colds and fever.

Boots decided to delve deeper into the psychology of a cold.

Involving a psychologist, the company set out to meet consumers, cold sufferers, those who treated their colds and those who did not. They discovered that the consumer was used to the idea of getting the common cold once or twice a year. Someone even said, 'If you treat a cold, it will go away in seven days. If you don't treat a cold, it will go away in a week.' What the psychologist was able to discover was that cold was a minor illness, but it was a major botheration. When you are suffering from a cold, you find it impossible to work. And the company latched on to the trigger that could help it sell Coldarin: why suffer through your cold, when you can take Coldarin and work well. The film that was made by Prahlad Kakkar for Clarion Advertising in the late '70s had a chemist working in a laboratory – the film was shot in the Boots development lab at its Sion factory, now an apartment complex. The chemist is suffering from a cold and is sniveling as he works. Suddenly, he sneezes and drops the glass beaker from his hand. The beaker falls and shatters. He sits with his hand on his head, deeply disturbed. His boss, a gentle old man walks up to him, puts his arm on his shoulder and says, '*Kya haal bana rakha hai? Kuch lete kyun nahin?*' To which our young hero replies, '*Bahut si dawaiyan li, sir, kuch farq hi nahin pada*'. The old man offers Coldarin, '*Coldarin li? Yeh sardi ke liye banaya gaya hai.*' ('What has happened to you? Why don't you take medicine?' 'I did take a lot of medicines, but no difference.' 'Did you take Coldarin? It has been made to treat the cold'). The young man takes Coldarin and the brand promise is heard, '*Sardi se aaram, chusti se chale kaam. Coldarin.*' The ad worked like magic and the company continued with this formula of advertising for almost two decades and managed to thwart deep-pocketed competitors.

OTC drug brands were trying to convert consumers from traditional home remedies and were starting to taste success. One brand that managed to break through the 'home remedy' syndrome was Woodwards Gripe Water, which is given to babies who have colic pain – modern day paediatricians do not encourage the use of this brand, though I remember running to a Santa Cruz chemist on a rainy night in Mumbai in 1986 to get this magic potion to relieve my son who couldn't sleep due to colic pain. Woodwards had an ad which featured a baby crying due to colic pain. The mother announces that she will give the child Woodwards Gripe Water. Then the baby's grandmom tells the baby's father, 'Give the baby Woodward's Gripe Water, when you were a baby I gave you that.' Then the baby's great-grandmother comes on the scene and says to the grandmother, 'Give the baby Woodwards Gripe Water. I used to give you that when you were a baby.' She in turn goes to the baby's great-great-grandmother to tell her about the baby crying. The great-great-grandmother then says: 'When YOU were a baby, I used to give you Woodwards Gripe Water too.' And so on, to show how like an allopathic remedy, even Woodward's is a quasi-home remedy, used for many many decades. Yet another early victor were rubs and balms. Brands like Amrutanjan, Iodex and Zandu succeeded to build traction.

Vicks Vaporub entered the advertising arena and decided to focus its brand in the cough-cold area. One of its most famous ad films of the '70s featured the love of a young kid for his mother. The house bell rings and the pretty lady of the house, played by model and actress Radhika Bartake, opens the door to see her son soaking wet, who sneezes as she opens the door. She admonishes him, 'You went out in the rain again. You will catch a cold. How many times have I told you not to go out in the rain.' To this the boy produces a bunch of flowers he was holding behind his back and says, 'Happy Birthday, Mummy'. The mom hugs him and you can see her moved to tears. The films cuts to night and the mom is liberally applying Vicks Vaporub all over the young boy's chest and throat. The next day, he is fit to go to school.

Iodex around the same time did a very catchy film that used

the terms '*Ooh, aah, ouch*'. Zandu balm decided to not just focus on back pain or cold or headache but to offer itself as a universal remedy, the brand's jingle captured the promise '*Zandu balm, Zandu balm, pida hari balm*'. The brand took the high ground of not just pain relief but '*pida hari*' which is 'relief from all troubles'.

There were also brands that were trying the humour route. Hamdard's tonic Cinkara had a catchy tune that spoke about how hard work can kill you, but thanks to Hamdard's Cinkara Tonic you can continue merrily. Starring the actor Javed Jaffrey doing a sort of robot dance, the film was a big hit.

Cough drops too were a big category those days with the battle raging between Halls, Vicks Cough Drops and Strepsils.

Vicks Cough Drops had a charming film with a father in the middle of narrating a story to his daughter but is not able to continue due to throat irritation. The brand used the catch line '*Gale main khich khich*' – an idea that was tested out in one of the Asian countries as the 'Ahem Bug'. The little kid winks and does a throat irritation sound to cadge a Vicks tablet from her dad.

Strepsils ran an ad which was one of the most loved on television in the 1980s. The films starts with the Metro-Goldwyn-Mayor lion coming out of its ring to roar, but he emits a 'meow'. The brand is offered to the lion, '*Gale mein kharash? Mazedar Strepsils*', then the lion roars!

Indian consumers were slowly giving up their home-remedy obsession. This was enabled by the rapid growth of the television medium in the mid-'80s. Conservative family-owned companies started advertising on television. Products which were till then seen as cottage industry products started getting branded and advertised in media.

The floodgate was opened with the launch of Dabur Chyawanprash through the Shriram Lagoo film which had the grandson asking him, '*Dada ji, badminton?*', to which Dada ji, played by Shriram, replies, '*Pehle Dabur Chyawanprash*'. The advertising in its own way managed to create a bridge between the older and the younger generation, with one strong statement. I am told the ad was a big success prompting Dabur to start advertising its digestive tablet, Hajmola, on television.

Television helped Indians rediscover ayurvedic remedies once again. Dressed in modern packaging, supported by strong consumer-insight-based advertising, ayurvedic products from companies like Dabur, Zandu, Emami, Baidyanath, Vicco started getting seen in shops all over India. Vicco Vajradanti along with Nirma was probably one of the most recalled brands in the '80s.

The government, in its wisdom, decided to allow all ayurvedic formulations to be retailed without a restricted drug license. So a small pan-bidi retailer would need a license to sell a brand like Saridon but could sell Hajmola. Realizing the potential, brands decided to adopt a unique strategy of 'ayurvedic labelling'. All the major rubs and balms quickly started declaring their ingredients in ayurvedic terms, so 'camphor' became '*karpoor*', 'menthol' became '*pudhina ki phool*', 'eucalyptus oil' became '*nilgiri ki tel*' and so on. In addition, they also decided to go into smaller and smaller packs. Vicks Vaporub got a big fillip with its ₹1 tin. Even Halls Cough Drops got re-labelled as an ayurvedic medicine. But of course, not all brands could go the ayurvedic route but they did benefit from the rapid growth of television and pharma retail outlets.

A savvy young marketer from Ahmedabad realized the potential offered by television and soon launched a series of brands. The company Paras tasted huge success with its Moov balm, which subversively repositioned Iodex as a pain balm that stained clothes due to its colour. The company followed that with yet another blockbuster, Krack Cream, aimed at heel repair. Once again the company managed to go razor sharp at one segment of the market and create a winner. Paras followed these two successes with two more brands, Itch guard and Ring guard, but I am not sure how successful they were. Paras managed to sell these brands to private equity companies just a decade after they were launched, and have given every Indian ayurvedic brand owner dreams of untold wealth.

Himalaya is a unique company among all ayurvedic product manufacturers. It is the only company that has a brand that is prescribed by almost all allopathic doctors in the country. Its brand Liv52, launched in 1955, is ranked among the top ten prescribed brands in the country reports *Business Standard*, 19 January 2015[5]. An amazing achievement. The company launched a range of ayurvedic products under the brand 'Ayurvedic Concepts' which did not succeed, and the name was dropped and the umbrella brand name 'Himalaya' was adopted in the 2000s. The Himalaya brand is today present in ninety countries and is a rather visible brand in the Middle East.

We saw that in the 1950s, British pharmaceutical companies advertised to build the credibility of the allopathic medical practitioner. It was an attempt to wean the reluctant Indian consumer from the grips of their grandmothers, the local Hakim or Ayurvedic doctor or even the magic of the local temple priest. It is not as if these genres of healthcare have vanished, but the last fifty years has seen the relentless rise of the allopathic doctor, to the extent that some think tanks are worried that we may lose the gems that are present in the ancient Indian texts such as Sushruta Samhita, the Sanskrit text on medicine, written more than 2500 years ago.

The rise of allopathic medicine has triggered yet another phenomenon where brands which were Rx – prescription-only – moved to become OTC. Some of them, such as Gelusil and Digene, continue to be promoted by doctors and advertised on TV. Some others like Revital, the multivitamin capsule, used Bollywood star Salman Khan to promote itself.

However, marketers do feel that Indian consumers are

not willing to commit themselves to OTC medicines like the consumers in more affluent countries. What is stopping the rise of OTC brands?

If we were to look at the growth of OTC brands, we will see that they have had problems convincing Indian consumers to switch from home remedies to an orally ingestible product. The biggest successes have been topical applications like Vicks Vaporub, Moov, Krack etc. Tonics have had limited success. If at all, it is the malted beverages like Horlicks, Pediasure and Complan that have had some level of success since they managed to straddle the food and medicine ladder together. Research shows that we are not a 'pill-popping nation'. Even in affluent segments of society, the habit of taking daily vitamins is very low.

The second affliction is the inherent faith in the doctor. Be it rich or poor, in most cities, a doctor is consulted for the smallest of complaints. Among the poor, there is blind faith – transferred from the traditional pujari of the temples – in the 'Doctor Saab'. And many Indian allopathic doctors also dispense medicines. So why would you spend ₹50 on an OTC brand, when for the same money you can meet a doctor, get a liquid mixture and also an injection – placebo, most likely.

My other hypothesis is that the lack of a suitable retail environment has also had its impact on self-medication. If you analyse the growth of self-medication in neighbouring countries, you may find that they got a big fillip when consumers started seeing the display of OTC medicines on modern self-service retail shelves. They could pick up, examine, read and interact with self-medication brands. Unfortunately, in India, modern retail trade is yet to gain ground, but, given the high margins in the business, the classical chemist outlet population is growing and consumers end up at best interacting with the the shopkeeper and his assistant, both of whom often act as semi-doctors themselves.

Dr Hasit Joshipura, former CEO of GSK, India's largest pharma company, laments at the state of Indian healthcare: In a country which prides itself on being the 'pharmacy to the world', the government's report on Macroeconomics & Healthcare of 2005 suggest that even today there are parts of the country where one has to travel two kilometres to buy a tablet of paracetamol, six kilometres for a blood test and twenty kilometres to a hospital bed. Public investment in healthcare is at an incredibly low 1.2 per cent of GDP. For a population of 1.2 billion, we have a doctor population of 600,000 and similar inadequacies with respect to hospital beds. Besides, 80 per cent of these capacities are urban centric, whereas 65 per cent of the population is rural[6]. If we juxtapose the urban fixation to visiting a doctor for every ailment, you can imagine the lack of interest in young doctors to set up practice in rural India.

While challenges remain, it is not as if nothing has been achieved in the healthcare arena. In some states in southern and western India, the primary healthcare system and dispensation of free medication is among the best. While challenges remain, advertising has played a role in spreading word about the problem of HIV/AIDS. The high impact advertising, using themes of 'delay sexual intercourse', 'stay with one partner' and 'use condom protection', have helped reduce the threat.

India won the battle against small pox a couple of decades ago. It is difficult to imagine that even one generation ago, it was common to have someone in the family who has suffered from small pox.

The year 2014 was momentous for India's fight against polio. The last known polio case was reported in January 2011. And, as recently as in 1978, there were 500 children paralysed with polio every single day. The launch of oral polio vaccine and the relentless campaign have helped eradicate this scourge in less than three decades. I believe mass communication played a very important role in building the momentum behind the campaign. The promise of 'just two drops' was amplified through mass media advertising. The creation of Polio Drop Days brought immediacy to the vaccination campaign. And over the last three decades, several advertising agencies, celebrities and film makers have played a useful role. In the year 2001, FCB Ulka was involved in making an ad where the superstar Shah Rukh Khan said that he was taking a day off from shooting to take his kid to the polio vaccination camp in order to give him the vital 'two drops'. The superstar did the film pro bono. In later years, Amitabh Bachchan played a big role in building momentum behind the polio immunization drive, lending his time and voice selflessly, ably guided by the agency, Ogilvy & Mather[7].

The growth of mass media will open up new avenues for healthcare service brands. One of the early movers who capitalized on the power of mass media television advertising is the Chennai-based Vaasan Eye Care institutions. Powered by private equity money, they have been able to build a formidable brand. Interestingly, Tamil Nadu is the breeding ground for eyecare institutions with Madurai-based Arvind Eye Care, Chennai-based Shankara Netralaya and Coimbatore-based Sankara Eyecare institutions. While Vaasan is using advertising, the others depend solely on word-of-mouth and have a strong social angle to their operation with less or no focus on profit-making.

We are now seeing the rise of hair transplantation and hair treatment services around India. Many of these hair treatment centres are funded by private equity firms. Big business has also entered the hospital arena with a vengeance and they are adopting all the marketing communication arsenal at their disposal. For instance, in the movie *3 Idiots*, Aamir Khan takes his friend's sick father to the hospital on a scooter; the hospital that featured in the film was Fortis and it was a great example of seamless brand integration into the film narrative.

Advertising, over the last fifty years, has tried to play the role of an information disseminator, attitude-change catalyst and behaviour-change driver in the healthcare space. Over the coming decades, the role of advertising may have to get a lot more nuanced to tackle the many new issues that healthcare will throw up. We will have to go beyond selling cold remedies and go back to seek the help of ethnographers, anthropologists and psychologists all over again.

Asli Swad Hai Cricket Ka

COMPLAN WAS FORMULATED by the pharmaceutical company Glaxo. Launched in 1954, it was promoted as a pharmaceutical nutritional supplement. In the '70s, Glaxo moved the brand to its family products division and wanted take on the might of Horlicks. In terms of formulation, each spoon of Complan contained a lot more nutrition than a spoon of Horlicks. But its early days as an advertised brand were not very promising. The brand had been positioned against milk and it claimed that a glass of Complan contained a lot more than a glass of milk. The campaign did not create the desired impact and Horlicks which had almost mythical properties, especially in Tamil Nadu and West Bengal, was not touched by Complan.

The brand then moved to FCB Ulka in the early '80s. When the advertising agency started engaging with the client team and the consumers, they realized that the brand needed a sharper focus. Just a broad theme of better than milk, aimed at all and sundry was not going to cut ice. Further, milk is seen as the gold standard of nutrition, a brand which is often used as a milk additive is just damaging itself by going against milk, said the consumer expert. A lot of brainstorming from the agency side led to the conclusion that the brand will succeed only if it is positioned as an expert nutritional supplement for the young. The first ad in the series featured the national swimming champion, Anita Sood, with her international coach explaining why she recommends Complan for champions. The brand finally had a voice, that of confidence and success. Anita Sood went on to become the fastest Asian woman to swim across the English Channel and set yet another record.

The brand Complan went on to become a formidable player in what is known as the milk food drinks category, but the ad done by the brand using the teenaged swimming sensation was a first for Indian advertising, especially since sports like swimming were not all that popular across the country.

Lifebuoy from Hindustan Lever used the more popular football and hockey to sell itself as the 'health soap'.

I intentionally started the chapter on sports with something other than cricket, since most of this chapter is about cricket after all.

Ramachandra Guha, bestselling historian and an IIM-C alumnus, points out that cricket was first played on Indian soil in 1721 by British sailors near Cambay. It was only in the 1830s that Parsis started playing the game. The formation of Hindu Gymkhana in 1866 and the Muslim cricket club in 1886 saw all communities embracing cricket[1].

Growing up in the '60s, cricket match tickets were truly prized possessions. Five-day test match tickets were difficult to obtain; often a ticket was shared between many friends, brothers and cousins. I remember bunking school and spending a day at the Chennai Test between India and England only to watch Bapu Nadkarni bowl thirty-two maiden overs and Ken Barrington bat right through the whole day! We did have a Nawab as the captain of the Indian cricket team. The discourse around sports and cricket changed dramatically in 1983 after Kapil Dev and his boys won the World Cup Cricket Tournament, unseating Clive Lloyd's formidable team.

Suddenly, there was a young man from Haryana, not to the manor born, leading the country to what was a fairytale victory.

Most of the Indians who are fifty-plus will remember where they were when the final West Indies wicket fell.

Advertising soon started reflecting this new social truth. Reliance started using international cricketers Vivian Richards and Ravi Shastri in their advertising. Many other brands followed, and one brand literally danced its way into millions of hearts using cricket.

Cadbury Dairy Milk Chocolates was facing a challenge in the early '90s. The brand needed a fresh consumer insight to break out of its traditional 'father-daughter' routine which had worked its magic through the '80s. Their campaign with the tag line 'Sometimes Cadbury can say it better than words' was well known, but the brand needed something more. The company, its advertising agency Ogilvy and its research agency IMRB went on a hunt to find out how to build new energy into the brand. They figured that if the brand, which was premium priced, had to grow, it had to attract a new set of users. The 'kids only' strategy had its limitations. How to target adults without alienating the core kid audience? It is rumoured that the agency team that was tasked to work on the brand remembered something they had seen on a cricket field and converted that into a Cadbury story.

A club match is in progress. The batsman has a ninety-nine score on the board. The crowd is well-dressed. We see a young woman eating a Cadbury Dairy Milk bar and the music starts. When the bowler bowls, the batsman goes for the big hit. The ball rises high, the crowd is wondering if it will find the hands of the fielder. We see the girl close her eyes and pray. The ball flies over the ropes and the fielder to become a sixer. The girl – dressed in a floral purple dress, purple being the Cadbury colour – is ecstatic. She leaps out of the stands with the chocolate in her hand, dodges the guard, runs on to the ground while performing probably the most absurd dance moves ever recorded in a television commercial. The product is shown and we hear the final pay off *'Asli swad zindagi ka'* (The real taste of life) as she hugs her batsman friend. The ad, written by Piyush Pandey of Ogilvy & Mather and directed by Mahesh Mathai, would go down as one of the most remembered ads of the decade, maybe even several decades.

This advertisement did its magic for Cadbury, but also, more importantly, it broke the Cricket–Nawab–Suiting nexus. Though the Cadbury film showed ladies and gents in their Sunday best, sitting appropriately, the final dance broke that mirage. The final dance was purely animalistic and an expression of joy. After her famous dance, Shimona Rashi was permanently referred to as the Cadbury girl. In fact, even the late model-VJ-turned-film star, Sophia Haque had been, mistakenly, referred to as the Cadbury cricket model.

When I was speaking about this with my friend, columnist and market researcher Satyam Viswanathan, he pointed out that while the Cadbury ad may have changed some rules of the way cricket as a game is presented in advertising, the Nike Cricket film done in 2007 changed the discourse in many newer ways. Created for a brand that celebrates sporting excellence, this film took what we know as gully cricket and executed it at a totally different level. Done by Agnello Dias, the film starts with one of those crazy Indian traffic jams. The bus carrying a cricket team is stuck in traffic and one of the bowlers climbs on to the roof of the bus to look around. The game starts when another player climbs out with a cricket bat and asks him to bowl. The old and young start watching the match from their window, cheering the

> COLOUR CODING: Have you noticed how the Cadbury girl is dressed in purple? Or the Santoor mom is dressed in orange? We call that 'colour coding', where the primary character in a film is dressed in the brand colours. This old custom continues though we are seeing exceptions too.

players along. Many passers-by join in, including an elephant. We also see Sreesanth and Zaheer of the then Indian cricket team stuck in the traffic as spectators. Finally, the biggest sports brand in the world acknowledged the real cricket that Indians play on their streets, with or without the traffic. The brand and its agency had been able to mine the Indian urban kitsch to create several such masterpieces.

While cricket and cricketers have been used to promote all kinds of products including apparel, face wash, engine oil, energy drinks and colas, it is not as if Indian advertisers have totally avoided supporting and showcasing any other sports.

Cricket started out as the sport of the nawabs, but with the big World Cup victory of Kapil and his boys and the growing adaptation of cricket with tennis balls, the game grew new wings and flew right down to rural India. As cricket was travelling to rural India, urban India was discovering new games to play.

In one of the visionary long-term sponsorships, NIIT, India's leading computer training institute has been supporting chess grandmaster, Vishwanathan Anand right through his meteoric rise. Vishy Anand appears in an occasional print advertisement, but is always photographed wearing a T-shirt with the NIIT logo up front.

Tata Group too had a film featuring kids and football which aired in 2005. Here, a group of kids are playing football in the pouring rain. In the final minutes, the goal keeper who is a kid afflicted by polio, leaps to save a goal. The film showcased the various aspects of the game like leadership, teamwork, grit, courage, respect, fearlessness and how they are relevant to a large corporate group like the Tatas.

India got its first marathon, organized as per the standards set by AIMS, the global marathon organization, in 2004. The Mumbai Marathon was a fun affair in the first year. I had managed to find myself at the finish line to see the Nigerian runners finish from close quarters. But big sponsorships came on board in 2005 when it became the Standard Chartered Marathon. Tata Consultancy Services too came on board as a joint sponsor. It is reported that there are probably more than a 100 marathons (42 km), half marathons (21 km) and 10 km runs in the country. Tata Consultancy Services also became the title sponsor of the New York City Marathon in 2014.

The metro city kids are now big fans of soccer and you can see them have many a serious argument about which English Premier League team is better, Chelsea or Man U. And in 2015, Tata Motors signed up the soccer superstar Lionel Messi as their global brand ambassador.

While new sports were gaining traction in urban India, it was cricket all the way for the whole country. Sociologists speak of three gods of India, the Film God, the Cricket God and the Religious God. Indians worshipped in front of these three deities.

Except for Kerala, sports in India was always a boy's preoccupation; Kerala produced India's first women athletes who could compete in the Olympics.

The narrative on cricket was also set to change with Sony bagging the telecast rights of World Cup Cricket 2003, 2007 and a host of ICC tournaments, for an astronomical amount. As Suman Srivatsav, who was then working at the ad agency handling the business, points out, the challenge facing Sony was to bring a new host of affluent viewers to watch the cricket World Cup. Till then, cricket telecast was seen as an all-male affair. Except for using Ruby Bhatia for a small role, no cricket telecast had really tried to woo the female viewer. Sony figured out that if they could get both men and women to watch the World Cup, they would be able to attract a whole host of new viewers and also charge higher ad rates. They hit on the idea of using Mandira Bedi as one of the commentators. Mandira Bedi had a fairly big fan following after her stint on several television serials, such as *Shanti*, and was quite articulate in both Hindi and English. Her energy was palpable and, as Tony Greig observed, like the Indian cricket fan, Mandira is 'Sometimes up, sometimes down, but never in the middle'. Sony used all its entertainment chops to make sure they hit all the right buttons. Mandira Bedi played her role to perfection, getting Charu Sharma to smile and Barry Richards to say things he may not have in any other circumstance. The ladies loved these comments, but they also loved Mandira's dress sense. She virtually invented the 'noodle-strap' blouse on prime-time television. Mumbai *Mid Day* had a daily review on her dress sense and they called it the 'Mandir-o-metre'. No wonder Sony managed to hit bullseye with their strategy. Cricket suddenly had hordes of women viewers.

If the stage had been set, it took yet another form of cricket to ramp it to the next level – the launch of the Indian Premier League (IPL) in 2008. It is true that the original Indian 20:20 cricket league was launched by the Zee Group as Indian Cricket League. However, BCCI with its tremendous power over players, officials and grounds took the domestic league to a level many would not have visualized. By bringing in Bollywood film stars, big business, international cricket stars and domestic cricket players together, IPL presented a heady mix. If USA has its Super Bowl, India has its IPL. Many brands create special campaigns to run for the forty-five-odd days of IPL. Brands such as Vodafone and Tata Docomo have even attempted to make over thirty commercials to run during the course of the IPL. And the audience is no longer just men. IPL too did its own advertising to get viewers to tune in and fans to get to the stadiums. While the man who orchestrated the whole parade, Lalit Modi, is a man of mystery, his creation, IPL, is bound to live on. George Bernard Shaw once reported to have said, 'Cricket is a game played by eleven flannelled fools, watched by 11,000 fools.' Well, the players are no longer in white flannels, and the audience is in millions and not thousands including women in large numbers.

Taking a leaf from IPL, we saw the launch of two other leagues in 2014. The Indian Super League (ISL) was presented as India's answer to the major soccer/football leagues of the world. In yet another coup in 2014, we saw the launch of Pro Kabaddi League (PKL). Played in fancy new indoor stadia, the game hitherto played in dusty small towns of the country got a heavy dose of glamour and style. Here too, Bollywood stardust was added to bring in the eyeballs. It is said that the Kabbadi League almost broke even in the first year itself.

Both ISL and PKL can succeed if they replicate the IPL strategy of high-power advertising, exciting content, a heavy dose of glamour and online buzz. From what we saw in 2014, they are well on their way to becoming national obsessions. For both men and women.

If we have seen new leagues sprout all over, we also saw something arrive and disappear. Formula One racing came to India in 2011 with the opening of the Buddh International Circuit in Noida, UP. The racetrack, designed by global experts, is a masterpiece, and a far cry from the Sholavaram racetrack I used to visit as a school kid to see motorbike and car races. After organizing the Formula One races in Buddh for three years – 2011, 2012 and 2013 – the global Formula One organization pulled out. So we have not had any Formula One races since 2013. But the wonderful Buddh track has been used for several car launches and exciting test drives of new models. Tata Motors smartly brought truck racing to India at the Buddh racetracks in 2014 and had an even bigger event in 2015.

What has triggered all these new movements? And will we see more such developments?

India has been seen as a single sport country and this was even more accentuated after the World Cup Cricket win in 1983.

The spread of television has made cricket stars recognized figures all over the country. However, as affluence has increased, there has been a growing desire to look at other sports. In some sense, cricket has become a game for the masses. The affluent want more types of games to follow and play. Football is growing in stature in the bigger cities. Badminton too has gained new traction with the success of Indian girls in the international arena. Games like golf and squash are finding niche appeal. Tennis, which was once in favour with Vijay Amritraj as the Indian face, is once again rising thanks to Leander Paes and Sania Mirza. Running, thanks to the marathon movement, has become a big sport. Unfortunately, hockey, a game Indians excelled in, has somewhere been left by the wayside despite the launch of the Indian Hockey League. Hopefully, it will get a second wind.

What does the future look like? Will India become a nation of sports lovers and not just cricket lovers? Will our kids be encouraged to play games and not just be textbook wonders?

With the growing penetration of mobile phones and smartphones, I suspect kids will be playing on their mobile phones and not in the playgrounds. An ad by Maggi done in 2014, starring Madhuri Dixit, has mothers playing football while the kids are playing video games and lazing about. The kids seeing their moms play join the real game. The film ends with the message and hashtag '#HealthIsEnjoyable'. Unfortunately, pressing the health button in its advertising did not help Maggi much as it got embroiled in a controversy regarding the contents in its pack in mid-2015. Fortunately for Madhuri Dixit and Maggi lovers, the brand seems to have recovered its mojo after dealing with the crisis.

Sports journalist Boria Majumdar writes about how Indians look across the border and lament at how backward we Indians are as compared to China when it comes to sports. He also says that the Indian sports machinery and organizations are a bit too complicated for India to adopt a unilinear approach to reviving Indian sports from its current stupor[2]. Therein lies the other big problem when we speak of India and sports. Unlike most parts of the developed and developing world, the emphasis placed on sports in Indian society is still abysmal. Many schools don't even have playgrounds. Admission to institutes of higher learning have no emphasis on sports or extracurricular achievements. The latest formula seems to be the addition of big money, big business and media glamour; this may, in fact, give Indian sports and sportsmen their much-needed spot in the limelight.

While as a kid, most of us in the fifty-plus generation used to play in our neighbourhood streets. I wonder if this is possible in any Indian city today, even during the weekends. Finally, as we saw in the Nike cricket ad, we may have to let our kids play cricket on top of buses stuck in traffic. I hope and pray it does not come to that.

Section Four
AD NARRATIVES

Doodh Doodh Doodh, Wonderful Doodh

'Sir, I am thinking of immigrating to Australia. What do you think?'

The question floored me. I was sitting outside the recording studio of a young music director who I knew as Dilip Kumar. I had heard that he was once part of Ilayaraja's group but had decided to try his own hand at music direction. I was trying to make a low-cost ad film for an ultra-low-cost roofing brand Literoof and my film producer had strongly recommended Dilip. I had heard some of his tracks and was impressed as hell. This was the year 1992. The country had just started tasting the winds of liberalization. We were waiting for the singer, Subha – who went on to become famous as Malgudi Subha – and were whiling away time outside the studio. I had no ready answer for Dilip, but managed to say that he would make a mistake by moving out of India just as it gets ready to grow drastically. Dilip did not sound convinced, but the singer arrived and we got busy.

If you were wondering who this young Dilip was, it is none other than music maestro AR Rahman. Let me assure you that many a film music director cut their teeth in crafting the perfect thirty-second jingle. From Shankar Ehsan Loy to Ram Sampat, all of them have had their first innings in ad films. I am sure many more will follow their illustrious steps.

Indian advertising is today a cornucopia of innumerable types of music. We also have film music coming at us from all directions – radio, television, Internet radio stations and even mobile radio stations. But it was not this way some six decades ago.

BV Keskar, who headed the Ministry of Information and Broadcasting from 1952-1962, disliked film music because he believed that it corrupted Indian classical music. In 1952, he made sure that All India Radio would not play any film music[1]. He put in motion moves to encourage and nurture classical music on radio with events like the Akashvani Sangeet Sammelan. Interestingly, even today TM Krishna, the Carnatic music virtuoso continues the same tradition of being dismissive of film songs and their claims of classical (Carnatic) music lineage[2].

Ameen Sayani, the radio advertising legend, recalls, 'This happened at a time when Indian film music was the best medium for the spread of the national language and for the spread of togetherness … This was the golden period when the giants of Indian music were creating some great music'. If AIR did not play their favourite songs, there were others who did.

Keskar's move gave birth to Radio Ceylon which started a thriving commercial broadcasting service aimed at the Indian sub-continent and aired one of the biggest hits on radio, *Binaca Geetmala*. The first broadcast of the programme in 1952 garnered an astounding 9000 letters when they were expecting just about fifty.

The government of India had an epiphany after the rise of Radio Ceylon. It launched Vividh Bharati Service in 1957 to broadcast film music and other popular formats, though radio advertising was allowed only in 1967. This helped Radio Ceylon continue its merry journey of compiling hit parades and tantalizing the film-music-hungry Indians. Finally, in 1970

Vividh Bharati started allowing recorded sponsored programmes, but Radio Ceylon had had a clear run for almost twenty years[3]!

Hindi film music was indeed the lifeblood of the country for many decades. The voices of Lata Mangeshkar and Mohammad Rafi captivated millions. Sanjay Srivastava explains the magnetic power of Lata Mangeshkar in his essay 'The Voice of the Nation and the Five-Year Plan Hero: Speculations on Gender, Space, and Popular Culture' saying that she has '…an aura of the cult of Meera – the medieval princess-poetess and an iconic figure in the Bhakti movement – about her. Like the Bhakti poets, Lata too has forsaken her sexuality and domesticity for devotion to a greater cause, namely the endowment of national pleasure through a redefinition of modern Indian feminine identity … in the process, she became the icon of virgin mother (sister?) (sic) of the nation'. Srivastava also says that there were other contrasting figures. 'The most obvious contrast is with the ghazal singer Begum Akhtar … made no effort, even in old age, to project the image of either an asexual mother figure or a generically "respectable" grandmother'[4].

The early ads in Indian cinema halls did borrow from the popularity of Hindi film songs. Lifebuoy with its anthemish jingle, '*Lifebuoy hai jahan, tandurusti hai wahan* (where there is Lifebuoy, there is health)' comes to mind as the most vivid example.

Around the mid-'70s, Indians were getting exposed to western popular music thanks to Radio Ceylon and Radio Kuwait, and the weekly dose on AIR. This led to the emergence of another voice from Kolkata, Usha Uthup. Her jingles for brands like Gold Spot and Nescafe are widely remembered. The Gold Spot cinema spot featured a girl walking down a beach carrying a bottle of Gold Spot as Usha crooned 'Livva little hot, sippa Gold Spot'; created by the legendary ad agency MCM, the film and print advertising featured a young girl who later became the superstar

Rekha. In yet another spot, which was shot in the Kaziranga Forest reserve where a group of youngsters were taking a ride on an elephant, sipping coffee to Usha's song of 'Come alive to the taste of Nescafe'.

Indian ads were also using popular Hindustani ragas to create memorable tunes. The most memorable ad of the '80s would probably be the Hamara Bajaj commercial which was in the Hindustani raga Desh.

The most-loved musical piece on television at that time – you cannot call it an advertisement – was the *Ek Sur* or *Mile Sur Mera Tumhara* film on national integration. The film was first telecast after the Prime Minister's speech at Red Fort on Independence Day, 1988. The project, conceptualized by Suresh Mallik (Ogilvy & Mather) and Kailash Surendranath, film-maker, had as its cast a whole host of musicians from around India, movie stars, sports personalities and more. The lyrics were by Piyush Pandey of Ogilvy & Mather, music was composed by Ashok Patki and arranged by Louis Banks.

In a sense, this film lives on in advertising as an example of a 'national integration' story. Bajaj was one of the earliest to adopt this approach. Numerous other brands such as the American car brand Chevrolet, cement brands, fabric brands have all used this format.

It is not as if Indian advertising was held captive by film music or classical musical formats. In the '90s, Parag Trivedi – he passed away at a very young age – used to conduct day-long workshops to get mainly advertising agency creative executives familiarized with western classical music. He used to take the listeners through the emergence of various musical forms in the West, starting with the Gregorian chant to the rise of classical music during the Renaissance.

Parag had a colleague who used to conduct a workshop on Indian classical music or Hindustani music. As preparation for a workshop she was conducting at our agency FCB Ulka, she asked for ten of our jingle-based ads to understand what our pet tunes were. She later told me that we seem to be in love with the Raga Desh.

Gregorian chant is a form of monophonic music which is without any instrumentation, employing only human voices. Gregorian chants were traditionally sung by choirs of men and boys in churches of the western Roman Catholic Church. While conceptualizing the ad for Voltas Megalaundrette, which featured a set of ten men and kids singing in only their towels, the music style that brought alive the words *'Yeh ho nahi sakta'* (This cannot happen) was the Gregorian chant.

Titan watches was set up in 1984 as a joint venture between the Tata Group and Tamil Nadu government's TIDCO. The company went on to take on the hegemony of the public sector giant HMT to redefine watch habit in the country. Riding the quartz wave, the company proved all naysayers wrong by getting conservative Indians to switch from a manual-winding watch to a watch powered by a battery that needed change every year. The company launched its range of great-looking watches through captivating catalogue-type advertising in newspapers and magazines. Indians, who till then were only exposed to such watches when they travelled abroad, were now spoilt for choice. The company also pioneered the retail end of the selling game by setting up its own company-authorized retail stores which were staffed with people who helped the Indian consumer make the leap from manual to battery-powered watches. When the brand started advertising on television and cinemas, it decided to once again showcase its great-looking watch range – shot with much love and affection. The managing director of the company then, Xerxes Desai, was a western classical music aficionado. The story goes that he picked a musical interlude from Wolfgang Amadeus Mozart's Symphony No. 25 in G minor. The company did not question the logic of using a musical piece that was over two hundred years old to help sell a modern quartz watch. But the gambit worked. Titan's choice of Mozart set it apart from the other jingle-based ads on television. The company has wisely stayed with the same musical piece, though it has been rendered in many different ways in the last thirty years. The lay public and buyers of Titan watches, at least most of them, think that it is Titan music, and not Mozart. This is not unique to India. Brands everywhere have used bits of classical music to sell their wares. Even for mundane products like Quaker Puffed Wheat and Puffed Rice, Tchaikovsky's finale to the 1812 Overture was used[5].

> AUDIO SIGNATURE: Brands can create and nurture its special feel by using a musical signature. It calls for careful crafting of a tune that can live a long life. Titan managed it. Britannia has lived with its little ditty for decades. Tata Docomo created a signature and built on it. So did Airtel.

If we were to look at ads produced in India over the last twenty years, we will get to meet numerous musical forms and they can be a great quick-guide to music. Let us take a quick tour.

Popular western music is a staple for Indian advertising. Till the copyright rules changed in the 2000s, ads were allowed to use a bit of any popular tune by just getting a written approval from an association. When we made our first Tata Indica film ('More Dreams Per Car') the film-makers, Namita Roy Ghose and Subir Chatterjee of White Light films used a short piece from the popular track by Lobo 'I'd love you to want me'. The film was such a big hit that when the music company that owned the track released a cassette featuring ten 'for the road' tracks, they even had a sticker on the cover saying 'Featuring the Indica Song'.

That was in the year 1999. A few years later when we were working on a film for the car Indigo Marina, we were keen on using the song by the jazz legend, Louis Armstrong, 'What a Wonderful World'. But our film-maker friend, Rajesh Saathi could not identify the title holder in India. Being an enterprising young film-maker, he came up with a great idea. He said he would get a song written about a man and a woman in love, get it composed and have a guy, whose voice was similar to Louis Armstrong, perform it. When the film was made, featuring the super model Sheetal Mallar being taken out on a date by a handsome young man, who pulls out a whole array of things from the cavernous boot of the Indigo Marina, all to the tune of the new song, we all fell in love with the film. Though the client team did not fully endorse our idea of a gravelly voice singing a love song, they relented after we played an optional track. The film ran on national television and the car sold well. Some months after the film went on air, I received a letter from a lady who said that her octogenarian father was an ardent fan of Louis Armstrong and had every single album, single sung/played by the great musician. After combing through his collection – it must have taken days – the old man could not locate the song that was used in the Indigo Marina film. So the lady said that her father was curious to know how we got the track and which album can she find it on. I had to write to her that we had fooled her, and her dad, by creating our own version of a Louis Armstrong song.

If that was jazz, can reggae be far behind.

When National Dairy Development Board, under the guidance of the Milkman of India, Dr V Kurien, wanted us to create an ad to popularize the consumption of milk, the team wrote a snappy jingle that used the Hindi word for milk – 'Doodh' – as the musical refrain. The jingle which touted the many benefits of milk – *'Doodh doodh doodh doodh, wonderful doodh, piyo glassful'* – was set to a reggae tune. This type of music derives its origins from Jamaican dance music. Till date, the

'Doodh Doodh' jingle and ad continues to be so popular that when a video production company decided to create an anthem for Indian advertising, it started with the 'Doodh Doodh' film. The jingle for Kingfisher Mineral Water too used a reggae tune for their meaningless jingle '*Ooolalala Ooleyo*'.

It is not as if Indian ads are besotted with western musical formats. Of late, we are seeing numerous relatively less-known Indian musical genres getting their time under the spotlight.

A boat is being rowed down the river. It is loaded with brand new wooden chairs. The boatman spots a nubile young woman waiting for a ride to get to the other side of the river. She asks him shyly and indicates with her eyes that his boat is full. He quickly pushes some of the chairs overboard – later we see that they are all tied to the boat – and creates space for the nubile wench. What fascinated me was the music that accompanied this love story. It was a particular type of music sung by the wandering minstrels of West Bengal, known as Bauls. Created by Ogilvy for its client Fevicol, the writer of the ad, Abhijit Awasti admitted that the choice of the music was by his uncle, the director of the film, Prasoon Pandey; just as several other talented ad film-makers of India, he too has a great range of musical knowledge.

In addition to using music in advertisements, brands also use music or musical notes as their signature. We saw how Titan usurped Mozart. Britannia biscuits have used a ditty, '*ting ting di ting*', as the last sound for their ad films for decades. Doordarshan's signature music composed by Pandit Ravi Shankar was once the most recalled musical tune. In recent times, Airtel has got music director AR Rahman – not Dilip this time – to compose a special musical track for them which they have used consistently, even if it is as an end note in every ad they have released. Tata Docomo too has its own musical signature – *do do do, do do do* – composed by Ram Sampath. Internationally, brands have used music in new ways and experts like music composer Joel Beckerman have been roped in to create 'sonic branding' for AT&T, Mercedes, Disney, Coca-Cola and others. Tyler Gray explores the new role of sonic branding and its role in brand building in *The Sonic Boom: How Sound Transforms the Way We Think, Feel and Buy*[6]. Brands are now figuring out how to engage with their customers better by creating and owning a bit of sound, music or even sound effect which can make the brand more evocative and sticky. This 'sonic branding' can play in all the advertising, in showrooms, as telephone hold tunes and even when the website is getting loaded. Rajeev Raja, a veteran creative director and a musician of great repute, has reinvented his career in 2012 to become a 'Brand Mogo' expert; mogo standing for 'musical logo'.

The usage of various forms of music in Indian ads fascinated me so much that I got a musically talented young man from our agency to try and catalogue various types of music that have been used in Indian advertising. In this chapter, till now we have seen Hindi film songs, Hindustani classical, western classical, western popular, Gregorian chant, jazz, reggae, baul. In our analysis, we also located Italian operatic music, gazals, sufi music, Indian Carnatic music, Indo-Jazz fusion music, Qawwali, African drums, scatting etc.

This should come as no surprise. All popular Indian art forms have a liberal dose of music. All Indian films till date have had songs; National Film awards are given not just for the film with the best music, but also for the best song, best male singer, best female singer etc. In his book *Hindi Film Geet Kosh*, Harminder Singh Hamraaz has indicated that JJ Madan's *Indra Sabha* (1932) had sixty-nine songs, the maximum for any Hindi movie; pointing this out, TJS George offers the musical crown to the Tamil movie *Lava Kusa*, which reportedly had seventy-two songs[7].

All Indian television soap operas have a song in the beginning. Song-based reality shows like Zee SaReGaMaPa continue to thrill audiences.

With the emergence of Internet as a separate medium, Indians' thirst for music is going to get even more diverse and hopefully will be even better served.

Coke Studio is an experiment of combining various musical forms and started in Brazil in 2007. It was adapted in Pakistan and became a digital video sensation clocking millions of views. Combining western rock-style music with Sufi music, Coke Studio Pakistan gained cult-like following in the sub-continent. Coke India along with its media agency Lodestar UM under the able guidance of Shashi Sinha decided to turn up the heat one more notch by partnering with MTV. Coke Studio India was offered on MTV and also on the Internet and has found great fan following. Not only has the programme used the genres of music that we all know, they have also managed to unearth relatively unknown musical formats like the folk music of Tamil Nadu by a singer called Chinnakannu. Absolutely fascinating stuff that!

> **SOUND VISUALS:** Radio experts tell us that sound needs to be presented in such a way that it will make the listener visualize what is happening. So using sound creatively is a part of great radio advertising. Listen carefully the next time, see if the radio production company is able to get you to visualize the situation.

As India becomes more and more prosperous, I believe there will be a growing appetite for various musical forms. Already in a city like Mumbai, we have Hindustani classical concerts, Carnatic music festivals, Sufi, gazal, blues, jazz, rock, EDM and other forms of music concerts.

In modern-day India, while other musical forms are gaining traction, Hindi film music continues to rule and is getting new life with the increasing need for songs to perform at wedding sangeet ceremonies. In addition, across the country there is a demand for live performers to belt out Hindi songs at events ranging from product launches, birthday parties, shop openings, wedding anniversaries, etc.

Keskar tried banning Hindi film music. But instead he ended up creating a pent-up demand for the genre of music he was keen on restricting. It is quite possible that the very same songs he tried banning on AIR in the late-'50s are finding new life in a remixed manner as wedding sangeet songs, not just in India but wherever Indians live.

Meri Khubsurti Ka Raaz

IT WAS THE biggest advertising event of the year, the Abby Awards Show of the Ad Club at the National Sports Club of India (NSCI) grounds at Worli, Mumbai. The special guest at the awards was the reigning superstar of Bollywood, Shah Rukh Khan. Ad Club had managed this coup thanks to the friendship of Pradeep Guha, the then President of Ad Club, with the superstar. I think the year was 2002. As was the custom, SRK was requested to say a few words at the event. His extempore speech, and Pradeep confirms that it was extempore, just floored me.

In short, SRK said: I am here at an advertising function to thank all of you for getting me those wonderful endorsement contracts. I make a packet endorsing brands and I have all of you to thank you for that. Please remember that the funding I get helps me try out new roles and experiment with the kind of stories I am picking to act in.

Asoka had just released. He went on like this for a few minutes. Then he started reeling out the brands he was endorsing, including Pepsi, Hyundai Santro etc. He ended his light speech with a call for action: he still had a few slots open and was looking for endorsements in headache pills, pain balms, hair oil, undergarments, socks and shoes!

SRK may have said it in mirth, but the truth is that in the year 2016, it is quite a task not to see a film star endorsing a brand when you switch on the TV set.

But it was not like this, even three decades ago. Stars endorsing brands is a mania we have seen in the 1990s and 2000s.

Did this western phenomenon of celebrity madness travel to India along with the concept of advertising?

The award for the most amusing episode relating to celebrity endorsements should go to this anecdote: In the 1920s, Harrods, the London departmental store, asked three literary luminaries, George Bernard Shaw, Arnold Benner and HG Wells to write testimonials for their store. All three declined for a variety of reasons, but their refusals were so evocative that they ultimately ran as advertisements[1].

> CELEBRITY COSTS: Hiring a celebrity costs a bomb and often they are particular about giving eight hours and nothing more. The hidden costs of hiring a film star could include special allowances for the star's driver, make-up man, hair stylist, dress designer, vanity van driver and more. Factor these in when you plan to hire a film star for your next launch.

While those learned gentlemen refused, many attractive Hollywood stars have willingly obliged and many have starred in Lux advertisements from the early twentieth century. No wonder filmographers say that the oldest film star endorsement in Indian firmament was possibly the Hindi star Leela Chitnis modelling for Lux. As the reader may know, Lux soap from Unilever is positioned globally as the 'beauty secret of film stars'. UK born ad historian Nigel Rees says that Lux even used a more emphatic claim – 'Nine out of ten screen stars use Lux toilet soap for their priceless smooth skins' – in the US in 1927 and continued to use it for twenty years[2]. The brand entered India over 100 years ago and used famous Hollywood stars to promote itself to the affluent Indian consumer. It was in the 1940s that the company decided it needed to use Indian actresses to help the brand connect with Indian women. What Leela Chitnis started was then followed up by almost all the leading film stars of India. It is rumoured that leading actresses in Indian cinema used to see the Lux contract as something that announced to the world that they had 'arrived'. Hindustan Lever for years used a single-point contract person who managed these star arrangements. Apparently, the fee was very low and the endorsement was sold as a sign of recognition. Leading Bollywood film stars including Waheeda Rehman, Rekha, Hema Malini, Sridevi, Madhuri Dixit, Zeenat Aman, Aishwarya Rai have all featured in Lux advertisements. In the south, all the major stars including Padmini, Savitri, Sharada, Jayanthi and others have followed suit. The first Indian male film star to have featured in a Lux advertisement is SRK. In 2005, to celebrate a special anniversary, Lux made an ad that had SRK in a bathtub surrounded by the former and current endorsers of the brand: Hema Malini, Sridevi, Juhi Chawla and Kareena Kapoor. In fact, till then, the only other male star to have featured in a Lux ad was the indomitable Paul Newman.

While female film stars have appeared in Lux advertisements for decades, the appearance of an Indian male film star in ads was a rarity. Archives tell us that in 1955, Kishore Kumar appeared in a print advertisement of Brylcreem, a product that was alien to the Indian male haircare regimen. There was even a Dilip Kumar-branded range of table tasties with products such as Royal Chutney, Mango Pickle and Lime Pickle from a company called Mother India Products. Brands like Bagpiper soda and Charminar cigarettes too used film stars in the '70s. Shatrughan Sinha featuring in a Bagpiper soda print advertisement says, *'Khoob jameg rang jab mil baithenge teen yaar – aap, hum aur Bagpiper Club Soda'* (The party will flow when we three friends sit together – you, me and Bagpiper Soda). Charminar used Jackie Shroff before he had joined the movies.

One of the most interesting use of a celebrity, or should one say a film character, was the 1976 ad of Britannia Glucose-D biscuits. Departing from the norm of using a film star as a film star, the brand boldly used Amjad Khan as the character he had played in the superhit movie *Sholay*: Gabbar Singh. The brand was presented as '*Gabbar ki asli pasand*'. The ad film which ran in movie halls all over the country was shot in the same location as the original *Sholay* film, featuring the characters from the movie (Samba, Kalia and others) and captured the exact ethos of the dacoit-infested Chambal valley in Uttar Pradesh (recreated near Mysore in Karnataka). The ad played off the familiar scene and dialogues from the film and was a great hit with the movie-going audience. It should be said that it was a very bold move by a brand to use a negative film character to sell a product aimed at children. The clincher in the ad comes at the very end, again playing off a famous dialogue from the original film '*Gaon ka har bachcha jaanta hai, ki Gabbar ki asli pasand kya hai! Asli cheese, samjhe! … Britannia Glucose-D biscuits, Gabbar ki asli pasand*' (Every kid knows Gabbar's real choice! The real thing, Britannia Glucose biscuits! Gabbar's real choice).

The fact that the campaign created by Lowe Lintas was well-loved and the brand went on to gain market share was indicative of the changes in the way Indian consumers were perceiving and decoding advertising messages. It also proves how enduring a film character can be, especially when the film is a big hit. I cannot recall any other such bold use of a negative character to endorse a brand, at least one where the film got embedded in the collective memory of the consumers.

In the '80s, the brand Pan Parag used veteran actors Ashok Kumar and Shammi Kapoor to enact a familiar scene between the father of the bride and the father of the bridegroom in a typical North Indian wedding.

Around the same time, we also had Vinod Khanna featuring in a Cinthol soap advertisement, running down a beach alongside a horse.

From the '50s to the '80s, if at all a male star featured in an advertisement, it was an exception. Dilip Kumar rarely featured in an ad – the pickle ad was an exception that proved the rule – neither did Raj Kapoor nor Dev Anand. In the south, NT Rama Rao, Shivaji Ganesan, MG Ramachandran, Raj Kumar or Prem Nazir never did advertisements. I suppose they felt that their fans would see them as pure 'commercial artists' if they did endorsements for money. You should remember that in the south, the film stars had socio-political leanings which may have prevented them from embracing capitalistic brands.

All this was set to change in 1995. Amitabh Bachchan was the ruling deity in Bollywood. Brand BPL was facing competition from international majors such as Sony, Toshiba as well as Indian players such as Videocon and Onida. In a coup of sorts, the brand roped in the Big B to endorse it. Amitabh had taken a break from films and was involved in building his company ABCL. The brand used him in a series of ads where he never openly endorsed the brand, but did speak of his passion for excellence and how one brand reflected this passion. In one of the ads, he named the various favourite characters he had played in his movies and how behind all of them was the passion for doing the best. The campaign went on to win accolades from both critics and consumers. BPL did get a leg up and went ahead, in image terms, of all Indian brands. Interestingly, in mid-2015, Pothy's, a Tamil Nadu-based large garment retailer roped in Kamal Haasan for the first time to do an ad for them; the message was about 'trust', echoing what Big B did for BPL. Unfortunately, BPL did not sustain its brand-building efforts and virtually vanished in the 2000s in the face of fresh attack from the Korean majors such as Samsung and LG. At one time, BPL was the leader in frost-free refrigerators and washing machines; difficult to even imagine it today. But campaigns like the one featuring Big B created by the Delhi-based boutique Dhar & Hoon did keep the brand ticking in the late '90s.

If we do a flash forward to the 2000s, you cannot watch three ads without spotting a celebrity. Big film stars like Amitabh Bachchan, SRK, Aamir Khan, Ranbir Kapoor and Salman Khan have been used to sell colas, biscuits, hair oil, shampoos, creams, suitings, shoes, cars, motorbikes, mobile services, mobile handsets, undergarments – yes, SRK endorses Lux Cozi. If male film stars are ruling the air waves can cricket stars be far behind? Dhoni and Sachin have a list of brand endorsements that can rival that of the Khans. Female stars too are no spring chickens in the endorsement game. When the FCB Ulka team was looking for a female star to endorse a hair oil brand they could not find one among the top ten heroines who was free to do the endorsement. Stars like Katrina Kaif, Kareena Kapoor and Aishwarya Rai have a long list of endorsements. Even stars who entered the fray in the 2010s, such as Sonakshi Sinha, today have endorsements that run in to pages.

> **BODY DOUBLES:** Like in feature films, when using stars, body doubles are routinely used in ads as well. Sometime they are needed to perform special stunts like jumping off a cliff, car or bike.

The South is now starting to resemble the North. The biggest star of the south, Rajnikanth, continues to dodge the brand bullets, but all the others are ready to play the game. Tamil stars like Vijay, Surya and Telugu superstar Mahesh Babu are today seen endorsing a variety of brands from two wheelers to tractors, biscuits to banyans, mobile services and more.

Why this celebrity obsession, you may ask.

The answer may lie somewhere else. Professor Arvind Rajagopal of New York University has been studying the changing

Indian media scene, advertising and consumer perceptions. He points out that brands started using totems from the bazaar to connect with consumers. In the 1950s, it was common to see brands like Pears using images of gods to sell themselves. In fact, an old poster of Pears claims: '*Pears soap, pure as the lotus, learn without sorrow, the eternal truth that youth is godlike and beauty is youth*'. Burmah Shell, a multinational petroleum company used to distribute calendars featuring Hindu gods and godesses. The practice of using gods in the calendar continues to this date. Professor Rajagopal says that brands borrowed from bazaar art to connect with the consumers when selling products the consumer was not familiar with.

It is likely this is happening at a larger scale in the 2010s. Brands are trying to drive usage down the socio-economic pyramid. Products like face wash and skin creams are now being targeted at the lower-middle classes. Shampoos and two-wheelers are also aiming to go down the pyramid. Mobile services too are targeting the lower classes. In all these cases, using a celebrity makes the message a lot more appealing and credible to the uninitiated. Consumers do know that the film star is not doing the endorsement for free, but still the celebrity face makes the story more aspirational and also maybe more credible.

As a case in point, when Cadbury had to face negative reports about worm infestation – which happened in the shops, not in their factories – it used the power of Amitabh Bachchan to send out the message that their packages have been revamped to take care of any such problem. Reports say that they bounced back to their original market share in a few months.

The second reason is that compared to the cost of running a campaign on mass media, the cost of a celebrity is today a lot more approachable. Many large brands look at a media spend in the region of ₹100 crores. In this context, paying SRK or Big B an amount equal to ₹10 crores does not seem too high, especially if their face will help the brand gain a few market-share points. As a related point, the corporatization of the Indian film industry has also played a role in the increased use of film stars. The days of income tax raids on film stars are all but over. Either they are no longer dodging taxes like they used to or they are managing to keep the news out of the media. Now there are more negative reports about corporate India's tax troubles than film stars and their tax fiddles.

The nature of using film stars is also changing. Most brands have figured out that just saying 'I use Lux' is no longer going to work, if all brands are using film stars. Savvy ad agencies have figured out that you need to 'cast' the film star as a character in a film rather than as a 'star'. In the ad film for TVS Scooty, Priety Zinta was used as just a girl having fun on her scooter.

In the film made by FCB Ulka for the two-wheeler Hero Pleasure, Priyanka Chopra plays a role of a smart young woman in a village, out at the railway station to meet the boy who her parents have chosen for her. Without revealing who she really is, she offers him a ride on her Hero Pleasure and when he speaks disparagingly about the girl his parents have chosen, who he thinks will be a 'silly village girl', she takes him for a merry ride only to drop him back at the station saying that 'That's your train and I'm Manjeet, your "silly village girl"'. The remorseful young man mutters to himself about what a mistake he had made.

Films like these are becoming the norm, where the film star is not someone who is a star to be worshipped, but an actor playing out a role.

One final reason film stars are becoming the staple in Indian ads is the fact that many marketers are resorting to pre-testing the ads. While pre-testing an ad, using a celebrity often helps the brand score many extra points. So for an additional cost of around 5 to 10 per cent of the annual media budget, if you can get a good score in the pre-test, the marketing manager is not going to let that go.

From using film stars in ads, today brands are trying to get into films and television programmes. The corporatization of movies has also opened up the new avenue of brand placement in films. So a Hyundai car gets featured in an SRK movie and Nescafe in a Hrithik Roshan film. Thus, the film industry, film stars and brands have come together to make a nice threesome to sing the 'buy me' song to the enchanted moviegoer. This is not unique to India. Michael Schudson speaks of how producers of Steven Spielberg's film *ET* contacted Mars candy company to ask if they would be interested in featuring M&Ms as the candy that cements the relationship between the alien and the human kid. The company did not show any interest. The producer, unbeknownst to Hershey, makers of Reese's Pieces, decided to use their brand in the said place. They, however, requested Hershey before the movie release for a tie-in promotion. Hershey loved the idea and invested a million dollars in promotion. The sales of Reese's Pieces reportedly jumped by 70 per cent in a month[3]! In India too, we have seen some very successful tie-ins – the oldest being Raj Kapoor's *Bobby* with Escorts; recently, Tata Salt and *Mary Kom*; *PK* with Hero Cycles, Duracell and Cycle Agarbatti seem to have spelt magic in the marketplace – and more will follow as brand managers get to understand how to leverage the connection.

Studies have been done to help marketers use celebrities better. Newspapers run articles featuring the star-power rankings every month.

FCB Ulka's Cogito Consulting's study done in the year 2002, points towards three key dimensions: Trait Fit Index, how the traits of the brand fit with those of the celebrity; Compatibility Index, consumers perception of suitability of brand with celebrity and, finally, Aura of the celebrity[4]. The study showed that brands will do well to pick the star with the biggest aura; the rest are not as important as the aura of the star. No wonder there is a mad rush to sign the most popular star. The report concludes: 'In sum, some celebrities can actually work if we make them work! To make a celebrity work harder, either choose one who is the latest craze or if you don't have those kinds of money, get a personality who is a mirror image of your brand (be sure that he/she has at least some aura about him/her or at least has strong personality traits). But if you are a youth brand, then make sure that the latest heartthrobs are included in your portfolio. You cannot do without them. On the other hand, if you are a serious category, heartthrobs be damned! Choose someone who radiates maturity and credibility. So before you write that cheque worth crores, just think twice'[5].

Bole Mere Lips,
I Love Uncle Chipps

I THOUGHT I had escaped the world of chemical engineering when I entered the exciting world of advertising in 1979. But lo and behold, the first account I was asked to handle when I joined Rediffusion Advertising was a Pune-based engineering company called Wanson. My then colleague, Ashok Kurien – who later went on to start the enormously successful ad agency Ambience – was delighted to hand over the account to me and focus his energies on the exciting Garden Sari account. Though I cursed him squarely then, I later realized it was a godsend opportunity for me to work on an emerging B2B brand. Soon after the agency was briefed about the change in the name of the company from Wanson to Thermax. I immersed into reading about the achievements of Wanson India and, to my delight, discovered numerous innovations the company had pioneered such as thermal heating systems, waste heat recovery systems, pollution control systems etc. The six-ad press campaign the agency created had a strong emphatic headline that proclaimed 'Thermax Does It' and each ad had a case study to support the innovation claim. The then managing director of Thermax, Mr RD Aga, loved the approach and the way the company's new logo was integrated into the campaign – Creative/Art Director Arun Kale's masterstroke again – and offered to personally flesh out the copy matter of the ad. The original headlines and concept had been penned by Kamlesh Pandey and I thought it was an honour that the MD, also an Oxford English graduate, himself offered to help with the writing of the cases. The ad that came back from Thermax to the agency had the most perfect copy possible. Though Kamlesh Pandey tried his hand, he could not improve on what Mr Aga had written. He protested that I was supporting the client's copy and not his version. Battle raged for a few days, but Mr Aga's copy won the final vote.

Kamlesh Pandey was one of the first of the new breed of copywriters to enter advertising in the mid-'70s. He was bilingual and could write a copy-heavy Hindi ad with equal alacrity as a copy-heavy English ad. He was also a genius at television scripts and went on to realize his dream of becoming one of the most celebrated Hindi movie scriptwriters – the superhit film *Tezaab* was written by Kamlesh. I got my first look at a screenplay when he proudly showed off his copy of the *Casablanca* screenplay to me!

The Indian advertising scene was largely dominated by convent-educated boys in the '60s and '70s. They took over the task from the British admen who exited the country in the '50s. Indian language writers were confined to the 'Language Department'. That was set to change. Kamlesh was one of the first to break this thick wall with his ads for brands like Red Eveready, Red & White cigarettes, HMT bulbs and more, all originally created in Hindi. Piyush Pandey, Balki, Prasoon Joshi and others have continued to blaze new trails for Hindi and non-English-medium writers in the '90s and 2000s. Creating a unique path just as Indian born English copywriters like Alyque Padamsee, Arun Kolatkar, Kersy Katrak and Frank Simoes did in the '60s and '70s.

It was not as if Indian agencies had no competency in writing copy in Indian languages. Gerson da Cunha recalls that in the '50s, Lintas was tasked to create print ads in fourteen different Indian languages by their client Lever Brothers for Dalda vanaspati. The agency did not attempt to write one ad and translate it into the various languages. It actually wrote each ad from ground up to reflect the food ethos of each linguistic community of India.

Coming to the '70s, while Kamlesh was writing Hindi copy, yet another linguistic revolution was taking place in the English film journalistic world. Devyani Chaubal, who used to be with the now defunct film magazine *Star & Style*, was bringing Hindi words into English journalism. Shobhaa Kilachand (De) soon started building on this at *Stardust*, the gossipy film magazine she edited for many years with great success.

In advertising too, the divide between Hindi and English copy was falling rapidly. The first big national campaign that used what we today call 'Hinglish' was the campaign for Uncle Chipps created by Contract Advertising, Delhi. The jingle and line went on to be on the lips of many Indians, not just because the line literally was *'Bole mere lips, I love Uncle Chipps'* (My lips say, I love Uncle Chipps). The brand from Amrit Agro Ltd was launched in 1992 and had a jingle that, for the first time, used English and Hindi words together. The language wall had finally fallen. The brand went on to become the biggest-selling branded chips in the country and was finally sold to Frito-Lays (Pepsico Foods) in 2000.

> LIP SYNC: Ad films are often shot in two versions. The Hindi version and the Tamil/Telugu version. All other languages are then dubbed on to the two originals. This is especially required when there are a lot of dialogues to be delivered. So the less dialogues to be delivered to camera, the better your language adaptations will be.

Yet another ad captured the imagination of the young in the mid-'90s by using a mix of English and Hindi words. This was the milk promotion ad done by FCB Ulka for NDDB. The jingle ran '*Doodh, doodh, doodh, wonderful doodh, piyo glassful...*'. This ad gets mentioned as one of the all-time favourites of young and old across India. But it is difficult to imagine in 2010s that this was one of the first ads to systematically use a mix of Hindi and English words. Interestingly, if we were to look at Bollywood dynamics, we see some interesting parallels. Hindi films in the early years, pre-post-independence, have a strong dose of Urdu to the extent that poet Sahir Ludhianvi once caused controversy by asking why Hindi films were not certified as Urdu films as all of them were in Urdu anyway, observed Professor Harish Trivedi, who has looked at how the Hindi language has evolved in Hindi cimema[1]. Historian and novelist Mukul Kesavan is also reported to have said that there exists a singular relationship between Hindi films and Muslim-ness, which is not only reflected in films with Muslim characters and themes, but has determined the very nature of this cinema. But Harish Trivedi points out that a random analysis of film titles indicates that Urdu titles account for less than 10 per cent, Hindi and Hindustani titles dominate with a couple of English titles. But this analysis was done for the period upto 1998. Till then you had Hindi films using different types of Hindi: Dialect Hindi (eg. *Do Bigha Zamin, Ganga Jumna*); Sanskritic Hindi (eg. *Aakrosh, Maya Darpan*); Bambaiya Hindi (eg. *Rangeela, Amar Akbar Anthony*). But the 2000s have seen Hindi movies embracing Hinglish with full vigour. As Harish Trivedi has commented, even on home ground, Hindi cinema is now acquiring a new, elite variety of Hindi in Hinglish, which could perhaps be seen in terms of cultural classification and moving it far from the social spectrum of a rural dialect.

The phenomenon of Hinglish is now all-pervasive, from ads to movies to television serials. Even an illiterate villager today knows a smattering of English words he has heard in movie songs and ads. Words like 'OK', 'love', 'perfect', 'tip-top' and more are part of rural dialects today. The brand Fair and Lovely is referred to as 'Lovely' in the villages of UP. The spread of Hinglish and the awareness that English can open up new doors of employment and success is spurring the growth of English-medium schools across India. Unfortunately, even the teachers in many of these schools do not know how to read or write English beyond the basic few sentences.

A few years ago, a publisher in Chennai approached me to see if one of my brand management books could be translated into Tamil. I was curious to know why they thought there was a potential for a Tamil book on branding. The smart publisher explained that there were over 500 business schools in Tamil Nadu and the students enrolled in over 300 of them could not read English fluently. This publisher had spotted an opportunity to provide them with Tamil translations of management books, which they could read in Tamil, understand the principles and maybe then answer their test papers in their own version of broken English.

It is to be noted that India is probably the only country in the world where readership of newspapers is continuing to rise, as confirmed by the Indian Readership Survey 2014. This has been driven by the growth of Indian language newspapers and the growing literacy in rural India. English language newspapers are in slow decline, though the desire to learn English is palpable across the country. Some Indian language newspapers have experimented with offering one page in English. *Rajasthan Patrika* experimented with this approach and tasted success. There are many more such experiments that should be tried out to bridge the Hindi-Hinglish-English divide.

We should thank the Tamils for keeping the English flag flying in India. Author Bala Jeyaraman writes that it was EV Ramaswamy who launched the first ever Anti-Hindi Agitation in 1937 across the then Madras constituency[2]. In a repeat of this, in 1968, the DMK party led the Anti-Hindi agitation against the Bhakthavatsalam-led Congress government in Madras state. That widespread agitation in a sense led to the electoral victory of DMK and the continued domination of DMK/AIADMK in Tamil Nadu, now running for over forty years. Interestingly, while Hindi agitation has kept English alive and kicking, you may have to know Hindi to order idly at the Saravana Bhavan restaurant in KK Nagar, Chennai.

Here is an interesting anecdote. My good friend Srini was at the said restaurant ready to have a hearty breakfast after an exhilarating motorbike ride. So he asked the waiter who was at his table, '*Sooda enna irruku?*' (What is available, fresh and hot) in Tamil and the waiter is reported to have asked him '*Kya bola?*' (What did you say?). So while Hindi has been kept out of the compulsory part of education in Chennai, the citizens of that city are today served by immigrant labourers from the Northern states of India. So if not to get government jobs, Tamils may just have to learn Hindi to get their dosas at the nearby Saravana Bhavan.

As advertising gets created in Indian languages and as television penetration goes deeper and deeper into the country, we are seeing yet another phenomenon developing. Cogito Consulting of FCB Ulka decided to analyse advertising of popular consumer products picked from the '80s, '90s, 2000s and 2010s. A total of 120 ads for consumer products like soaps, shampoos, detergents etc. were analysed. The researchers decided to count the number of words used in each ad. The words could be dialogue spoken by a character, jingle or a voiceover announcement. What they found was indeed interesting. There has been a steady increase in the number of words employed

> VOICEOVER: Advertising voiceover artistes are an interesting breed. Often they can provide the voice of a film star or sports star even better than the star himself.

in advertising over the forty-year period. From an average of forty-one words in an average thirty-second advertisement, the number has steadily climbed to fifty-three in 2010s. What has led to the increase in the word count? According to global ad guru Professor John Philip Jones, an effective ad is generally more visual than verbal, the number of words in a thirty-second commercial should be restricted to thirty or less; the picture should tell the story[3]. If this is true, why are marketers thrusting more and more words into advertising for mundane products like toothpastes and beverages? What could have happened in the last forty years?

Compared to the 1980s, television has become an even more of a mass market media in the 2010s. In the '80s, just about 15 per cent of homes across India had access to television. The number is set to cross 70 per cent in 2015. As a result of this, ads beamed through television are reaching a much larger percentage of the consuming public – in fact, the pet peeve of the Indian Broadcasting Foundation is that by using television rating points as the measurement metric, the advertising community is not considering the fact that 5 per cent viewership in 30 million homes is not the same as 3 per cent viewership in 100 million homes. The growth of television penetration has given mass market consumer brands a big thrust in terms of attracting new users to their brands. Many of these new users need to be told the full story, since they are probably semi-literate. As a result of this, brands are today including elaborate product and ingredient descriptions. Compare a 2010 ad for soap to the Liril ad from the 1970s. You will be surprised to see how the ad for the simple product has an elaborate description of the ingredients, how they act on the skin and keep you glowing etc. The same could be said of a shampoo or a detergent powder. The second phenomenon is the growth of advertising pre-testing across all FMCG marketers. The ads are first created in an animation format and are tested with the target audience. Agencies and brand managers often work together to ensure the ads pass this test. Adding more words helps the process, so does the addition of a celebrity, a baby or a dog. The third reason is the proliferation of brands and brand extensions. From the simple offer of Lux available in pink, white and green, now you have numerous sub-brands and variants with exotic ingredients like strawberry, peach, olive, chocolate, even sea minerals. All this means that the ad needs to have what is known as a 'product window' or 'freight section' to explain the logic of what sea minerals have to do with a simple soap.

Professor Gerald Zaltman of Harvard Business School lists six marketing fallacies and one of them happens to be that marketers tend to think that 'consumers think in words'. He explains: Marketers also believe that consumers' thoughts occur only as words. Thus, they assume they can understand consumers' thinking by interpreting the words used in standard conversations or written on a questionnaire[4]. This excessive focus on words and ignoring the non-verbal cues from consumers leads to an overload of verbal content in advertising as well, ignoring the importance of other cues that may be more effective. In India too, marketers are adding words to their advertising, hoping to communicate better with their target consumers.

Linguistic experiments are being tried out even in television. Educationalists are today advocating same language subtitling as a way to speed up literacy. Hindi songs with subtitles have enabled semi-literate viewers to develop the courage to start reading. Zee Studio and Zee Café, two English-language channels from the Zee Group experimented with same language subtitling of English programming. This move, which may sound rather daft, ended up creating a new trend. Today almost all English-language channels are resorting to same-language subtitling. The English subtitling and Hindi subtitling serve different objectives. English subtitling is needed by most Indian viewers due to their inability to decode the diction of Hollywood films and serials. In the case of Hindi subtitling, the objective is more educational. Sociologists have shown that literacy levels can be driven up if Hindi programming is subtitled in Hindi!

What has led to all these experiments and why are consumers being subjected to these?

India is often described as a continent connected through shared values. Our languages separate us but our culture keeps us connected. The country, over the last fifty years, has seen some dramatic migratory trends. As generations move out, they are also trying to keep in touch through popular media. As the world-reknowned columnist and author Thomas Friedman points out, while we all desire the Lexus in our garage, we are also looking for that specific brand of olive oil from our hometown to add that special flavour to our cooking[5]. This desire to drift apart and at the same time keep links to the mothership has led to numerous media and linguistic experiments. As the cost of creating content in different languages keep declining, we will see the emergence of numerous types of media content. For instance, we have seen the birth and growth of Oriya and Bhojpuri television channels in the 2000s, just as we saw the growth of Tamil and Telugu private channels in the early '90s. Digital media will help boost this further as we see various dialects having their own channels of delivery. So as this changes media consumption, there will also be a growing demand for content that unites us as one country. So the future of Hindi, English and Hinglish is also relatively safe.

As we drift apart, we will also develop an ability to appreciate something that is alien to our cultural sensibilities. Take, for example, the top-grossing film of 2014, *Chennai Express*. The film starring Shah Rukh Khan and Deepika Padukone used Tamil dialogues for the Tamil characters without any subtitling. The director of the film, Rohit Shetty, decided that film is a visual medium and can be understood even without the spoken words. And that is what happened. One of the songs from the film is today a must-dance-to number in every North Indian wedding. The 'Lungi Dance' song must have sold several million dollars worth of lungis, and sunglasses, across wherever the Indian diaspora lives.

That we are finally one country was brought out wonderfully in an ad done for Nestle by McCann in 2014. A young couple are adopting a little girl who is from a different ethnic group at an adoption centre. Their son does not take well to his new sister who also looks so different from him. He fights with his mother to keep her attention. But one day the two kids are in the garden digging. The little girl, quite bravely, pulls out an earthworm with her hands. The young boy is quite amazed at her courage but does not show it as she puts the worm in a glass jar. We then see her leading him to raid the kitchen, climbing up to the top shelf to pull out a jar of cup cakes. He is now her fan. The film ends with the two of them cozily sharing cake. The film poignantly presents the potential of adoption to change this country. And I do hope the film got a few more couples to adopt children who are not from their own neighbourhood.

So from pristine pure English to Hindi to Hinglish, the language of Indian advertising is now a cacophony of many languages. On an average show, you may see ads done in English, Hindi, Hinglish and maybe even in yet another Indian language. With this ever-expanding palette of languages, our country continues to enthrall all of us, while becoming a bigger and bigger puzzle for foreigners to unravel.

No Squeeze, No Wheeze, No Navel Please!

IN THE EARLY '80s, Boots Company was rated as one of the top ten pharmaceutical companies in India. In addition to making several fast-selling pharmaceutical brands such as Digene, Brufen, Cremmafin, Entamizole, the company also had a very successful OTC range consisting of Strepsils throat lozenges and Coldarin cold tablets. It was around 1984, as a Group Product Manager at Boots, when I was tasked to see if the company could revive any of the other brands in its archives. The attention soon focused on Sweetex, an artificial sweetener brand the company had launched in the '70s but had withdrawn due to negative press about its key ingredient, saccharine. But this was the '80s, saccharine no longer had such a bad halo and calorie control was in the news. The company was keen that Sweetex becomes its fourth brand – in addition to Strepsils, Coldarin and Burnol – in the fledgling OTC division. An inter-departmental committee was formed to ensure that the packaging was in attractive plastic, leakage of the liquid pack was near-zero and supplies were certain. It then took up the job of creating demand. Boots decided to hire the ad agency that was making waves in the mid-1980s, Trikaya, to handle this launch. Television was expected to be the key medium, and so the agency was briefed to create a television advertisement which would position Sweetex as the perfect complement to a healthy, low-calorie diet. The film made by Prahlad Kakkar showed a svelte young girl getting into skin-tight jeans and cavorting as the jingle went: 'No squeeze, no wheeze, no sugar in my coffee, please. Sweetex, Sweetex, a sweeter life without calories'.

Those were the days of Doordarshan. Before an ad is made at great cost, the agency always gets a 'storyboard', which is a pictorial depiction of the ad, approved by the Doordarshan authorities.

The agency had done its job, the film was made and all of us loved the film and its energy. The next step was to get the final film approved by Doordarshan. The agency did not see any problem since the storyboard was already approved.

Then came the bombshell. Doordarshan rejected the film on the grounds of obscenity. We were shocked and angered. The film did not violate any norms laid down by the authorities, unless there were any that we did not know of. So I was told by the company to go to Delhi, to the Doordarshan Head Office at Mandi House, plead the case and not come back without a 'yes'!

The agency team accompanied me to Doordarshan and we met the person who had rejected the ad. When we started discussing the film, we were told that the film showed the 'navel' of the model in a close-up shot right at the beginning of the film. And that was seen as obscene. The film-maker had shown the model dressed in a halter top and jeans, so her midriff was exposed and when the words 'No squeeze' was said in the audio track, the model measures her midriff with a tape. I tried explaining how it was a dress style and we had not tried to show a navel for the sake of cheap titillation.

I then had the temerity to tell the Doordarshan official how I did not consider the display of a navel as 'obscene'; I even mentioned that the previous day on the popular film-song programme *Chayageet* on Doordarshan I counted not less than five different navels of film stars on show, with one such midriff serving the purpose of a table in the hands of a handsome hero. I even tried the argument of how our temples and places of worship show gods and goddesses with their midriffs exposed.

Soon I was told to stop and was given a lecture on how all such exposure will be abolished and Doordarshan will not show anything that is even remotely obscene. We were told to change the visual and reapply for permission. Case dismissed!

I came back to Mumbai pretty upset since the film would have to be reshot at considerable expense, but fortunately the film-maker figured out a way of doing a low-cost shoot of only one visual. The film went on air a fortnight later. Unfortunately, the brand did not perform to the expectations of the company, it was a little too ahead of its time, and television advertising stopped after the first year. So I was spared any more encounters with the DD authorities and their obsession against bare navels.

If we were to dial back to the days before commercial advertising on government-owned television, the primary mode of audio-visual advertising was through cinema halls. Brands made shorts of roughly 100 feet length (30.4 metres). These films which ran for one minute, had to be shown to the censor authorities and a censor certificate had to be obtained. Till date, this practice continues, as you would have noticed if you have been in any movie hall. I believe censor authorities were probably a lot clearer about what they wanted to stop and their process was a lot less arbitrary than the 'navel-hating' Doordarshan of that time. The censor authorities had approved a bikini-clad girl cavorting under a waterfall for Liril soap in the mid-'70s and, if we were to believe Alyque Padamsee, the model had ingested good quantities of rum to face the cold waters in winter.

Doordarshan had its own set of rules and these kept changing. It was not just Sweetex that had to tread the treacherous slopes of the Mandi House office. Hindustan Lever, which was launching its fairness cream, was prevented from using the Hindi word for 'fair' or gori. They found a way around it by using the word nikhri and over time managed to get it established as an equivalent word for 'fair'. Though nikhri in Hindi literally means 'improved'. Even sanitary napkins were not permitted to be advertised on prime time.

Indian advertising legend, the late Bal Mundkur, founder of Ulka Advertising, has an interesting story to narrate about fairness obsession from his early days in advertising in the 1950s: 'I once said to John Thurman, Country Head BOAC (airline), a client I serviced, "John, why do we not replace European stewardesses with Indian models in saris?" He replied, "Rubbish. Spray them a bit dark and put a tikka on their foreheads"'[1].

Sometimes the most innocent of lines provoke violent reactions. 'Does she ... or doesn't she? Hair colour so natural only her hair dresser knows for sure' was the line written by Shirley Polykoff of Foote Cone & Belding [FCB] in 1955 when the Clairol account moved to FCB. This seemingly non-acceptable phrase turned a non-acceptable commodity into the highly respected industry that hair colouring is today. But when *Life* magazine saw the ad, it did not want to run it. Finally research amongst their female staff, as suggested by Shirley Polykoff[2], showed that none of them saw any double meaning in it. Many years later, the ad for Calvin Klein jeans featuring the teenage-sensation Brooke Shields with the line, 'You wanna know what comes between me and my Calvins? Nothing'. Either because of her age or the skin-baring commercials, the ad came under a lot of fire. But the jeans were a huge hit.

In order to bring about some method to this censorship madness, the advertising agencies, advertisers and media decided to create a body that would help bring about a level of 'self-regulation' in Indian advertising. Advertising Standards Council of India (ASCI) was born in 1985. Modelled after the UK Council, it had sixteen members on its Board of Governors and a twenty-one-member Consumer Complaints Council.

ASCI came out with elaborate codes on 'Self-Regulation in Advertising'. These rules have been modified over time and extended to cover new categories of advertisers. Complaints received by ASCI were put up to the CCC and were either upheld or rejected. If the complaint was upheld, the company was told to make modifications to the advertising and resubmit the ads to ASCI for their record. Most large companies, advertising agencies and media owners (television and print) were members of ASCI, and almost always complied with the directives. Non-member companies were wont to disregard the ruling. As a final shot in the arm of ASCI, the government of India in 2007 modified the Cable TV Network Rules to ensure that no ad found objectionable by ASCI could be aired through any cable network.

Taking a leaf out of the ASCI code, television broadcasters too set up two self-regulatory bodies, News Broadcasting Standards Authority (NBSA) and Broadcasting Content Complaints Council (BCCC). These bodies are, by and large, concerned with the content that is broadcast and not the advertising.

While ASCI had been set up in 1985, a condom ad managed to make headline news in the parliament in 1991. JK Chemicals, a part of the Raymond Group, decided to enter the condom category. The company wanted to see if it could give this product a new image, far removed from the Nirodh-family-planning aura. The agency tasked with the job, Lintas, turned the argument on its head and decided to brand this condom 'KamaSutra', and position not on the family-planning platform, but as a enabler of better lovemaking – 'For the pleasure of making love'. The brand offered a range of condoms such as textured and other special interest condoms – dotted, ribbed, contoured, long-lasting, superthin, intensity (multi-textured), smooth (plain, extra-lubricated), extra-large, flared and flavoured/scented condoms. KamaSutra was priced at a significant premium to the government brand, Nirodh, and even the imported condoms, which were retailed in sleazy cartons.

Commenting about this campaign, William Mazzerella, Professor of Antrhopology at University of Chicago, has surmised after speaking with the creators of the campaign that once the big idea of the sexy condom had been arrived at, the name KamaSutra seemed particularly fortuitous to the agency team because it instantly satisfied three crucial requirements: maximum reach/intelligibility, an erotic connotation, and cultural legitimacy[3].

The print ads released for KamaSutra featured the model Pooja Bedi – daughter of Kabir and Protima Bedi – that added to the buzz value of the campaign. Industry observers lauded the campaign since it was extremely upfront about sex, but was at the same time rather elegant. In a rare first, the brand took over the entire advertising of the September 1991 issue of the Men's magazine *Debonair*. The film made for KamaSutra got stuck in the Doordarshan red tape, though cinema halls did carry the film. The campaign attracted enough positive and negative press. Among the first to attack was the Women and Media Committee of Bombay Union of Journalists who lodged a complaint with ASCI. At the upper house of parliament, Rajya Sabha, member Dinesh Trivedi complained to the then minister of social welfare, Margaret Alva, requesting she calls for a ban. Trivedi also complained to the Press Council saying that the ad portrayed women as sex objects and it sought to promote 'sex itself' instead of family planning and prevention of sexually-transmitted disease. ASCI ruled that the brand modify some aspects of the advertising, the parliamentary question got lost in an inter-departmental file movement, and Doordarshan quietly withdrew the storyboard approval they had given. Having created enough buzz and publicity around the brand, the company quietly went back to using shop displays to support the brand.

If KamaSutra, or KS as it was called in short, created a long run soap operatic drama, another brand got shot in its head the day the ad broke. In mid-1995, Tuffs shoes ran a half-page ad in the *Times of India* featuring supermodels Milind Soman and Madhu Sapre in the nude except for their shoes and a strategically positioned python wrapped around them. The brand, the advertising agency Ambience, the founder of the agency, Ashok Kurien, the models and all involved with the ad were taken to court for obscenity. *India Today* reported in September 1995: When Soman and Sapre admitted on 27 July that they had posed in the nude for the Tuffs shoes campaign, the moral mafia descended on them. They were charged with violating the Indecent Representation of Women Act, 1986, and subsequently under Section 292(A) of the Indian Penal Code[4]. Ashok Kurien recalls how the case dragged on and the judges kept changing and in one such hearing, when the judge asked, 'Who has seen these two people during the photography session and can say that they did not indulge in any sexual activity?', a voice from the back shouted, 'The python'.

Even the Wild Life Protection Act was invoked to fight the case for the poor python. The ad, which was done in a tasteful manner, ended up being in a long drawn court battle, only to be dismissed fourteen years later. *Times of India* has this amusing anecdote of what happened outside the courtroom in 2004: The crowd overflowed outside the court as bystanders gathered for a peek at the duo. The final gem came when an old woman who was present in court and did not recognize the models, asked

Soman, 'Who are all these people waiting with you? What have they done?' *'Koi chor log honge* (Must be some thieves)', he replied with a smile.

If nude models and a python caused a furore, yet another ad saying 'Nude Models Wanted' was a big hit, this time with mothers. This small ad written by Chris Rosario for Trikaya's client Johnson & Johnson in 1993 was a call for baby models. The copy of the ad is a work of art: 'Figure: Chubby; Hair: Preferably; Chin: Double; Eyes: Brown; Skin: Peachy; Age: 8-12 months. Candidates should be carried to Trikaya Advertising on Sunday, 12th September, 10 am to 2 pm.' This small ad was rated as the ad of the decade by the advertising fraternity. Fortunately, it did not provoke any court case.

> ANIMAL PHOBIA: Using real animals in ad films is today highly regulated by the Animal Welfare Board. They can appoint a supervisor to oversee the shoot and more. So before you approve a script featuring a python, a dog or a cat, just find out how you are going to manage the Animal Welfare Board.

In addition to dragging brands, models and ad agencies to court, the mid-'80s also saw the government levying a tax on advertising. Companies were told that 20 per cent of the amount spent on advertising would be disallowed. Fortunately, the industry rallied around and this draconian law was later repealed as the economy opened up.

In the 2000s, ASCI has been facing a lot of flak from consumer advocates for excessive use of sex for selling two particular types of products: undergarments and deodorants.

It is a village water tank. Women are having a bath, washing clothes as the music starts. *'Yeh toh bada toing hai'*, and in walks an attractive shapely young woman. She is curvaceous with a look of a cat that had eaten a bowl full of cream – played to perfection by Sana Khan who went on to star in Bigg Boss with Salman

Khan. To the astonished looks of her fellow villagers, she opens her bag of dirty clothes to pull out a pair of blue men's briefs. She then starts washing them erotically, pounding them on the rock as the women around shriek in mock terror. She finally holds the clean pair for all to see and the clincher promise flashes: 'Amul Macho. Crafted for Fantasies.' The ad caused a great deal of excitement till ASCI ruled that it was obscene. *'Yeh toh bada toing hai'* went into popular lexicon.

Brands such as Axe have used man-woman attraction to sell the world over. An Indian brand Wild Stone decided to add an Indian twist to its sales story. Indian language porn literature is full of illicit sex with ones neighbour's or brother's wife – the eponymous sexy Bhabhi. There was a very popular soft-porn website called Savita Bhabhi. As an ode to Savita Bhabhi, the Wild Stone ad is set in a locale where there is celebration underway, for example the Durga Puja. The attractive young woman, obviously married, is carrying a tray of flowers. She collides with a young man who had just emerged from his bath fully drenched in Wild Stone deo. The smell of his deo sends her into a world of fantasy, she is rolling in bed with him … the film cuts back to her collision and the brand name flashes: 'Wild Stone. Wild by Nature.' The brand sublimely offers the promise of illicit sex with attractive strange women if you use the deodarant.

This ad too was hauled in front of ASCI and was told to amend its storyline.

While we have seen brands trying to push the boundary of decency to attract eyeballs, we have also seen several new categories pushing the limits of societal acceptance.

i-pill was launched as a product that could be taken by women after a night of unprotected sex. The brand was aggressively promoted on television and this led to gross misuse by young women. Doctors started getting patients who had taken i-pill several times a week. And this led to a whole new set of complications. Finally, the brand was told that it should not advertise on mass media. The brand by then had changed hands, and fortunately, the new owners decided to abide by the guidelines and have smartly extended the brand name to a category that is of relevance: Pregnancy Testing.

Yet another product category that burst into infamy is the category that goes by the name 'vaginal cleaners'. A brand called Clean and Dry offers a whole range of products including vaginal whiteners.

From the days of Doordarshan questioning the exposed navel to Doordarshan permitting sanitary pad advertising only post-10 p.m., we are now in an age where everything is out in the open, enabled by cable TV and Internet. Given the intense competition among television channels for advertising, chances are there will be some television channel that is willing to take the *toing* or the Wild Stone or the Clean and Dry advertising.

As Hindi movies and television serials are becoming more and more comfortable with the exposure of skin and discussing till-now forbidden topics, brands too are starting to embrace interesting subjects.

One of the brands that has tried to push the limits of societal understanding of difference has been the brand Fastrack. In an ad creatd by Lowe Advertising which ran in 2012, the brand shows a closet shaking vigorously. When it opens, out walks a young girl adjusting her clothes, and if you thought you would now see a young lad coming out, you were mistaken. Out walks yet another girl, again adjusting her clothes. 'Getting out of the closet', demonstrated in very explicit terms. The brand has spoken in the past of moving on! In June 2015, social media went abuzz over an ad by the online retailer brand Myntra which showed a lesbian couple getting ready to meet one of their parents.

Also in 2015, jewellery brand Kalyan decided to feature film star Aishwarya Rai in an ad reminiscent of the era of rajas; where they showed a dark-skinned kid fanning the film star. Social media went agog over this faux pas. Child labour. Social class discrimination. Colour discrimination and more such criticism were showered upon the ad. The brand quickly issued an apology. The film star feigned ignorance and apologized.

So from the days of Doordarshan, today we have social media playing the role of the jury. We can expect more brands to start looking at dimensions that may have been seen as too liberal in the past. The challenges of the kind faced by Tuffs and KS will continue to remain. But if societal mores are changing, brands can stay rooted in the past or can try and stay one step ahead of the consumer. As Harish Bhat, Member Group Executive Council, Tata Group, observed when I discussed the Fastrack campaign with him: 'Just as good writers capture the fringes of society very well and bring them to life, does advertising have the courage to do that? Or will advertising stay in the middle of the road?'

Last Word

Consumption Era Cometh

INDIAN ECONOMY TOUCHED $2 trillion in the year 2014 in real dollar terms, making India the ninth largest economy; in purchase power parity terms, Indian economy is estimated at $7.3 trillion making it already the third in the world.

But look around you. Does India really seem all that prosperous? The broad GDP numbers tend to hide one big truth, the per capita consumption capacity of the nation. If we were to factor that in, India may not feature anywhere in the top ten, unfortunately.

For all the readers who are less than forty years of age, the story is bound to get better in the coming years. As Indian GDP continues to clock over 7 per cent growth, as prosperity trickles down, India and Indians will shake off their poverty blues and start embracing the consumption culture. Marketing and advertising have to play a big role in the forthcoming transformation of India, from a country of penny pinchers to a country of consumers who love consumption.

Advertising expenditure as a percentage of GDP is still hovering around 0.4 to 0.5 per cent in India. This compares rather unfavourably with almost all other developed and even developing economies where ad spends are often in the 0.9 to 1.2 per cent league. The low ad spend ratio is due to several reasons.

In many categories, we did not have too much competition and therefore not much advertising even till the year 2001; as new brands enter the market, we will see advertising spends shoot up. Secondly, the cost of advertising in India, whatever marketing managers may say, is still very low. These costs will go up, as we will see later. Thirdly, several categories of products and services do not get enough ad support in India.

If ad spends move up to even 0.8 per cent, what can we expect to see around us? For one, we will see the emergence of a consumption era. Antropologists talk of potlatch as a way indigenous peoples of Canada and American Indians show off their wealth and reaffirm their status, through exhaustive and exhausting display of food and gift-giving. We are seeing some signs of this in India, we may see more of this in the years ahead.

Advertisers and ad agencies will play a major role in driving this consumption culture in India. And in numerous categories, the head room for increasing consumption is immense. In mundane categories like packaged foods, per capita consumption is miniscule. In services like health insurance, the Indian market is yet to gain good traction as penetration numbers are infinitesimally small. And if we were to go to the top of the consumption pyramid, and look at a product like luxury handbags for women – as against a Chinese working woman who owns at least five luxury handbags, the Indian working woman owns just one, if at all.

Let me now try and present what I think would be ten mega trends for the Indian advertising and consumer market:

1. The way we define markets will dramatically change in the coming two decades. The classical rural/urban divide is fast disappearing. According to Hindustan Unilever and their Chairman's speech, India can be segmented into fourteen zones which can be targeted with specific products and

services. These zones are a mix of rural and urban areas. It is to be noted that both Indian Readership Survey (IRS) and Broadcast Audience Research Council (BARC) have adopted the new NCCS (New Consumer Classification System) which is geography neutral, considering only the education of the chief wage earner and the possession of durables, as against occupation of the CWE. Till recently, we used the SEC System that classified urban households as A/B/C/D/E and rural households as R1/R2/R3. The adoption of the NCCS is a seismic move, in my opinion. The use of NCCS will encourage marketers to start looking at consumers across rural and urban India without blinkers. Why should you discriminate a rural consumer just because she or he is living in a small village, as long as his/her aspirations are similar to her city cousins?

2. Moving to the next seismic shift: the definitions of gender may also undergo dramatic change. The role of women in Indian society is changing rather rapidly, driven by the increasing rate of women moving into higher education systems. The entry of women into jobs and businesses will put a reverse pressure on the men of India. Men will have to seriously start re-evaluating their role, not just out of charity but because women will not tolerate a husband who will not cook or change nappies. So men of India will have to not just start using cosmetics, but also learn to cook and clean.

3. The third seismic shift will be the rise of new categories of products and services. Who would have imagined twenty years ago that automobiles will become such a big advertised category in the 2000s? And who would have imagined in 2000 that telecom and mobile will be such a money spinner for ad agencies and media companies in the 2010s. In 2015, we are seeing the rise of e-commerce; while experts expect this party to end in a year or two, we may be in for a much

longer ride on the e-commerce bandwagon. There are several other categories that are yet to get the power of advertising fully behind them. Areas like healthcare and education are waiting to unleash the power of advertising.

4. In the coming twenty years, what we call advertising may undergo dramatic change. Nowhere in the world has the consumer's media cost been as badly subsidized by advertising. Indian newspapers are among the cheapest in the world. Indian cable and satellite television is again among the cheapest. All due to the ubiquitious presence of advertising. In the coming years, we will see brands entering the narrative not just in what we call 'advertising' but also into the editorial text. This could be in the form of product placement in films and television programmes or even brand integration into the storyline of films. All this will drive up advertising costs, with an added benefit of better targeting metrics.

5. The media landscape and the advertisers who dominate these spaces in India will undergo major transformation. For instance, someone from Europe or USA visiting India in the early '80s may have wondered why industrial products and heavy-duty equipment were advertised in daily newspapers. But as we moved to the 2000s, those categories have all but disappeared into technical journals and digital/direct media. Classified advertising, which was a big money spinner, is a pale shadow of itself, thanks to the growth of digital media offerings. However, print and television today occupy roughly equal spends at about 45 per cent each, and this has been steady for over a decade. During the 2020s, this media landscape will change with increasing literacy. This in turn will drive Indian language print, digitization of television which will create niche opportunities, and the Internet boom which will get further enhanced by the dominance

of the mobile, 3G, 4G and more. Similarly, the increased urbanization and destruction of urban and rural community facilities will lead to the continued growth of the shopping mall as the new village square and that will also offer new avenues for advertisers. The categories that advertise in these media will also change, just as they changed during the last three decades.

6. Global pundits speak of digital revolution and technology enabled marketing. All the global award shows are full of such wonders; an armband that calls out to a child that runs far from its mother, an app that you can run with, a staircase with an embedded piano keyboard and such like. In India, we will see all that, but given our craze for movies, I predict the blossoming of millions of small film-makers. They will be able to exploit the downward cost spiral of making movies. In a reverse logic, all of them will be open to partnering with brands to create content that will be of use to consumers and brands. Imagine a series of 100 films on child nutrition, or fifty films on different hairstyles; I suspect many of them are already out there and a million more will follow. As smartphones become the screen for consuming media, we will see the uptake of these videos boom.

7. Leading from the above point is the other key issue that will face brands in the coming decade. The rise of advertising costs. From the days of one television channel that could reach the whole of India in the late '80s, today all channels put together reach only a fraction of television-owning homes. However, the pie has dramatically grown. In this decade, almost all 250 to 280 million homes will have television. So reaching all of them will cost an astronomical amount. Help will be at hand with media channels offering ways of segmenting the market and reaching only those big or nano segments you want to reach for a fraction of the

cost. This ability to deploy media into smaller and smaller segments will help numerous new Indian brands to enter the world of advertising. If the '80s saw Nirma, the '90s saw Paras and Emami, the 2020 will see hundred such new companies bloom all over India.

8. The use of advertising by brands and services will undergo a change and I would expect a stronger social narrative coming into brand presentations. This is a global trend but it is catching on in India rather fast. If we dial back, we saw how the national integration campaigns and films played a role in building a sense of national unity. The song 'Mile sur mera tumhara' continues to echo in many minds.

As far back as 1952, the Indian Cancer Society used advertising to spread the cause of testing. In the late '70s, they ran a very successful print campaign that presented 'Life after Cancer – It is worth living'.

Lifebuoy's 'Help a Child Reach 5' has been a globally-recognized campaign that espouses the cause of handwashing. The Gundappa film by Lowe has not only won awards, it has also moved millions of mothers to ensure that their wards wash their hands before eating.

The silent National Anthem film by Mudra has shown how even the deaf can sing the national anthem in their own unique way.

Times of India's Lead India and Teach India initiatives have had such a strong public following that they have become annual phenomena.

In a first, Ulka's campaign for the Bangladesh relief fund raiser was the Campaign of the Year Award winner in the year 1973, probably the only time a public service campaign was awarded this high honour.

HTA's campaign for Tata Steel, 'We also make steel' presented the human side of entreprise that would have made management gurus like Peter Drucker proud.

If you were under the impression that the government never gets good advertising from Indian agencies, you should be informed that HTA's campaign for Indian Army won the Campaign of the Year Award in 1998.

9. The coming decade will see brands adopting a more humane approach to advertising. In a parallel move, we should see the government adopting an aggressive advertising posture to get its citizens to change their ways. The BJP government that came to power in 2014 used high-power advertising and the Modi government is no slacker when it comes to using catchy slogans and campaigns. With the socialist halo fast disappearing, the government will emerge in the 2020s as the biggest advertiser, using advertising for all kinds of purposes, from refusing gas subsidy to paying taxes to opening bank accounts to buying health insurance.

10. With the emergence of consumption culture, Indian consumers will come out of their shell to buy and spend more. Encouraged by advertising, we will see a quicker onset of product obsolescence. From the days when a car was used for ten years, we are already seeing cars being traded in every five years or less. Mobile phones too are facing rapid recycling. The same is true with other household durables. Unfortunately, the emergence of the potlatch culture will also be a part of the modern Indian reality. Bigger and bigger weddings, bigger and bigger expenditures on weddings and birthdays are going to be a part of modern India. This will lead to a bigger set of problems.

As India becomes a consumer economy, driven by advertising, the large section that is unable to participate in this largesse is going to adopt various types of behaviour, some not so savoury. Childhood undernutrition was once identified with poor women giving their babies highly diluted baby foods whose ads they saw on television instead of giving them mother's milk. This incidentally led to the total ban of television advertising of all types of baby and weaning foods. Will the coming era of consumption also create such monsters? The drive towards higher education may devalue technical skills and trade skills leading to imbalances in the job market. The fast-fashion culture could lead to unnecessary expenditure by the poor on fashion goods that they can least afford. One element of Indian society may prove to be a saviour and that is the trickle-down system that has been in vogue for centuries. In the past, it used to be clothes and utensils. Now it has become television sets, mobile phones and even two wheelers. Tomorrow it will be laptops and more.

Our journey has taken us through how advertising has looked at society through numerous lenses; presentation of women, men, kids, senior citizens, marriage, jobs, education, teenagers. We have also looked at how various products and services have shown society, be it cars, mobiles, foods, sports, dresses etc.

We saw how depiction of habits, rituals and roles have changed. In some of the cases, advertising merely reflected society as it is. In some cases, advertising predicted a social norm. And in some cases, advertising harked back to a forgotten custom.

Advertising's role will have to evolve with the times. How can we reflect societal trends? How can we ride the social media boom?

Should advertising be a predictor of societal trends or should we stay one-step behind? Should we stick to the 'hyper-ritualization' routine or should we embrace a 'neo-ritualization' trend?

As India changes, its advertising will also change and become a force multiplier. That is the power of advertising. And that is what advertising can achieve. These questions and more will keep advertising men and women awake at night. And that is not entirely a bad thing.

Acknowledgements

I GOT INTO advertising thanks to Ajit Balakrishnan and Subhas Chakravarty of Rediffusion, and I left after three years for a ten-year stint in marketing and sales. I returned to advertising, thanks to the invitation from Anil Kapoor who had taken over as the CEO of an ailing Ulka Advertising. Over the thirty-five-plus years I have spent in advertising and marketing, I was fortunate to work with truly passionate people and I owe a deep debt of gratitude to them for having tolerated me and also for educating me on the finer aspects of advertising and marketing communication.

When I floated the idea of the book with Anish Chandy, my literary agent, he did not hesitate for an instant to say 'yes'. And over the course of the last twelve months, we have met several times, discussed chapters and topics over calls and emails. He is the first to pull me back when I digress into the realm of academia. He is also to be blamed if you found too many personal anecdotes from my life in advertising.

I owe a special debt of gratitude to many experts who were generous with their time. Gerson da Cunha, the grand old wizard, called me home and spent over two hours telling me tales about the wonderful old days of advertising. Many others such as Professor Arvind Rajagopal, Subhas Chakravarty, Satyam Viswanathan, Arun Kale, Anvar Ali Khan, Vikram Doctor were kind enough to share their thoughts. The final draft was reviewed by Suman Srivatsava, Savita Mathai, Kinjal

Medh, Sharon Picardo and Dorab Sopariwala. A special thanks to them for their valuable comments. Industry experts who have taken the time to write books about their views on consumers and advertising, namely Subroto Sengupta, Piyush Pandey, Alyque Padamsee, AG Krishnamurthy, Ramesh Narayan, Anand Halve, Jayanta Sengupta, Rama Bijapurkar, Ramanujam Sridhar, RV Rajan, Dheeraj Sinha, Santosh Desai et al were always present within arms-length for consultation as I started writing the book. I also reached out to numerous industry captains for their approval to use images from their campaigns. Every single one of them gave me their enthusiastic nod and these include Ashok Kurien, Goutam Rakshit, Mukul Upadayay, Madhukar Kamath, Madhukar Sabnavis, Tarun Rai, Prasoon Joshi, Joe George, Dhunji Wadia, Piyush Pandey, Rahul DaCunha, Alok Nanda, Sanjay Behl et al. Special thanks to all of them.

Pan Macmillan India has been a very supportive publisher. Pranav Kumar Singh, who started with us on this journey, Rajdeep Mukherjee and, later, Diya Kar Hazra, who has been forthright with her views on many aspects of the book, have had a very important role in shaping this book. If you found the book easier to read it is thanks to Diya's efforts. The copy editor on the book, Sushmita Chatterjee, has done an awesome job in going through the text in meticulous detail, spotting errors that had missed my eyes. The cover design by Samia Singh is a showstopper. Special thanks to Ratna Joshi and Peter Modoli for their work in marketing the book.

Finally, my wife Nithya has been extremely supportive of my literary excursions. She is subjected to go through the first draft and in return she is ruthlessly critical in her views. I am notoriously bad at rewriting. But she got me to rewrite many of the chapters. So if you enjoyed the book, you know whom else to thank.

My colleagues at FCB Ulka, the place I called home for the last twenty-seven years have tolerated me and supported me right through all my writing adventures. All my past senior colleagues, Anil Kapoor, Nagesh Alai, Shashi Sinha, Arvind Wable and Niteen Bhagwat, have been silent supporters. They and many of our colleagues, film-maker partners and clients feature in the book. My past assistants, Jensy George, Mincy Fernandes and Amrita Keny, and the superb FCB Ulka production team under Hemant Ranadive have been a big help as well.

This book is a result of what I have learnt from my many colleagues, partners and clients. If you found it of value, the credit goes to them. The faults are entirely my own.

Notes

Introduction: Divining Societal Trends Using Advertising

1. J Lears, *Fables of Abundance: A Cultural History of Advertising in America* (New York: Basic Books, 1994).
2. N Mehta, *Behind a Billion Screens: What Television Tells Us about Modern India* (New Delhi: HarperCollins, 2015).

SECTION ONE

The [In] Complete Man

1. N Mehta, *Behind a Billion Screens: What Television Tells Us about Modern India* (New Delhi: HarperCollins, 2015).
2. C Moog, *Are They Selling Her Lips? Advertising and Identity* (New York: William Morrow and Company, 1990).
3. McKinsey & Company, ed., *Reimagining India: Unlocking the Potential of Asia's Next Superpower* (New York: Simon & Schuster, 2013).
4. 'Man Mood 2014', *Cogito Journal*, Cogito Consulting, vol. 21, 2014.
5. R Bijapurkar, *A Never-Before World: Tracking the Evolution of Consumer India* (New Delhi: Penguin Books India, 2013).

I am a Complan Girl! I am a Complan Boy!

1. See under 'Our Commitments': 'Responsible Marketing & Advertising to Children', *International Food & Beverage*

    Alliance, 2015, https://ifballiance.org/our-commitments/responsible-marketing-advertising-to-children/
2. JU McNeal, *Kids as Customers – A Handbook of Marketing to Children* (New York: Lexington Books, 1992).

The Tingling Freshness of Teens

1. A Padamsee, *A Double Life: My Exciting Years in Theatre and Advertising* (New Delhi: Penguin Books India, 1999).
2. Isabel Ortiz and Matthew Cummins, 'When the Global Crisis and Youth Bulge Collide: Double the Jobs Trouble for Youth', *United Nations Children's Emergency Fund (UNICEF)*, New York, February 2012, http://www.unicef.org/socialpolicy/files/Global_Crisis_and_Youth_Bulge_-_FINAL.pdf
3. M Gladwell, *Blink: The Power of Thinking without Thinking* (New York: Little, Brown and Company, 2005).
4. R Bijapurkar, *We Are Like That Only: Understanding the Logic of Consumer India* (New Delhi: Penguin Books India, 2007).
5. D Sinha, *Consumer India: Inside the Indian Mind and Wallet* (New Delhi: Times Group Books, 2011).
6. R Titus, *Yuva India: Consumption and Lifestyle Choices of a Young India* (New Delhi: Random House India, 2015).

Jo Biwi Se Kare Pyaar...

1. R Dwyer, *Picture Abhi Baaki Hai: Bollywood as a Guide to Modern India* (Gurgaon: Hachette India, 2014).
2. SC Dube, *Indian Society* (New Delhi: National Book Trust, 1990).
3. See Census of India, http://www.censusindia.gov.in/ and http://censusindia.gov.in/Census_And_You/age_structure_and_marital_status.aspx
4. 'The Parenting Group and Edelman Partner To Provide Insights on The Modern Dad at the First Dad 2.0 Summit', *Edelman*, 8 March 2012, http://www.edelman.com/news/the-parenting-group-and-edelman-partner-to-provide-

insights-on-the-modern-dad-at-the-first-dad-2-0-summit-82-percent-of-men-who-became-a-parent-in-the-past-two-years-feel-there-is-a-societal-bias-ag-2/
5. P Underhill, *What Woman Want: The Science of Female Shopping* (New York: Simon & Schuster, 2011).

Ab Main Bilkul Boodha Hoon, Goli Khake Jeeta Hoon!

1. S Kakar and K Kakar, *The Indians: Portrait of a People* (New Delhi: Penguin Books India, 2007).
2. P Chamikutty, 'A Country for Old Men and Women, Anybody?', *The Economic Times*, 8 August 2012, http://epaper.timesofindia.com/Repository/getFiles.asp?Style=OliveXLib:LowLevelEntityToPrint_ETNEW&Type=text/html&Locale=english-skin-custom&Path=ETM/2012/08/08&ID=Ar03100
3. R Edgley, 'The Rise of Viagra Abuse: Doctors Warn against Worrying 'Sextasy' Trend - Where Ecstasy Is Mixed with Drug to Enhance Euphoria', *Mail Online*, 13 February 2014, http://www.dailymail.co.uk/health/article-2558502/The-rise-Viagra-abuse-Doctors-warn-against-worrying-sextacy-trend-ecstasy-mixed-drug-enhance-euphoria.html
4. 'Riding the Wave', *The Economist*, 27 June 2015, http://www.economist.com/news/business/21656190-worlds-enthusiasm-cruising-lifting-europes-shipbuilders-riding-wave
5. 'Over 60 and Overlooked', *The Economist*, 8 August 2002, http://www.economist.com/node/1270771

Twacha Se Meri Umar Ka Pata Hi Nahi Chalta

1. AG Krishnamurthy, *The Invisible CEO: My Mudra Years Including AGKspeak* (New Delhi: Tata McGraw Hill, 2005).
2. A Padamsee, *A Double Life: My Exciting Years in Theatre and Advertising* (New Delhi: Penguin Books India, 1999).
3. E Goffman, *Gender Advertisements* (New York: Harper & Row, 1976).

4. McKinsey & Company, ed., *Reimagining India: Unlocking the Potential of Asia's Next Superpower* (New York: Simon & Schuster, 2013).
5. R Bijapurkar, *A Never-Before World: Tracking the Evolution of Consumer India* (New Delhi: Penguin Books India, 2013).
6. 'Woman Mood I', *Cogito Journal*, Cogito Consulting, vol. 22, 2015.
7. Centre for Social Research Report, 'In Search of a Suitable Girl', *India Today*, 6 April 2015.
8. howindialives.com, 'Young Wives, Young Mothers', *Livemint*, 18 March 2015, http://www.livemint.com/Politics/HW6UN51zR85FWM3oGwdBRM/Young-wives-young-mothers.html
9. 'Mothers India', *The Sunday Guardian*, 10 May 2015.
10. howindialives.com, 'Women in Decision-making', , *Livemint*, 9 March 2015, http://www.livemint.com/Politics/1Vik7Ud6SL0b8WRgXS5QNM/Women-in-decisionmaking.html
11. V Dehejia and R Subramanya, *Indianomix: Making Sense of Modern India* (New Delhi: Random House India, 2012).
12. G Zaltman, *How Customers Think: Essential Insights into the Mind of the Market* (Boston: Harvard Business Review Press, 2003).

SECTION TWO

Only Vimal

1. R Majumdar, *Product Management in India* (New Delhi : PHI Learning, 2007).
2. M Schudson, *Advertising, the Uneasy Persuasion: Its Dubious Impact on American Society* (New York: Basic Books, 1984).
3. AG Krishamurthy, *If You Can Dream* (New Delhi: Tata McGraw Hill, 2013).
4. See interview with AY Noorani, *Fibre2Fashion*, 25 June 2007,

http://www.fibre2fashion.com/interviews/face2face/zodiac-clothing/ay-noorani-interview/10-1
5. V Mehta, *The Sanjay Story* (New Delhi: Harper Collins, 2012).
6. J Pudussery, 'The Dying Art of the Sari', *Time*, 25 June 2009, http://content.time.com/time/magazine/article/0,9171,1912430,00.html
7. S Tharoor, *The Elephant, the Tiger and the Cellphone: Reflections on India, the Emerging 21st-Century Power* (New Delhi: Penguin Books India, 2007).

Bachhe Toh Bachhe, Baap Re Baap!

1. VS Pinto, '40 Years Ago … And Now: How Dalda Built, and Lost, Its Monopoly', *Business Standard*, 5 March 2015, http://www.business-standard.com/article/management/40-years-ago-and-now-how-dalda-built-and-lost-its-monopoly-115030501153_1.html
2. SL Rao, 'Maggi Lesson for Regulation', *The Financial Express*, 9 June 2015, http://www.financialexpress.com/article/fe-columnist/column-maggi-lesson-for-regulation/81906/
3. T Talukdar, 'Increasing Demand for Olive Oil in India, Consumption Expected to Exceed 60 Per Cent in 2012', *The Economic Times*, 23 June 2012, http://articles.economictimes.indiatimes
4. *Amul's India: Based on 50 Years of Amul Advertising* (New Delhi: HarperCollins India, 2012).
5. V Dave and S Das, 'Amul Plans to Market Camel Milk', *Business Standard*, 19 March 2015 http://www.business-standard.com/article/companies/amul-plans-to-market-camel-milk-115031800782_1.html
6. Agence France-Presse, 'Traditional Nepal Cheese a Hit Overseas — as Dog Snack', *NewAge*, 18 March 2015, http://newagebd.net/103893/traditional-nepal-cheese-a-hit-overseas-as-dog-snack/
7. AB Halve, *Planning for Power Advertising: A User's Manual for Students and Practitioners* (New Delhi: Sage Response, 2005).

8. S Desai, *Mother Pious Lady: Making Sense of Everyday India* (New Delhi: HarperCollins, 2010).
9. R Bijapurkar, *A Never-Before World: Tracking the Evolution of Consumer India* (New Delhi: Penguin Books India, 2013).
10. P Iyengar, 'Chicken A La South', *Outlook*, 10 December 2007, http://www.outlookindia.com/magazine/story/chicken-a-la-south/236231
11. McKinsey & Company, ed., *Reimagining India: Unlocking the Potential of Asia's Next Superpower* (New York: Simon & Schuster, 2013).
12. 'The Food Show Craze', *The Economist*, 25 June 2015, http://www.economist.com/news/asia/21656240-epicurean-entertainment-luring-korean-men-kitchen-food-show-craze

Hamara Bajaj, Hamara Bajaj

1. CP Chauhan, 'Road to Resurgence', *Business Today*, 20 December 2015, http://www.businesstoday.in/magazine/features/resurgence-of-scooters-in-indias-two-wheeler-market/story/226493.html
2. A Padamsee, *A Double Life: My Exciting Years in Theatre and Advertising* (New Delhi: Penguin Books India, 1999).
3. J Hegarty, *Hegarty on Advertising: Turning Intelligence into Magic* (London : Thames & Hudson, 2011).
4. MG Parameswaran and K Medh, eds., *India 2061 – A Look at the Future of India* (Mumbai: DraftFCB+Ulka Publication, 2012).

Ghar Ghar Ki Raunaq Badhani Ho

1. 'Spending Patterns across SECs', *Marketing Whitebook 2010-11* (New Delhi: Business World Books, 2010).
2. J Lears, *Fables of Abundance: A Cultural History of Advertising in America* (New York: Basic Books, 1994).
3. MG Parameswaran, *Understanding Consumers: Building Powerful Brands Using Consumer Research* (New Delhi: Tata McGraw Hill, 2003)

Jai Jawan! Jai Kisan!

1. P Kashyap, *Rural Marketing* (New Delhi: Pearson India, 2012).
2. RV Rajan, *Don't Flirt with Rural Marketing: The Handbook of Rural Marketing* (Chennai: Productivity & Quality Publishing, 2013).
3. P Kashyap, *Rural Marketing* (New Delhi: Pearson India, 2012).
4. EM Rogers, *Diffusion of Innovation* (New York: Simon & Schuster, 1962).
5. *RK Swamy BBDO Guide to Market Planning*, 2013.

Har Ek Friend Zaroori Hota Hai

1. P Verma, *The Great Indian Middle Class* (New Delhi: Penguin Books India, 2007).
2. AG Krishamurthy, *If You Can Dream* (New Delhi: Tata McGraw Hill 2013).
3. G Zaltman, *How Customers Think: Essential Insights into the Mind of the Market* (Boston: Harvard Business Review Press, 2003).
4. 'Halfway There', 29 May 2008, http://www.economist.com/node/11465558
5. See interview with Chris Houghton, *The Times of India*, 6 April 2015, http://blogs.timesofindia.indiatimes.com/the-interviews-blog/indians-spend-three-hours-daily-on-phones-and-25-check-phones-100-times-chris-houghton/
6. E Greenberg and A Kates, *Strategic Digital Marketing: Top Digital Experts Share the Formula for Tangible Returns on Your Marketing Investment* (New Delhi: McGraw Hill Professional, 2013).
7. MG Parameswaran and K Medh, eds., *India 2061 – A Look at the Future of India* (Mumbai: DraftFCB+Ulka Publication, 2012).

SECTION THREE

Baraatioyon Ka Swagat

1. M Schudson, *Advertising, the Uneasy Persuasion: Its Dubious Impact on American Society* (New York: Basic Books, 1984).
2. JB Twitchell, *Adcult USA: The Triumph of Advertising in American Culture* (New York: Columbia University Press, 1996).
3. K Jain, *Gods in the Bazaar: The Economies of Indian Calendar Art* (Durham: Duke University Press, 2007).
4. S Khilnani, *The Idea of India* (New York: Farrar, Straus and Giroux, 1999).

Tan Ki Shakti, Man Ki Shakti

1. B Obama, *The Audacity of Hope: Thoughts on Reclaiming the American Dream* (New York: Three Rivers Press, 2006).
2. MG Parameswaran and K Medh, eds., *India 2061 – A Look at the Future of India* (Mumbai: DraftFCB+Ulka Publication, 2012).
3. Ibid.

Zindagi Ke Saath Bhi, Zindagi Ke Baad Bhi!

1. S Sengupta, *Brand Positioning: Strategies for Competitive Advantage* (New Delhi: Tata McGraw Hill, 1990), p. 9.
2. S Varma, '22% of Households in Cities, 31% in Villages Are in Debt', *The Times of India*, 2 December 2014, http://timesofindia.indiatimes.com/india/22-of-households-in-cities-31-in-villages-are-in-debt/articleshow/45597822.cms
3. 'Ahmedabad, Jamnagar and Gujarat in Mukesh Ambani's AGM Speech', *DeshGujarat*, 7 June 2012, http://deshgujarat.com/2012/06/07/ahmedabad-jamnagar-and-gujarat-in-mukesh-ambanis-agm-speech/
4. 'Gold Losing Its Sheen, Price Slides on Akshaya Tritiya', *Hindustan Times*, 22 April 2015, http://www.hindustantimes.

com/business/gold-losing-its-sheen-price-slides-on-akshaya-tritiya/story-KO0ZJ4mzNkzfpLLDKMCVLM.html
5. 'Top of the Pyramid Report 2015', *Kotak Wealth Management Report*, Mumbai, 2015.

God's Own Country

1. A Halve and A Sarkar, *Adkatha: The Story of Indian Advertising* (Goa: Centrum Charitable Trust, 2011).
2. MG Parameswaran, *For God's Sake: An Adman on the Business of Religion* (New Delhi: Penguin Books India, 2014).
3. D Ogilvy, *Confessions of an Advertising Man* (London: Pan Books, 1987).
4. MW Lawrence, *A Big Life (in Advertising)* (New York: Touchstone, 2002).
5. A Kant, *Branding India: An Incredible Story* (New Delhi: HarperCollins India, 2009).
6. JWT Changing India Report, *Campaign India*, 7 October 2011.

Naukri: H for Hitler, A for Arrogant

1. A Chaudhuri, *Indian Advertising: Laughter and Tears* (New Delhi: Niyogi Books, 2014).
2. N Singh, 'Bosses, Not Money, Make Staff Stick to Company', *The Times of India*, 10 March 2015, http://timesofindia.indiatimes.com/business/india-business/Bosses-not-money-make-staff-stick-to-company/articleshow/46511067.cms
3. DH Pink, *Drive: The Surprising Truth About What Motivates Us* (New York: Riverhead Books, 2011).
4. S Ramadorai, *The TCS Story & Beyond* (New Delhi: Penguin Books India, 2011).
5. C Moog, *Are They Selling Her Lips? Advertising and Identity* (New York: William Morrow and Company, 1990).
6. W Isaacson, *Steve Jobs* (New York: Simon & Schuster, 2011).
7. 'Statoistics: Manufacturing Careers', *The Times of India*,

17 March 2015, http://timesofindia.indiatimes.com/business/india-business/Statoistics-Manufacturing-careers/articleshow/46593149.cms

Kyaa Haal Bana Rakha Hai

1. JB Twitchell, *Adcult USA: The Triumph of Advertising in American Culture* (New York: Columbia University Press, 1996).
2. M Schudson, *Advertising, the Uneasy Persuasion: Its Dubious Impact on American Society* (New York: Basic Books, 1984).
3. A Chaudhuri, *Indian Advertising: 1790 to 1950 A.D.* (New Delhi: Tata McGraw Hill, 2007).
4. A Chaudhuri, *Indian Advertising: Laughter and Tears* (New Delhi: Niyogi Books, 2014).
5. P Haydon, '40 Years Ago ... and Now: Taking Traditional Indian Medicine to the World', *Business Standard*, 19 January 2015, http://www.business-standard.com/article/management/40-years-ago-and-now-taking-traditional-indian-medicine-to-the-world-115011800514_1.html
6. MG Parameswaran and K Medh, eds., *India 2061 – A Look at the Future of India* (Mumbai: DraftFCB+Ulka Publication, 2012).
7. P Pandey, *Pandeymonium: Piyush Pandey on Advertising* (New Delhi: Penguin Books India, 2015).

Asli Swad Hai Cricket Ka

1. R Guha, *A Corner of a Foreign Field: The Indian History of a British Sport* (New Delhi: Picador, 2003).
2. A Appadurai and A Mack, eds., *India's World: The Politics of Creativity in a Globalized Society* (New Delhi: Rupa & Co., 2012).

SECTION FOUR

Doodh Doodh Doodh, Wonderful Doodh

1. A Halve and A Sarkar, *Adkatha: The Story of Indian Advertising* (Goa: Centrum Charitable Trust, 2011).
2. TM Krishna, *A Southern Music: The Karnatik Story* (New Delhi: HarperCollins India, 2013).
3. Ibid.
4. V Lal and A Nandy, eds., *Fingerprinting Popular Culture: The Mythic and the Iconic in Indian Cinema* (New Delhi: Oxford University Press, 2006).
5. JB Twitchell, *Adcult USA: The Triumph of Advertising in American Culture* (New York: Columbia University Press, 1996).
6. J Beckerman and T Gray, *The Sonic Boom: How Sound Transforms the Way We Think, Feel, and Buy* (New York: Houghton Mifflin Harcourt, 2014).
7. TJS George, *MS: A Life in Music* (New Delhi: HarperCollins India, 2004).

Meri Khubsurti Ka Raaz

1. J Lears, *Fables of Abundance: A Cultural History of Advertising in America* (New York: Basic Books, 1994).
2. N Rees, *Book of Slogans and Catchphrases* (London: Allen & Unwin, 1982).
3. M Schudson, *Advertising, the Uneasy Persuasion: Its Dubious Impact on American Society* (New York: Basic Books, 1984).
4. FCB Ulka's *Cogito Journal*, vol. 3, 2002.
5. Ibid.

Bole Mere Lips, I Love Uncle Chipps

1. V Lal and A Nandy, eds., *Fingerprinting Popular Culture: The Mythic and the Iconic in Indian Cinema* (New Delhi: Oxford University Press, 2006).

2. B Jeyaraman, *Periyar: A Political Biography of E.V. Ramasamy* (New Delhi: Rupa & Co., 2013).
3. JP Jones, *Brands as Engines for Profit: Universal Guidelines on How to Drive Growth* (New Delhi: Tata McGraw Hill, 2012).
4. G Zaltman, *How Customers Think: Essential Insights into the Mind of the Market* (Boston: Harvard Business Review Press, 2003).
5. TL Friedman, *The Lexus and the Olive Tree: Understanding Globalization* (New York: Picador, 1999).

No Squeeze, No Wheeze, No Navel Please!

1. A Halve and A Sarkar, *Adkatha: The Story of Indian Advertising* (Goa: Centrum Charitable Trust, 2011).
2. RM Thomas Jr, 'Shirley Polykoff, 90, Ad Writer Whose Query Colored a Nation', *The New York Times*, 8 June 1998, http://www.nytimes.com/1998/06/08/nyregion/shirley-polykoff-90-ad-writer-whose-query-colored-a-nation.html
3. W Mazzarella, *Shoveling Smoke: Advertising and Globalization in Contemporary India* (London: Duke University Press, 2003).
4. R Abreu, 'Moral Posturings', *India Today*, 15 September 1995, http://indiatoday.intoday.in/story/politics-and-law-snare-milind-soman-and-madhu-sapre-in-an-obscenity-case/1/289355.html

Suggested Reading

Amul's India: Based on 50 Years of Amul Advertising, daCunha Communications (New Delhi: HarperCollins, 2012).

Basham AL, *The Wonder That Was India* (New Delhi: Rupa & Co. 1981).

Bijapurkar, R, *We Are Like That Only: Understanding the Logic of Consumer India* (New Delhi: Penguin India, 2007).

Chaudhuri, A, *Indian Advertising: Laughter and Tears* (New Delhi: Niyogi Books, 2014).

Dehejia, V, and R Subramanya, *Indianomix: Making Sense of Modern India* (New Delhi: Random House, 2012).

Desai, S, *Mother Pious Lady: Making Sense of Everyday India* (New Delhi: Harper Collins, 2010).

Doctor, V, and AA Khan, 'Kyon Na Aazmaye', *The India Magazine of Her People and Culture*, January 1997.

Halve, A, *Planning for Power Advertising: A User's Manual for Students and Practitioners* (New Delhi: Sage Response, 2005).

Halve, A, and A Sarkar, *Ad Katha: The Story of Indian Advertising* (Goa: Centrum Charitable Trust, 2011).

Imam, S, *The Making of Advertising: Gleanings from Subhas Ghosal* (New Delhi: Macmillan India, 2002).

Kakar, S, and K Kakar, *The Indians: Portrait of a People* (New Delhi: Penguin Books India, 2007).

Kant, A, *Branding India: An Incredible Story* (New Delhi: HarperCollins, 2009).

Khilnani, S, *The Idea of India* (New York: Farrar, Straus and Giroux, 1999).

Krishnamurthy, AG, *The Invisible CEO: My Mudra Years Including AGKspeak* (New Delhi: Tata McGraw Hill, 2005).

Luce, E, *In Spite of the Gods: The Strange Rise of Modern India* (London: Little, Brown and Company, 2006).

Mazzarella, W, *Shoveling Smoke: Advertising and Globalization in Contemporary India* (London: Duke University Press, 2003).

Menon, A, *Media Planning and Buying: Principles and Practice in the Indian Context* (New Delhi: Tata McGraw Hill, 2009).

Narayan, R, *Reflections: The Marketing and Advertising World Around Me* (Mumbai: Cortlandt Rand, 2007).

Padamsee, A, *A Double Life: My Exciting Years in Theatre and Advertising* (New Delhi: Penguin Books India, 1999).

Pandey, P, *Pandeymonium: Piyush Pandey on Advertising* (New Delhi: Penguin Books India, 2015).

Parameswaran, MG, *FCB-Ulka Brand Building Advertising: Concepts and Cases* (New Delhi: Tata McGraw Hill, 2001).

Parameswaran, MG, and K Medh, *DraftFCB+Ulka Brand Building Advertising: Concepts and Cases, Case Book II* (New Delhi: Tata McGraw Hill, 2011).

Rajagopal, A, *Politics after Television: Hindu Nationalism and the Reshaping of the Public in India* (Cambridge: Cambridge University Press, 2001).

Rajan, RV, *Don't Flirt with Rural Marketing: The Handbook of Rural Marketing* (Chennai: Productivity & Quality Publishing, 2013).

Sengupta, S, *Brand Positioning: Strategies for Competitive Advantage* (New Delhi: Tata McGraw Hill, 1990).

Sengupta, S, *Cases in Advertising and Communication Management in India* (Ahmedabad: IIM Ahmedabad, 1976).

Sinha, D, *Consumer India: Inside the Indian Mind and Wallet* (New Delhi: Times Group Books, 2011).

Sridhar, R, *One Land, One Billion Minds: Insights on Branding in India* (Chennai: Productivity & Quality Publishing, 2006).

Srinivas, MN, *Indian Society through Personal Writings* (New Delhi: Oxford University Press, 1999).

Tiwari, S, *The [un]Common Sense of Advertising: Getting the Basics Right* (New Delhi: Sage Response, 2003).

Verma, PK, *The Great Indian Middle Class* (New Delhi: Penguin Books India, 1998).

Index

A

Aakrosh, 237
Aamoksh, 54
Aar Paar, 129
Aashirvaad, 88
Abbott, 185. *See also* Boots Company
Abby Awards Show, 224
ABCL (Amitabh Bachchan Corporation Ltd.), 151, 228
ACC, 112
Activa, 99, 108
Ad Club, 224
Ad Factors, 159
Ador Consulting, 184–85
adult literacy, 152
adulteration, 84
Advertising Avenues, 6, 113
Advertising Standards Council of India (ASCI), 248, 249, 252
Afaqs, 32
Aga, RD, 234–35
Aga, Sanjeev, 135
Agarwal, Rajiv, 7, 148, 149
Agence France-Presse, 90
Aggarwal, Anuradha, 60
Air Deccan, 170
Air India Maharaja, 77, 169–70

Airtel, 33, 40, 55, 125–27, 128, 129–30, 218, 220
Akashvani Sangeet Sammelan, 214
Akhtar, Begum, 215
Aliens, 184
All India Radio (AIR), 120, 149, 214–15
Aloke Kumar, 109
Alva, Margaret, 249
Amar Akbar Anthony, 237
Amazon, 145
Ambani, Dhirubhai, 127
Ambani, Mukesh, 164
Ambassador, 100–1
Ambience, 30, 79, 234, 250
Ambuja, 111, 112
American Super Bowl, 105
Amrit Agro Ltd, 236
Amritraj, Vijay, 208
Amrutanjan, 192
Amul (Anand Milk Union Limited), xiv, 88–90, 142
Amul Macho, 252
Anacin, 190
Anand, Dev, 228
Anand, Viswanathan, 156, 157, 204

Andrew, 190
Angiers, 190
Annapurna, 88
Anne French, 62
anti-Hindi agitation in Madras, 238–39
apparel brands, 81
appearance anxiety, 13
Apple Macintosh, 184
Aptech, 185–86
Aramusk, 9
Ariel, 8, 44, 64
Armstrong, Louis, 219
Arrow, 77, 81
Arvind Eye Care, Madurai, 198
Ashok Kumar, 139, 227
Asian Games (1982), Delhi, xiv, 113
Asian Paints, 110, 111, 116, 144
Asoka, 224
Aspro, 190
AT&T, 125, 221
ATM, 162
audio signature, 218
auto sector in India, 97–102
Avanti Fellows, 36
Awasthi, Abhijit, 220
Axe, 252
Ayer, 116
'Ayurvedic Concepts', 195
Azim Premji Foundation, 154

B

Baade Ache Lagte Hain, 42
Babbar, Raj, 5
Bachchan, Abhishek, 39, 129
Bachchan, Aishwarya Rai, 29–30, 39, 63, 226, 229, 253
Bachchan, Amitabh, 60, 99, 151, 161, 198, 228–29, 230
Bagpiper soda, 226
Baidyanath, 194
Bajaj Bulbs, 48
Bajaj Chetak, 97
Bajaj scooter, 97–100, 216
Bajaj Sunny, 100
Balakrishnan, Ajit, 78, 148, 157
Balakrishnan, R (Balki), 235
Balu, 54
banking system in India, 164–66
Banks, Louis, 216
Barbie, 23
Barrington, Ken, 201
Bartake, Radhika, 192
Barthes, Roland, xi
Bartos, Rena, 43
Basu, Jyoti, 126
Bata, 20
Beckerman, Joel, 221
Bedi, Kabir and Protima, 249
Bedi, Mandira, 205–6
Bedi, Pooja, 249
Beiersdorf, 9
Ben Hur, 3
Benetton, 81
Benner, Arnold, 225
Bernbach, Bill, 105
Best Foods, USA, 88
Bhakthavatsalam, M, 239
Bhakti movement, 215
Bharat Matrimony, 44
Bhat, Harish, 254
Bhatia, Ruby, 205
Big Bazaar, 144–45
Big Boss, 251
Bijapurkar, Rama, 13, 35, 65, 92

Binaca Geetmala, 214
Binny, 80
Birla, Aditya, 129
Birla White, 111
Birlas, 95
Biswas, Basudev, 159
Blade Runner, 184
Bobby, 42, 232
Bollywood
and advertising, 10, 13, 27, 31, 42, 75, 76, 94, 139, 160–61, 195, 206, 224, 226, 228
and consumerism, 146
and international travel, 174
linguistic experiments in, 237
role of woman, 62, 68
Bombay Dyeing, 6, 75, 76, 79, 80
BookMyShow, 165
Boots Company, 184–85, 189–91, 244
Bose, Ardhendu, 6, 76
Boston Consulting Group, New York, 36
Bourdeau, Mary, 131
Bourdieu, Pierre, 157
Bournvita Quiz Contest, 148–50, 152
Bournvita, 16, 22, 149
BPL, 125, 228
brand equity, 52, 85, 162
brand justice, 52
Brides of India, 142
Brilliant Tutorials, 157
Britannia, 218, 220, 226
Britannia Glucose (Glaxo Biscuits), 92, 227; -D, 226–27
Broadcast Audience Research Council (BARC), 123, 257

Broadcasting Content Complaints Council (BCCC), 248
Board of Control for Cricket in India (BCCI), 206
Brooke Bond Red Label, 46
Brooke Shields, 247
Brufen, 244
Brylcreem, 226
Buddh International Circuit, Noida, Uttar Pradesh, 207
Bunge, 85
Buniyaad, 41
Burmah Shell, 230
Burnol, 244
Burnett, Leo, 170

C

Cadbury Dairy Milk Chocolates, 202–3
Cadbury India, 18, 142, 149, 230
Calcutta Chemicals, 9
calendar art forms, 144
Caliber, 76
Calvin Klein, 247
Campa Cola, 29
Cantata Carmina Burana, 5
Capital Advertising, 102
Captain Cook, 87, 96
Casablanca, 235
cash on delivery, 134, 165
celebrities, brand endorsements, 10, 31, 42, 75–76, 139, 145, 195, 206, 215, 224–33
costs, 225, 230
Center Shock, 31–32
Chakravarty, KS, 130
Chakravarty, Subhas, 13, 77, 93, 109

Chand Chhap urea, 119
Changavalli, Venkat, 133
Chaplin, Charlie, 184
Charminar, 5, 74, 226
Charms, 74–75
Chatterjee, Subir, 16, 218
Chaturvedi, Mahuya, 24
Chaubal, Devyani, 236
Chaudhary, Mahima, 29–30
Chaudhuri, Arun, 180
Chauhan, Ramesh, 30
Chauhans, 28
Chawla, Juhi, 226
Chayageet, 245–46
Chennai Express, 83, 242–43
Cherry Blossom, 5
Chetan Bhagat, *Revolution 2020*, 155
Chevrolet, 216
Chiat/Day, 184
Chief Wage Earner (CWE), 124
Chik, 19, 121
child labour, 254
Chinnakannu, 222
Chitnis, Leela, 225
Chopra, Priyanka, 231
Chopra, Yash, 174
Choudhary, Kavita, 61
Churpi, 90
Chutney Mary, UK, 172
Ciba, 78
Cinkara, 192
Cinthol, 227
Citi Bank, 162–63, 165
Clairol, 33, 247
Clarion Advertising, xiv, 116, 191
class and caste divisions, x
Clean and Dry, 253

Close Up, 26
Club Mahindra, 173
C-MARC, 119
Coca-Cola, 18, 27, 28, 30, 31, 74, 143, 221
Cogito Consulting, 22, 24, 232
cognitive development, 34
Coke Studio India, 222
Coke Studio Pakistan, 222
Coldarin, 189, 190–91, 244
Colgate, 4, 19, 121
Colgate toothpowder, 4
colour coding, 203
colour discrimination, 254
commercial culture and technology, 22
commodity mindset to brand mindset, 87
company-owned websites, 23
Complan, 16–17, 196, 200, 201
computerization, 156, 184–86
consumer behaviour, xiii–xv; changing, 10–13
Consumer Complaints Council, 248
consumption culture, 255–62
copywriters, xii
corporate and brand-owned websites, 23
corporate governance issues, 40
corporatization of the Indian film industry, 231–32
credit cards, 165
Cremmafin, 244
cricket and advertising, xiv, 30, 58, 63, 130, 200–9, 229
Cummins, Matthew, 28
Cycle Agarbatti, 232

D

da Cunha, Gerson, 84, 235
da Cunha, Rahul, 89–90
da Cunha, Sylvester, 89, 90
da Cunha, Uma, 78
Dabur, 194
Dabur Chyawanprash, 93, 193–94
DADA, 84
Dalda, 84–85, 236
Dalda Refined Oil, 85
Darth Vader, 105
Das, Nandita, 62
Dasgupta, Prabhudda, 173
DCM, 78
DCW Home Products, 88
Dean, James, 75
demographic shift, 53
department-store concept, 81
Desai, Santosh, 91–92
Desai, Xerxes, 217
Deshpande, Ravi, 173
Deshpande, Sulabha, 56
Dev, Kapil, 63, 201, 204
Dhar & Hoon, 229
Dhara, 16
Dharmendra, 99
Dheer, Sudarshan, 78
Dhoni, MS, 153, 229
Dias, Agnello, 40, 130
Diet Pepsi, 29
Diffusion of Innovation, 122
Digene, 195, 244
digital medium, 157, 242
Digjam, 75, 76, 80
Dilip Kumar, 226, 228
Dilwale Dulhania Le Jayenge (DDLJ), x, 31, 42
Dinesh, 75, 76, 80

Direct Money Transfer, 124
discount messaging, xiii
Disney, 23, 221
Dixit, Madhuri, 208, 226
Do Bigha Zamin, 237
Dole, Bob, 52
Dominos, 94
Don 2, 174
Dongre, Anita, 83
Doordarshan, xiii, 41, 48, 92, 114, 118, 139, 150, 220, 245–46, 249–50, 253–54
Doyle Dane Bernbach, 105
Drucker, Peter, 260
Dube, Shyama Charan, 46
Dubey, PK, 132
Dulux, 111
Duracell, 232
Dwyer, Rachel, 42

E

e-commerce, xiii
Economic Times Brand Equity Quiz, 152
economy, Indian, xiv, 53, 63, 67, 110, 122, 124, 165, 170, 174, 177, 179, 251, 255
education sector in India, 153–58
electronic cash, 165
Elpar, 6
Emami, 8, 9, 194, 260
Emergency, 27, 28
employee engagement, 182–83
Emulsion, 190
Enfield Bullet, 98–99, 100
English Premier League, 205
Entamizole, 244
Enterprise, 91

Ephazone, 190
equity culture in India, 160
Ericsson, 131, 133
Escorts, 232
ET, 232
Everest Advertising, 92, 140

F

Faber Castell, 24
Fabindia, 81, 83
Facebook, 134, 145, 177
FACT, 119–20
Fair & Handsome, 8
Fair & Lovely, 9, 59, 181, 238
fairness obsession, xiii, 8–9, 59, 247
Faraday, Michael, 135
Farex, 17
farm sector, automation, 119
Fastrack, xiii, 46
FCB (Foote, Cone & Belding) Ulka, 10, 15, 24, 33, 35, 55, 64–66, 88, 89, 98, 104, 110, 125, 140, 159, 177, 182, 198, 200, 216, 229, 231, 232, 236, 239, 246, 260
FCB New York, 165
FCB Ulka Futures, 159
Femina Miss India, 63
festivals (religious celebrations) and advertising/shopping, 142–47
Fevicol, 112–13
financial marketing and advertising, 159–68
'501 Blues', 7
Flipkart, 145
Flora, 15

font creation, 173
Food Bazaar, 87
food habits in India, 88, 91, 94–95
food photography, 88, 94
Football, 208
For God's Sake, 35, 147
Forhans, 19
Formula One races, 207
Fortis, 198
Fortune, 86
Four Square, 5
Fox, Michael J, 29
Frito-Lays (Pepsico Foods), 236

G

Gadkari, Kavita, 24
Gaitonde, Vikas, 172
Gandhi, Indira, xiv, 27, 100, 161
Gandhi, Maneka, 78, 130
Gandhi, MK, 85, 151
Gandhi, Sanjay, 78, 100
Ganesan, Shivaji, 228
Ganga Jumna, 237
Garden, 79
Garden sari account, 234
Garden Vareli, 79
Garnier, 9
Gavaskar, Sunil, 76
Gelusil, 195
gender
 defined roles, 62, 64
 discrimination, xii, 69
 equality, 47
 roles, 41, 66–67
 stereotyping, 63
George, TJS, 221
Ghosh, Namita Roy, 16, 218
Gill, Khushmeet Singh, 177

Gladwell, Malcolm, 34
Glaser, Milton, 172
Glaxo, 200
Global Dale Carnegie Consulting Organization, 182
Global Policy on Marketing and Advertising to Children, 23
globalization, 95
Glucose-D, 226
Glycodin Terp Vasaka, 190
Goa tourism, 171–72
Godbole, Avinash, 78
Godfrey Philips, 5
Godrej, 9
Godrej Expert, 9
Godrej Storwel, 140
Goffman, Erving, 61
Gold Spot, 28, 30, 78, 215
Golden Quadrilateral, 106
Goldfinger, 145
Goli Vada Pav, 94
Google, 55, 134, 149
Gopinath, GR, 170
Gray, Tyler, 221
Greig, Tony, 206
GSK, 197
Guha, Pradeep, 63, 224
Guha, Ramachandra, 201
Gujarat Co-Operative Milk Marketing Federation, 89, 90
Gundappa, 260
Gupta, Ravi, 78
Gwalior, 75

H
Haasan, Kamal, 228
Hajmola, 155, 194
Halls, 192, 194
Halve, Anand, 91
Hamara Bajaj, 97
Hamdard, 192
Hamraaz, Harminder Singh, *Hindi Film Geet Kosh*, 221
Hansa Research, 66
Happy Dent, 32
Haque, Sophia, 203
Harijan, 85
Harrods, London, 225
Havells, 44
HDFC (Housing Development Finance Corporation), 163
HDFC Life, 167
HDFC Standard Life, 50
Hegarty, John, 105
Hema Malini, 226
Hero Cycles, 232
Hero Honda, 98, 99, 100, 102
Hero Pleasure, 106, 231
Hero, 64, 99
Hershey, 232
Himalaya, 195
Hindustan Motors, 101
Hindustan Unilever (HUL), xiii, 9, 26, 59, 84, 85, 86, 93, 109, 110, 121, 123, 179, 201, 225–26, 256
Hindustan Vanaspati Manufacturing Corporation, 84
HMT, 217
Honda, 99
Hongkong and Shanghai Banking Corporation (HSBC) bank, 162
Horlicks, 16, 180, 196, 200
'Horseman' urea, 119

Houghton, Chris, 133
housekeeping, 11, 14
housing loans, 163–64
Hum Aap Ke Hain Kaun, 146
Hum Log, 41
#100sareepact, 81–82
Hyundai, 232
Hyundai Santro, 224

I
IBM, 27, 28, 78, 184
ICI (British), 111, 119, 190
ICICI (Industrial Credit and Investment Corporation), 34, 161
ICICI Bank, 161–62
ICICI Prudential, 186
Idea cellular, 129, 135
IIM Calcutta, 156, 157
Ilayaraja, 213
Imperial Tobacco Company (ITC), 15, 40–41, 86, 88, 118
Impressions, 116
'Incredible India', 174, 175
Indecent Representation of Women Act (1986), 250
India Parade, New York, 174
Indian Broadcasting Foundation, 240
Indian Cancer Society, 260
Indian Hockey League, 208
Indian Penal Code, 250
Indian Premier League (IPL), 130, 206–7
Indian Readership Survey (IRS), 107, 127, 257
Indian Super League (ISL), 207
IndiGo, 170–71

information dissemination through advertising, 199
Interface Advertising, 123
Interface Communication, 105
International Advertising Association, 66
International Food and Beverage Alliance (IFBA), 23
Internet, 23, 133, 134, 157, 174, 176, 222, 253
Internet banking, 162
Iodex, 192, 193, 194
i-pill, 252
IPO (initial public offering) advertising, 160
scams, 164
IRCTC, 173
Isaacson, Walter, 184
Itch Guard, 110, 195
Iyer, Arun, 141
Iyer, PS, 190

J
Jade Blue, 81
Jaffrey, Javed, 60, 192
Jaguar, 113
Jain, Nitish, 88
Jain, Panna, 78
Jaipur Literature Festival, 177
Jallikattu, 3
Jayanthi, 226
Jeevamurtham, 190
Jenson & Nicholson, 109, 111
Jeyaraman, Bala, 238
Jhaveri, Ankitha, 17
JK Chemicals, 248
Jobs, Steve, 184
John Player, 81

Johnson & Johnson, 251
joint-family business sagas, x
Jones, John Philip, 240
Joshi, Prasoon, 31, 32, 235
Joshi, RK, 173
Joshipura, Hasit, 197
Justdial services, 133
JWT, 163, 166, 169, 175, 180, 203

K

Kadam, Anju Maudgal, 81
Kahaani, 42
Kaif, Katrina, 229
Kakar, Sudhir and Katharina, 50
Kakkar, Ashwini, 178
Kakkar, Prahlad, 38, 99, 191, 245
Kale, Arun, 7, 78, 79, 109, 149, 234
Kalgutkar, Vilas, 6
Kalyan Jewellers, 145, 253
KamaSutra (KS), 248–50, 254
Kamath, KV, 161
Kant, Amitabh, 171, 174–75
Kapoor, Anil, 78, 189
Kapoor, Karan, 76
Kapoor, Kareena, 226
Kapoor, Kunal, 20
Kapoor, Raj, 161, 232
Kapoor, Ram, 42
Kapoor, Ranbir, 229
Kapoor, Shahid, 16
Kapoor, Shammi, 139, 227
Kapoor, Shashi, 76
Kapur, Shekhar, 76
Karbonn, 132
Kashyap, Pradeep, 119, 121
Katrak, Kersy, 78, 85, 235
Kaun Banega Crorepati (*KBC*), 150–52, 153
Kennedy, John F, 75
Kerala – God's Own Country, 171
Kesavan, Mukul, 237
Keskar, BV, 214, 223
Khan, Aamir, 29–30, 31, 198, 229
Khan, Amjad, 92, 227
Khan, Anvar Ali, 169
Khan, Colleen, 180–81
Khan, Mohammad, 75, 78, 91
Khan, Saif Ali, 75
Khan, Salman, 75, 195, 229, 251
Khan, Sana, 251
Khan, Shah Rukh (SRK), 8, 42, 127, 151, 198, 224, 226, 229, 230, 232, 242
Khanna, Vikas, 95
Khanna, Vinod, 227
khap panchayats, 43
Khatau, 78–79
Khilnani, Sunil, 146
Khote, Deven, 88
Kids Fashion Week (2015), 23
Kilachand, Shobhaa, 236
Kinetic, 99, 100
Kingfisher Airlines, 170
Kingfisher Mineral Water, 220
Kishore Kumar, 226
Knoll. *See* Abbott
Kolatkar, Arun, 78, 235
Kooka, Bobby, 169–70
Kotak Wealth Management, 166
Krack Cream, 110, 194, 196
Kraft, 95
Krishna, TM, 214
Krishnakumar, T, 18
Krishnamurthy, AG, 58, 76, 127, 155

Krishnan, Rajesh, 182
Kurien, Ashok, 30, 234, 250
Kurien, Verghese, 89, 90, 219

L
L'Oréal, 9, 53
Lacoste, 81
Lagoo, Shriram, 193–94
Lakme, 63
language and linguistic experiments in advertisements, television and cinema, 234–43
Lava Kusa, 221
Lava, 132
Lawrence, Mary Wells, 172
Lazear, David, 34
Lears, TJ Jackson, xi, 116
legal battles and brands, xiii, 98, 250–51
Lehar Pepsi, 29
Lever Brothers, 84, 236
Levi Strauss & Company, 7
Levi's, 81
Levi's jeans, 74
LG, 228
liberalization, x, 7, 114, 213
Liberty, 77
Life Insurance Corporation of India (LIC), 160–61
Lifebuoy, 4, 201, 215, 260
'Lifestage Marketing' 165, 166
Lijjat Papad, 92
Limca, 28, 30
LinkedIn, 134
Liril, 26–27, 240
Literoof, 213
Liv 52, 195

Lloyd, Clive, 201
Lodestar UM, 222
Louis Philippe, 81
Lovely University, Punjab, 157
Lowe Lintas, 4, 32, 44, 60, 84, 97, 98, 104, 112, 116, 123, 141, 179, 227, 235, 248, 253, 260
Ludhianvi, Sahir, 237
Lunel, Karen, 26–27
Lux advertisements, 9, 225–26, 241
Lux Cozi, 229

M
Macaroni & Cheese, 95
Madan, JJ, 221
Madhwani, Ram, 32
Mafatlal, 80
Maggi 2-Minute Noodles, 17–18, 85, 93–94, 208
Magic, 126, 128
Magnusson, Magnus, 150
Mahabharat, 98
Mahesh Babu, 123, 229
Mahindra & Mahindra, 99, 100, 105–6
Mahindra Arjun tractors, 123
Maidenform, 6
Maine Pyar Kiya, 75
Majumdar, Boria, 208
MakeMyTrip, 177
Malabar Jewellers, 141–42
male grooming products, 9, 13
Malhotra, Arun, 101
Mallar, Sheetal, 219
Mallik, Suresh, 216
Mammen, Ravi, 104
Mangeshkar, Lata, 109, 215

Mani, VSS, 133
Manusmriti, x, 68
Manyawar, 81, 142
Maratha Mandir, Mumbai, 42
Marico, 86
marital relationships, depiction in advertisements, 38–47
Mark McCrindle, 36
Marks & Spencer, 81
Maruti, 100–4
Maruti 800, 100
Maruti Esteem, 20
Mary Kom, 232
masculinity, Indian, 13
mass appeal and prestige, 83
Mass Communication and Marketing (MCM), 78, 85, 215
mass communication, role in health care, 197–98
MasterCard, 165
Mastermind, 150
Mathai, Mahesh, 203
Mathan, Ahalya, 81
Mathew, Robby, 123
Mauritius Tourism, 172
MaxTouch, 125
Maya Darpan, 237
Mazzerella, William, 249
Majumdar, Ramanuj, 75
McCann, 31, 32, 243
McDonalds, 74, 94
McNeal, James, 24
Mehta, Harshad, 164
Mehta, Vinod, 78
Menon, Rajiv, 111
Mentos, 155
Mercedes, 221

Mercury Travel, 178
Messi, Lionel, 205
MICA, 155
Micromax, 131
Mile Sur Mera Tumhara, 97, 216, 260
'Mind & Mood', 10, 45
Mind of Market, 131
Mirza, Sania, 208
Mishra, Vasudha, 33
Mitra, Chitta, 118–19
mobile banking, 34, 134, 162
mobile cash transfer, 134
mobile phones, xiii, 125–35
mobile service operators/providers, 125–27, 135
Modern, 93
Modi, Lalit, 206
Modi, Narendra, xiv, 81, 167, 261
Mohenjo-Daro, 3
Monsoon Wedding, 132
Mood Studies, 10
Moog, Carol, 7, 184
Moov, 110, 194, 196
Mother India Products, 226
Mother India, x, 42, 68
Mountain Dew, 10
Mouthshut.com, 59
Mozart, Wolfgang Amadeus, 5, 217–18, 220
Mr Paek's Home Cooking, 95
MRF Zigma, 104
MTV, 222
Mudra Communications, 16, 17, 58, 127, 155, 260
multiplex movie screens, xv
Mumbai Marathon, 204
Mundkur, Bal, 247

Murthy, Narayana, 158
musical forms in advertising, 213–23
Myntra, 253

N
Nadkarni, Bapu, 201
Nagarkar, Kiran, 78
Nair, Rajan, 7
Nair, Sameer, 150–51
Nanda, Alok, 172
Nanda, Arun, 27, 78, 148
Nanda, Ritu, 161
Nanji, Elsie, 79
Nano, 107
nano-segmentation, 177
Narayanan, R, 22
National Dairy Development Board (NDDB), 219, 236
National Egg Coordination Committee (NECC), 91
National Film awards, 221
National Industry Targeted Aptitude Test (NITAT), 156
National Institute of Information Technology (NIIT), 156, 185, 186, 188, 204
Naukri.com, 182
Nazir, Prem, 228
Nerolac Paints, 109–10, 116
Nescafe, 215–16, 232
Nestle, 93, 243
New Consumer Classification System (NCCS), 124, 257
Newman, Paul, 226
News Broadcasting Standards Authority (NBSA), 248
Nexus Advertising, 149

Nexus Equity, 7, 131
Nike Cricket, 203, 209
1984, 184
Nirma, 61, 63, 69, 121, 179, 194, 260
Nirodh, 248–49
Nivea, 9
Nokia, 131, 132
Noorani, AY, 77
NRI Parents Services Package, 54

O
O Kadhal Kanmani, 46
O'Brien, Derek, 149
O'Brien, Neil, 149
Obama, Barack, 153
Oberoi Hotels, 178
obscenity, xiii, 245–47, 250
Ogilvy & Mather, 111, 112, 130, 156, 175, 198, 202–3, 216, 220
Ogilvy, David, 172
Ola, 107
old age, depiction in advertisements, 48–56
Old Spice, 5–6
Omnicom, 123
Onida, 113, 228
Operation Flood, 89
Orchard Advertising, 170
Ortiz, Isabel, 28
Orthopaedic Association, 55
Orwell, George, 184
OTC brands, 191, 195–96

P
Padamsee, Alyque, 27, 61, 104, 235, 246
Padmini, 101, 226
Padukone, Deepika, 27, 242

Paes, Leander, 208
Pan Parag, 139–40, 227
Panag, Gul, 106
Pandey, Kamlesh, 4, 109, 235
Pandey, Piyush, 49, 111, 131, 156, 203, 216, 235
Pandey, Prasoon, 131, 220
Paras Pharma, 110, 194–95, 260
Park Avenue, 77
Parle, 28, 30
Parle G (Parle Gluco), 92–93, 94
Pataudi, Nawab Mansur Ali Khan, 75
Patel, Darshan, 109, 110
Patel, Karsanbhai, 109
patent medicines, 189, 190
Patki, Ashok, 216
Pears, 230
Pediasure, 196
Pepe, 81
Pepperfry, 117
Pepsi, 29–30, 31, 224
Pester Power, 20–21
Peter England, 81
Pfizer, 52, 53
Philips, 144
Piaget, Jean, 34
Piagio, 99
Pidilite Industries, 112–13
Pieces, 232
Pink, Daniel, 183
Pitch fees, 159
Pitroda, Sam, 132
PK, 232
Pleasure, 64
Polio Drop Days, 198
polio immunization drive, 198
Polykoff, Shirley, 247

Ponds Dreamflower Fragrant Talc, 9, 180–81
Ponds, 9
Pothy's, 228
Premier Automobiles, 101
prescription-only brands, 52
Pressman, 159
Prestige, 38–39
'Priceless', 165
pricing, xiii
print advertising, 23, 39, 40, 52, 81, 84, 102, 128, 157, 163, 171–73, 180, 190, 204, 215, 226, 235, 248, 249, 258, 260
Pro Kabaddi League (PKL), 207
Procter & Gamble, 9, 44, 142
product marketing communications, 23
product placement, 31, 62
Punjabi, Camellia, 171–72
Punjabi, Namita, 172

Q

Quaker, 218
quick-service restaurants (QSR), 93

R

Radio Ceylon, 214–15
Radio Kuwait, 215
Rafi, Mohammad, 215
Raghunath, M, 7
Rahman, AR (Dilip Kumar), 130, 213, 220
Rai, Aishwarya. *See* Bachchan, Aishwarya Rai
Raj Kumar, 228
Raja Hindustani, 42

Raja, Rajeev, 221
Rajabali, Anjum, 62
Rajagopal, Arvind, 60, 229, 230
Rajan, RV, 120–21
Rajnikanth, 229
Raju, Ramalinga, 133
Rakshit, Goutam, 6, 113
Ramachandran, MG, 228
Ramadorai, S., 183
Ramaswamy, EV, 238
Ramaswamy, Venkat, 126
Ramayana, 98, 114
Ramkumar, Krishna, 36
Rana, Dhanji, 77
Ranaut, Kangana, 229
Rangeela, 237
Ranjekar, Dileep, 154
Rao, BV, 91
Rao, NT Rama, 228
Rao, PV Narasimha, 114, 179
Rao, Rajiv, 130
Rao, SL, 85
Rashi, Shimona, 203
Rasna, 17, 21, 114
Ratnam, Mani, 46
Ravi Verma, Raja, 144
Ravichandran, RL, 98, 100
Ray, Satyajit, 116
Raymond, 6–7, 75, 77–78, 81, 82, 149, 156, 248
Rebel Without a Cause (1955), 75
Red & White, 5, 235
Red Eveready, 235
Red Lamp, 119
Redbus, 173
Rediff.com, 148
Rediffusion Advertising, 4, 27, 62–63, 79, 102, 109, 127, 130, 148, 234
Rees, Nigel, 225
Reese, 232
Rehman, Waheeda, 226
Rekha, 215, 226
rekla race, 3
Reliance Industries Ltd, 76, 164, 202
Reliance Mobile, 127–28
religious mythologies, x
religious symbols, use in advertising, 144
religious tourism, 171
reservation (affirmative action), 152
reservation system, 154
responsive web design (RWD), 134
retirement solutions, 186
Revital, 195
Richards, Barry, 206
Richards, Vivian, 76, 202
righteousness, x
Ritu Kumar, 83
Roadies, 32–33
Rogers, Everett, 122
Rosario, Chris, 251
Roshan, Hrithik, 232
Royal Chutney, 226
rural consumers, 4, 118–23, 257

S
S Kumars, 20
Saathi, Rajesh, 219
Saffola, 15, 85, 86
Saffola Masala Oats, 94
Sampath, Ram, 213, 220

Samsonite, 140
Samsung, 132, 228
Sankara Eyecare, Coimbatore, 198
Santayana, George, 19
Santoor, 57–59, 203
Sapre, Madhu, xiii, 250
Saridon, 190, 194
Satyam, 133
Savitri, 226
Saxena, Akshay, 36
Sayani, Ameen, 149, 214
Sayani, Hamid, 149
SBI Life Insurance, 49
Schudson, Michael, 143, 189, 232
Scorpio, 105
Scotch-Brite, 32
Scott, 190
Scott, Ridley, 184
SEBI, 160
Sehwag, Virendra, 128
Sen, Amartya, 69
Sen, Nandini, 5
Sen, Shunu, 61
Sen, Sushmita, 63
Senior Agency International, 55
Sentil Kumar, 203
Shakti Ammas, 121
Shankar, Pandit Ravi, 220
Shankara Netralaya, Chennai, 198
Shanti, 205
Sharada, 226
Sharma, Charu, 206
Sharma, Tara, 27
Shastri, Lal Bahadur, 124
Shastri, Ravi, 76, 202
Shaw, George Bernard, 206, 225
Sher Shah Suri, 105–06

Shetty, Rohit, 242
Shivaji, 228
Sholay, 92, 99, 227
shopping malls, 81
Shroff, Jackie, 5, 226
Simoes, Frank, 7, 78, 79, 171, 172, 235
Singh, Harpal, 100
Singh, Khushwant, 77
Singh, Manmohan, xiv
Singh, Satbir, 175
Sinha, Dheeraj, 36
Sinha, Shashi, 222
Sinha, Shatrughan, 226
Sinha, Sonakshi, 229
Sirolin, 190
Sistas, 99
Sita, 54
Siyaram, 76
skill development, 186–88
Skoda Superb, 107
smartphones, 24, 25, 28, 34, 133, 157
Snapdeal, 145
soap operas, 142, 222
social changes, x, xv
social class discrimination, 254
social justice, 52
social media, 134, 176, 177, 254
Socio Economic and Caste Census of India (SECC) 2011, 107
Socio Economic Classifications (SEC), 124
Sodhi, RS, 89
Soman, Milind, xiii, 6, 250–51
sonic branding, 221

Sony, 149, 151, 205–6, 228
Sood, Anita, 200–1
sound visuals, 222
Spartek, 112
Spielberg, Steven, 232
Sreesanth, 204
Sridevi, 226
Srivastava, Sanjay, 215
Srivatsav, Suman, 205
Standard Chartered Marathon, 205
Star, 30
Star Plus, 95, 151
Star TV, 150–51
Sterling Resorts, 173
stock photos, 8
Strepsils, 189, 192, 244
Subha, 213
Subramaniam, Prasad, 102
Subramanian, Ganapathy, 54
suiting advertising, 6
Sukh Ram, 126
Sundaram Finance, 163
Sundrop, 15, 85–86
Sunil, V., 100, 175
Super Bowl, 184, 206
Surendranath, Kailash, 216
Surf Excel, 61
Surya, 229
Sushruta Samhita, 195
Suzuki Corporation of Japan, 99, 100
'Swaach Bharat' movement (2015), 117
Swades, x
Sweetex, 244, 245, 246
Swish Blades, 78

T

Table Tasties, 226
Tagore, Sharmila, 62
Tahil, Dalip, 6
Taj Hotels, 171
Takia, Ayesha, 16–17
Tandon, Prakash, 85
Tanishq, 141
Taproot, 69, 130
Taproot Dentsu, 40
Tata Consultancy Service (TCS), 152, 183, 205
Tata Crucible – The Business Quiz, 152
Tata Docomo, 33, 128–29, 140, 206–7, 218, 220
Tata Group, Tatas, xiii, 152, 204, 217, 254
Tata Indica, 102–4, 218
Tata Indigo CS, 107
Tata Indigo Marina, 218–19
Tata, JRD, 169
Tata Motors, 106, 107, 205
Tata Salt, 36, 232
Tata Sierra, 87
Tata Steel, xiv, 260
Tata Tea, xiv, 32, 49, 60
Tchaikovsky, 218
Teacher Education Reform, 154
television, xiii, 21, 30, 32, 164
advertising, ix–xi, xiv, 6, 13, 18, 30, 38, 47, 52, 55, 64, 75, 79, 81, 92–95, 113, 128, 140–42, 149–50, 155, 189, 193–94, 198, 202, 214, 217–19, 244, 246, 252–53
cable and satellite, 115, 258
colour, 113–14

growth of, xiv–xv, 41, 78, 98, 121–23, 193, 208, 239–40, 259
linguistic experiments, 235, 237, 239–42
serials/soap operas, 41–42, 66, 205, 22
depiction of social changes, 41–42, 66
Tendulkar, Sachin, 229
Tezaab, 235
Thadani, Ramesh, 117
thali theory, 91–92, 94
Tharoor, Shashi, 80
Thermax, 234–35
3 Idiots, 94, 198
Thums Up, 10, 28, 30
Thurman, John, 247
TIDCO, 217
Tiger Moms, 21, 67
time share resorts, 173
Times Group of publications, 152
Titan, 5, 140, 217–18, 220
Titus, Ray, 36
'Tombstone' ads, 160
Toshiba, 228
tourism industry and advertising, 171, 172–78
transparency and accountability, 168
Trikaya Advertising, 29, 112, 159, 172, 244, 251
Trikaya Options, 159
Trivedi, Dinesh, 249
Trivedi, Harish, 237
Trivedi, Parag, 216
Tuffs shoes, xiii, 250, 254
TVS, 99–100
TVS Scooty, 231
Twitchell, James, 189
Twitter, 134
Tyagi, Amelia, 154

U
Uber, 107, 108
Ulka Kolkata, 77
Uncle Chipps, 236
Underhill, Paco, 47
unemployment, 27, 183, 186
UNICEF, 28
Unique Identification System (UID), 124
Universal Banking, 124
Upadyay, Mukul, 48
Urban Ladder, 117
urbanization, 43, 87, 119, 258
Uthup, Usha, 215–16

V
Vaasan Eye Care institutions, 198
Vaastu, 116
Vajpayee, Atal Bihari, 105, 175
value of values, 11
Van Heusen, 77
Vatsa Corporation, 159
Vazir Sultan Tobacco, 74
Velvette, 19
Venkateshwara Hatcheries (VH Group), 91
Verma, Pavan, 127
Veta, 188
Viagra, 52–53
Vicco, 194
Vicks Cough Drops, 192
Vicks Vaporub, 192, 194, 196
Vicky Donor, 68

Videocon, 114, 228
Vijay, 229
Vimal, 73–81
VIP Frenchie, 6
Visvanathan, Shiv, 51
Viswanathan, Satyam, 13, 152, 157, 203
Vites, 190
Vividh Bharati, 148–49, 214
Vodafone (Hutch), 130, 206
Volkswagen Beetle, 105
Voltas India Limited, 29
Voltas Megalaundrette, 217
VSNL, 133

W
Walker, Johnny, 129
Walmart, 145
Wanson, 234
Warren, Elizabeth, 154
Washes Whiter, 61
wedding theme in advertisements, 139–41
Wells, HG, 225
Wheel, 179
Whirlpool, 10, 21, 64
White Light, 16, 180, 218
White Revolution, 89
Who Wants to Be a Millionaire?, 150
Wieden & Kennedy, 100, 171
Wild Life Protection Act, 250
Wild Stone, 252, 253
Wills Filter, 41
Wills Lifestyle, 81
Wills Navy Cut, 40–41
Wilmar, Adani, 86
WIMCO, 78

WomanMood, 65
Women and Media Committee of Bombay Union of Journalists, 249
women,
changing aspirations, 57–60
depiction in advertising, x–xiv, 7–9, 13, 32, 40, 43–46, 57–68, 77–78, 80–81, 140, 166, 180, 201–2, 219–20, 231, 250–2, 256
role in Bollywood, 27, 62, 68
empowerment, 43, 66
concept of Missing Women, 69
working, 40, 43–45, 62, 64, 65, 68, 146, 256
Woodwards Gripe Water, 192
World Cup Cricket
(1983), 207
(1996), 30
(2003), and (2007), 205
World War II, 106
Wrangler, 81

Y
Yamaha, 99
Youth Mood, 35
YouTube, 132, 149

Z
Zaheer, 204
Zaltman, Gerald, 131, 241
Zandu, 192, 193, 194
Zanjeer, x
Zara, 81
Zee Group, 30, 149, 150, 206
Zee Khana Khazana, 95
Zee SaReGaMaPa, 222

Zee Studio and Zee Café, 241
Zeenat Aman, 226
Zindagi Na Milegi Dobara, 174
Zinta, Preity, 27, 231
Zodiac, 77, 81
Zozilla Engineering Works, Kargil, 101, 102
Zuari, 119